CW01082516

No Particula

BRITISH TRAVELLERS IN FINLAND 1830 1917

Tony Lurcock grew up in Kent, and studied English at University College, Oxford. He became lecturer in English at Helsinki University, and subsequently at Åbo Akademi. Returning to Oxford, he completed a D.Phil. thesis, and taught there, and in America, until his recent retirement. He is the author of *Not So Barren or Uncultivated: British Travellers in Finland 1760–1830* (CB editions, 2010), and numerous review articles, mainly on eighteenth-century literature and on biography.

MIDNIGHT HAVEN OF REST

Sketch by Mrs Alec Tweedie: frontispiece of the first edition of *Through Finland in Carts* (1897), showing 'all the necessaries and luxuries of Finnish humble life'. Hanging between the roof beams are the round loaves described by so many travellers. (See pp.156–7.)

No Particular Hurry

BRITISH TRAVELLERS IN FINLAND
1830–1917

Tony Lurcock

'Not being in any particular hurry, we lingered . . .'
Mrs Alec Tweedie

'. . . what demand is there for hurry
or punctuality in places like Riehki or Teerlä?'
Rosalind Travers

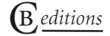

First published in 2013
by CB editions
146 Percy Road London W12 9QL
www.cbeditions.com

Front cover: Victor Westerholm (1860–1919), *A View at Ruissalo*
(*Maisema Ruissalosta*), 1903. Oscar Huttunen Collection,
Kuopio Art Museum

Printed in England by Imprint Digital, Exeter EX5 5HY

ISBN 978-0-9567359-9-7

Contents

Acknowledgements

Many people have given help and encouragement at different times and in different places, some of them long ago, some far away, and some both. In particular Silvester Mazzarella has read several versions over the years, and has, as ever, encouraged the whole enterprise, while on the home front Pontus has again contributed corrections, clarifications, and many insights and suggestions.

I thank Marjetta Bell for help with Russian War details; Jonathan Clark for producing the two maps of Finland; Larry Eldredge for deciphering certain words in the Evans ms; Eva Ennis for the loan of her precious *Finland Bulletin*; Tim Griggs for editing out most of my favourite parts in the Introduction; Philip Grover, at the Pitt Rivers Museum, for assembling all of Arthur Evans's drawings of Finland for me to see; Kevin Hart for making my naval terminology shipshape; Diana Kaley for information about her grandmother Sylvia Mac-Dougall; Bill Mead for sending me copies of useful articles; Gunnar Nyström for information about the Julin family; Ilaria Perzia at the Ashmolean Museum for generous help with the ms of Evans's Journal; Pasi Sahlberg for giving me perspectives on Finnish education; Roger Sell for general encouragement and particular help; Katherine Turner for explaining when ladies are women; and Angela Wilson for the map of Åland.

I have consulted many books in the course of producing one, and they are listed in the bibliographies. I am particularly indebted to Basil Greenhill and Ann Gifford, *The British Assault on Finland 1854–1855: A Forgotten Naval War* (1988).

Publication of this volume has been made possible by a grant from Konstsamfundet; thanks are due to Kaj-Gustaf Bergh, and also to Karl Grotenfelt for his help as an intermediary.

Any comments, corrections or additions would be welcomed by the author at 9 Monmouth Road, Oxford OX1 4TD, UK, or by email to tonylurcock@yahoo.com.

Place names in Swedish and Finnish

Archaic Swedish spellings are in parentheses. Places which are mentioned only once are usually translated in the text. There are a few places, almost all in Lapland, which I have not been able to identify. In a book of this size it has not proved possible to provide a map which shows every small village and settlement, but they can easily be found of the website http://kansalaisen. karttapaikka.fi. The site recognises only Finnish names.

Björneborg	Pori
Borgå (Bergo)	Porvoo
Brahestad	Raahe
Ekenäs (Eckness)	Tammisaari
Enare	Inari
Enontekis	Enontekiö
Fölisön	Seurasaari
Fredrikshamn	Hamina
Gamla Karleby	Kokkola
Hangö	Hanko
Helsingfors	Helsinki
Kajana	Kajaani
Kexholm	Käkisalmi
Lovisa (Louisa)	Loviisa
Nykarleby	Uusikaarlepyy
Nyslott	Savonlinna
Nystad	Uusikaupunki
Pyttis	Pyhtä
Raumo	Rauma
Seskar	Seiskari
Sibho	Sibbo

Sordavala	Sortavala
Sveaborg	Suomenlinna
Tammerfors (Tamerfers)	Tampere
Tavastehus	Hämeenlinna
Torneå	Tornio
Uleåborg	Oulu
Urdiala	Urjala
Vasa	Vaasa
Vyborg	Viipuri
Åbo	Turku
Övertorneå	Ylitornio

Beyond Finland

Reval	Tallinn
'Nargon' (Nargen)	Naissaar

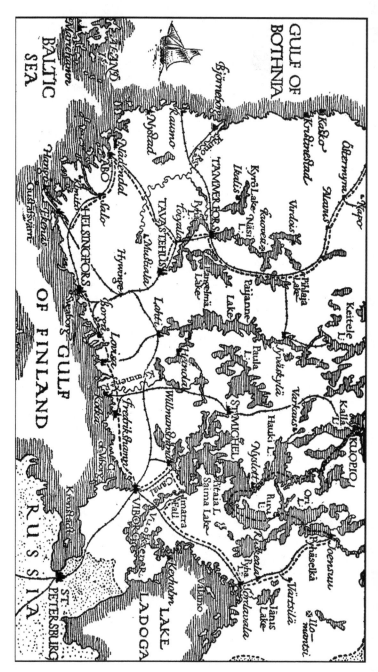

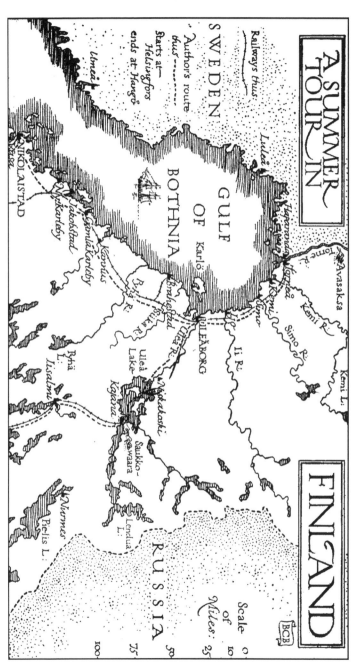

Map from Sylvia MacDougall ['Paul Waineman'], *A Summer
Tour in Finland*, 1908, with place names in Swedish

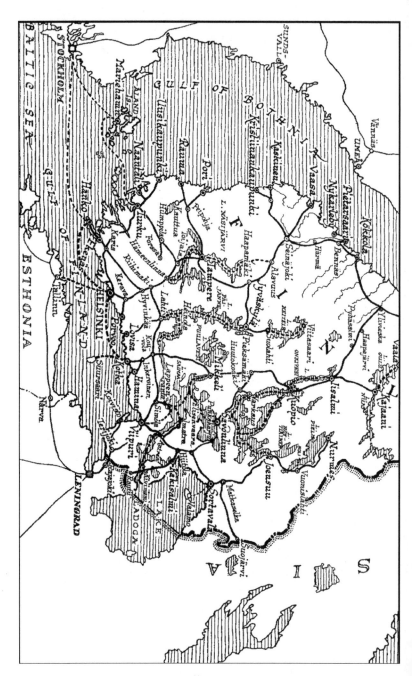

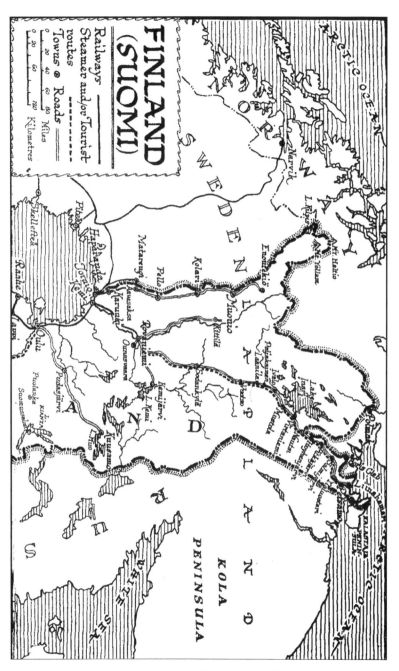

Map *c*.1930 with place names in Finnish

Preface

'Whether further volumes appear will have to depend on the reception of what follows' was how I rather timidly concluded the Preface of *'Not so Barren or Uncultivated': British Travellers in Finland 1760–1830* (CB editions, 2010). Though not widely reviewed, the book seems slowly to have made itself known, and there has even been a modest reprint. So here is the second volume. It is, obviously, a continuation, but is also a separate work, telling its own story, and not assuming knowledge of the earlier volume.

The title *No Particular Hurry* reflects what is perhaps the most persistent difference between the two volumes. Before the 1830s a dominant purpose of the travellers was to get through Finland to Russia or to Sweden as quickly as possible. This purpose is seen still in the first two travellers here, Robert Paul and Thomas Whatley. After 1840 there is a striking reversal; in 1901 Harry de Windt wrote 'I predict that, once in Finland, you will be in no hurry to leave it.'

The first volume traced a simple development: the transformation of the British conception of Finland from an unknown, even barbarous region into a picturesque country with some 'tolerable' hotels. The trajectory of *No Particular Hurry* is more complex, and the material more varied, but a unifying theme is that much of what is seen and described here shows Finland developing as a nation. '*Suomi* will rise to distinction, for this younger generation of Finlanders, as Ibsen says, is now "knocking at the door" of nations,' wrote Mrs Alec Tweedie in 1897. Twenty years later Finland declared independence.

The book is first and foremost an anthology, with extracts chosen from more than two dozen accounts. There is more material from this period than was available for the first volume; I have not always necessarily sought the 'best' passages for my extracts, but have attempted also to make the material varied, by avoiding duplication and by including descriptions of as many locations as possible. I give a short introduction to each writer, and make the book rather more than a chronology by linking some of the recurrent features. There is very little in the British accounts before 1830 which anticipates modern Finland; in the present volume we see modern Finland in the making.

I have again confined myself, with one exception, to printed material; all of the books and periodicals which are discussed and cited are by British authors, and published in Britain. I have corrected a few misprints in these sources, and have occasionally ventured to reform the paragraphing (usually in collections of letters). I am sorry that there has not been space for the American writer and diplomat, Bayard Taylor; his outstanding account of winter travelling in Lapland can be read on the CB editions website.

The nature of the material has presented a particular problem: the Baltic Campaign (1854–55), the part of the Crimean War which took the British and French fleets to the Baltic for two summers, is now little known in Britain, but it has an important part in the following pages. Although the war is an integral part of the whole book, I have separated it off with its own Introduction, rather than having it unbalance the general Introduction. Otherwise, I have followed customs established for the earlier volume.

During that earlier period few travellers took any account of the Finnish language; now they come across Finnish more and more, as it gains parity with Swedish, and as they travel inland, away from the Swedish-speaking coastal settlements. Most towns in Finland were still known by their Swedish names during this period (in fact 'Helsingfors' was still used by the British during the Second World War), and travellers use Finnish place names only occasionally. A straw in the wind was *The Illustrated London News* writing in 1855 of '[t]he city of Helsingfors, called in the Finland dialect Helsinki'. Several popular destinations – Imatra and Joensuu, for example – do not have Swedish names (in the Åland Islands it is the other way round: there are no Finnish versions of the Swedish names). I have kept the Swedish names in quoted texts, and the Finnish names in my own text. In the few places where this could be confusing I have made use of parentheses, and have again provided a list of names in each language. Several of the writers describe places such as Vyborg and Sortavala, which were lost to Russia in the 1944 armistice.

Introduction

During the first years of the nineteenth century many of the British travellers to Finland had still been genuine adventurers, heading for an unexplored country, and willing to journey without maps. Some of them had particular interests too, of course – among them agriculture, economics, ethnology, botany, the picturesque, and the midnight sun – but they were all, to different extents, heading into the unknown. By the 1830s all this was changing, as I wrote in the Epilogue of *Not so Barren or Uncultivated*:

> the extraordinary range of interests which had taken so many curious travellers to Finland in the later eighteenth century had evaporated. The tradition of the Grand Tour, or even its shadows and substitutes, had vanished . . . There was no more interest in Lapland magic, the vogue of the primitive had run its course, Rousseau had made way for Bentham, and artists had moved on from the picturesque and Romantic. When Murray published his first *Handbook for Travellers* in 1839 the last 'unvisited corner' of Europe had been mapped.

Finland was no longer just a remote location where visitors could exercise their romantic sensibilities: increasingly during the nineteenth century it attracted their socio-political interests. These interests were not confined to those who had visited the country; relations with Russia became a wider, recurrent concern. The Russian War in the Baltic, 1854–55, brought professional sailors and marines as well as journalists to Finland, and was widely reported in Britain. Later in the century there was a surge of political and ideological interest, with enthusiasm for the emergent Social Democratic Party, and for the advanced position which women held in society. From about 1890 there were many powerful advocates in England urging the Finnish cause against the process of Russification.

By the early nineteenth century genuine explorers were already giving way to travellers; what the present volume records is, essentially, the development of travel into tourism. As the practical problems involved in travelling both to and within Finland were steadily removed, tourists came to have time and leisure to see more, and to learn more about the country.

Travellers who write were joined by writers who travel; Elizabeth Rigby noted, and regretted, this development in an article as early as 1846, identifying

> that more systematic set of travellers who regularly make
> a tour in order to make a book, and have thus pretty well
> divided the tourable world between them.

The age of the Grand Tour had passed, and with it the upper-class gentleman with his servants. The new generation was broadly middle-class; several were semi-professional travel-writers, simply adding Finland to their list and writing for readers as comfortably middle-class as themselves. Many of the accounts of Finnish travel are by women, who saw and described all manner of things which earlier travellers had not seen, or had not noticed.

Most of the early travellers had regarded Finland only as an intermediate stage on their way to or from Russia. In 1902, wrote Henry Norman, you could travel by train 'from Charing Cross to St. Petersburg in fifty hours, with only one change of carriage where the gauge changes'. Since Russia could be reached so easily without even setting foot in Finland, those who went to Finland usually went by choice; for them the journey now mattered more than the arrival.

Murray's *Handbook*

In 1896, when Mrs Alec Tweedie was planning the journey described in *Through Finland in Carts* (1897), she found that 'no guide book was to be obtained in all London . . . No one ever dreamed of going to Finland apparently'. She may have been dramatising her own forthcoming adventure, or perhaps the seventh edition of John Murray's *Handbook for Travellers in Russia, Poland, and Finland* (1893) was already sold out: the earlier editions had certainly been successful enough to merit regular revision and expansion. A survey of the successive editions shows clearly the ways in which travel in Finland changed over a period of some fifty years. Travellers who genuinely wanted to find experiences worth recording could no longer simply follow the Great Coastal Road along the south coast; they had to head into the interior.

The first edition, *A Handbook for Travellers in Denmark, Norway, Sweden and Russia* (1839), included a twenty-eight page section on Finland. The Preface is signed simply T.D.W.; this was Thomas Denman Whatley, a Cambridge-educated barrister. Much of the Finland section is his own first-person narrative, and is a travel book quite as much as a guide:

> The principal object of the following pages is to afford such of my travelling countrymen as are disposed to quit the more beaten paths of southern Europe, and explore the less known, but equally romantic, regions of the north – some useful information as to time and distance, which at present they can only obtain by actual experience. Beyond Hamburg, all is an unknown land . . .
>
> The entire tour of the North can hardly be accomplished in a single summer, without hurrying over too much that deserves a more careful survey, or undergoing such a degree of bodily fatigue as would outweigh the pleasure.

'No journey of the same extent,' he concludes, 'can . . . be put in competition with it, either for variety or interest.'

Whatley gives the Baltic timetable for 1838: from early May to late October there were three steamers a month from Stockholm to Cronstadt via Turku, Helsinki and Tallinn (Tallinn was known as Reval until 1917). Ideally the voyage from Stockholm to Turku took about thirty hours, and onwards to St Petersburg about eighty hours more, but he describes a journey to St Petersburg made in late September 1838 which took eight days. 'There is little to make amends for this tedious voyage,' he writes, recommending instead the steamer to Turku, and posting east on the Great Coastal Road. In the 1849 edition of the Handbook; we learn that the post route from Grisslehamn through the Åland Islands, so graphically described by many of the earliest travellers, 'is but seldom taken since the introduction of *steam* navigation between Stockholm and Abo'. The steamer to St Petersburg is now considered to be reliable; there are no more descriptions of the horrors encountered on the Great Coastal Road. 'The most convenient and agreeable mode of travelling in Finland,' he now advises, 'is by sea.'

1865 saw a greatly expanded New Edition. The author was T. Michelle, 'Attache to Her Majesty's Embassy at the Court of Russia', and his name remains until the final edition of 1893. By this date Finland was recognised as a destination in its own right: we learn that 'Finland may be reached from Lubeck by steamer once a week to Helsingfors'. The most significant changes in this edition are those which imply a very different type of traveller. The section on Finland (now entitled 'Grand Duchy of Finland') provides tables of weights and measures, lists of Finnish words and phrases, and specimen dialogues. Previously, Swedish had been recommended as the language for travelling, with Finnish dismissed as 'their own perfectly unintelligible tongue'. This volume is recognisably a modern guide book, written with intelligent and inquisitive readers in mind.

Railways and lake steamers are mentioned for the first time, as part of the developing pattern of travel in central and eastern Finland:

> Route 55, only. 4. Tavesthus. – A rly. unites Helsingfors with the town of Tavasethus, 80 m. distant, in the interior of the country. Fare 3 roubles. Tavastehus is well worth visiting in summer time, as it is most picturesquely situated, and gives a good idea of Finnish lake scenery. Small government steamboats go once or twice a week from Tavastehus up the river and lakes to Tammerfors . . . Very good posting hence into the interior.

The 1865 *Handbook* was reissued in 1868, with a few minor corrections and changes. Finland is now correctly called Suomi, not 'Secomi', and we learn that that 'good Bavarian beer is to be had throughout the country'.

The Third Edition (1875) is substantially rewritten to reflect 'changes and improvements in the mode of travelling':

> The sections relating to . . . Finland, which have been much enlarged, may have the effect of attracting travellers, and particularly sportsmen, to those picturesque countries. The construction of railways has brought them within comparatively easy reach of Western Europe.

The new routes go further into the interior of the country; for example, Route 67 is 'Uleaborg to Kuopio', and Route 69 is 'Wiborg to Kuopio'. In addition, a number of excursions, supplementing these routes, are suggested. For the first time the Imatra falls are mentioned by name; by the end of the century they were probably the most popular tourist sight in Finland. The Fourth Edition (1888) lists steamers direct from England to Turku and Helsinki; Finland was now a chosen destination for the British.

Although the private carriage was still recommended in

1865, there are only a few accounts of it during this period. Joseph Sturge 'found that the only posting here is by one rough two-wheeled vehicle . . . We therefore bought a comfortable carriage in which we can sleep at night, for about £20.' He considered the posting arrangements efficient and cheap: 'it has cost us about £3 to come here [Tampere] from Helsingfors, or about 4½d. per mile for three horses, double fares for driving, and our meals on the road; in England it would have cost near £20'. Finland was now opening up to those who did not aspire to a private carriage. Murray's *Handbook* could be bought at any bookshop, and cheap public transport by water and rail was making even quite remote parts of Finland accessible, no longer the preserve of the rich or attractive only to the adventurous. As early as 1908 Sylvia MacDougall was disparaging popular tourism, writing in Imatra of 'tawdry wooden pavilions . . . from which countless kodaks can be levelled'.

The earlier travellers had usually had servants, guides and interpreters with them. Now they seem to have been much more independent; Whatley (1848) advised against 'taking English servants, particularly females', as they 'would prove a far greater trouble than comfort'. Timetables, maps, and later the telephone took many uncertainties out of travelling; some British tourists claimed to have managed without interpreters yet, puzzlingly, are able transcribe lengthy conversations with locals. Sometimes they got by with German – 'without German,' wrote Whatley, 'I really think we should hardly have reached St. Petersburg' – occasionally with French, and once, memorably, with Latin. Several spoke or learned Swedish; Finland was an obvious holiday destination for a Swedish speaker, especially when – like most of the women travellers – they were relatives, friends, or guests of wealthy Swedish-speaking families.

The most graphic descriptions by earlier travellers had been of winter travelling, but there are none in the present volume. Finland was becoming known, and promoted, for summer vacations. Several of the summer visitors are nonetheless aware that Finland is really a winter country. Selina Bunbury, for example, writing in mid-May, claimed that '[n]othing can be more delightful than this scene in winter. In fact in the north one gets to like ice and snow just as much as we dislike the misty and cold season called winter in England.' Anka Ryall notes Tweedie's focus 'on winter as Finland's defining season. Even in the heat of summer [she] views the country as '"ice-bound" by nature'. At times, some writers seem even a little ashamed of being in Finland in summer, when everything is so easy.

The creature comforts which tourists were now coming to expect could not yet be found in the far north, which is perhaps why Lapland remained largely unexplored during the nineteenth century. The only writers in this volume who could be regarded as explorers were in fact the three who went to Lapland: Edward Rae, Arthur J. Evans and C. J. Cutcliffe Hyne. The latter two were 'crusted characters' who, in their different ways, stood out against the superficial ease of tourism: Rae parodies at times the stance and style of pith-helmeted African explorers such as Stanley, while Hyne writes disdainfully that he has no interest in following 'future tourist routes', and sets off, against all advice, into 'the Land of Horrible Flies'.

Lapland reappears as a regular destination only after the railway reached Rovaniemi in 1909. It was eventually to be branded, for better or for worse, as 'The Official Hometown of Santa Claus', and is nowadays served by seasonal day trips by air from England. This tourist hype was anticipated more than a hundred years ago by Sir George Renwick, who discovered in Tornio Finland's 'Ultima Thule', a 'fairy-tale town', and 'Elysium'; there he spent 'golden hours', and found a hotel where '[t]he service was everything that one could require in fairyland'.

Back in the eighteenth century some travellers to Lapland had hoped to find a fabled race of virtuous beings living in a Rousseauesque 'state of nature'. By then Lapland had already been popularised by the Scottish poet James Thomson as a new Arcadia, and his descriptions were frequently quoted in travellers' accounts. It is surprising to find this earlier, prelapsarian picture of Finland echoed in Colonel Hamley's memoirs of the Russian War of the 1850s. Aware that primitive simplicity, 'without savagery or barbarism, has been ever a favourite topic of poets and pastoral romanticists', he locates this primitiveness firmly in Åland, which he sees as a northern Utopia invaded and corrupted by war. Hamley felt that the military operations in Åland had destroyed an earthly paradise. This sort of idealisation of Finland is an undercurrent in several narratives: Alexander MacCallam Scott, on a boat trip outside Helsinki, writes, 'we sailed straight into Arcady, back into the youth of the world and the primal age of innocence'; Tweedie describes 'a primitive dinner' at a post-station where the people 'were so honest and simple, so far removed from civilisation and its corrupting influences on their thoughts, that they and their life seemed to take us back a couple centuries at least.' It is revealing that while the earlier travellers use 'primitive' pejoratively, by the 1890s it is associated with charm rather than disgust. For all this emphasis on native innocence, though, many visitors found a society more advanced than England. By the early twentieth century Finland was, paradoxically, being idealised for primitiveness at the same time as it was being praised for progressiveness.

The picture of Finland found in the British accounts from the period of the Russian War (1854–55) is a remarkably attractive one. The Finns were well-regarded – and not only because they were not Russian. The British fleet was in the Baltic only during the best months of the year, returning to England as autumn set in, and we repeatedly come across descriptions which seem to belong not to a war but to a vacation, with bathing and excursions ashore to pick blueberries. 'The first few days in September were exceedingly fine,' writes William Gerard Don, 'and we made the most of them on shore in cricket matches, and other amusements'.

As a result of the war, different aspects of Finland were getting known in England. The name of Runeberg was heard, perhaps for the first time: in July 1854 the *Illustrated London News* published three of his poems in translation, claiming that 'Runeberg is not only the modern Homer of Finland, but of all the lands of the north'. In September it devoted a whole page to printing the 'Patriot Song of the Finlanders': 'Vårt Land' in Swedish, with English translation, and music by Pacius. The *Kalevala* was surprisingly well known in England; Crawford's translation was published in 1888, nineteen years before Kirby's Everyman edition. After this date almost all the writers refer to it; the poem seems almost to have been required reading for those writing on Finland, and quoting from it proof that they had done their homework.

'Embryo Qualities'

Several of the qualities for which Finland has become notable in recent times are seen in embryo, as it were, in the second half of the nineteenth century. Already in the 1850s writers are recording their surprise at finding that in Finland the fishermen and small farmers, and their wives, were all literate. Every household and boat, it seemed, contained a Bible and a prayer book. Captain Sulivan describes an episode near Degerby, in Åland, when he stopped and searched a small sloop, crewed by a couple and their young son. He was surprised to find a 'nice clean cabin' containing a 'Testament and Psalter', and reflected:

> It is certainly not creditable to us as a nation that we should be so behind in education those we have previously considered half-barbarous Finns. They can hardly believe that numbers of people in England cannot read.

Sturge noted during his visit in 1856 that 'every Finn of sound mind and adult age can read'. Even in 'isolated farms' in Lapland Evans found 'one or two books about, mostly Bible and Prayer books it is true, & a large proportion of them as far as we can test, can read and write'. 'They are,' wrote Renwick in 1911, 'undoubtedly the best educated nation in the world.' (See notes.)

Earlier in the nineteenth century several retired British naval officers had travelled between Stockholm and Turku on Swedish and Finnish boats, and had had little good to say about either the boats or their crews. Some of them simply felt fortunate not to have been drowned. Now British naval officers were full of praise for Finnish ships and Finnish seamanship. Ten years before the war Charles Fredrick Henningsen wrote: '[t]he only reasonable hope which Russia might entertain . . . would be in the prospect of eventually manning her fleets with her Finnish subjects, the only portion of the population of her vast empire containing sailors'. Sturge, viewing 'the school for merchant seamen' in Turku, asked: 'would not our merchant service be benefitted by similar institutions?'

The Commander of the Fleet, Sir Charles James Napier, admired all that he saw of naval activity in Finland, and gave this authoritative assessment of Finnish expertise:

> In most of the ports are excellent ship-building yards . . . The science of naval architecture is carried to a degree of perfection which will bear comparison with the state of ship-building in England. The Fins are indefatigable in producing the finest models from other countries, and their aim is, if not to improve upon them, at least to equal them . . . [To] a power like Russia, aiming every year more and more at naval excellence, the possession of Finland is invaluable; and the cordial co-operation of its artisans no less so.
>
> The Finnish seamen are equally good with their ships, and from them Russia draws her best supply for manning

her navy . . .They are sober, steady, and active, possessing all the good qualities of the English seaman. Hence their services are deemed desirable in British merchant ships wherever they can be obtained.

Higher praise could hardly be imagined. In 2012, Finland still has three large shipyards, and is a major builder of cruise liners.

Finland today is famous also as a nation of musicians, with Finnish conductors in charge of orchestras from Norway to New Zealand. S. S. Hill writes of the 'genius of the Finns for music and poetry', and much later Miss Clive-Bayley praises the singing on the steamer between Tampere and Rouvesi: '[t]he students on board our steamer sang some magnificent songs . . . The compass of the voices, and of the music sung, seemed to me greater than is usual in England'. Tweedie was perhaps the most judicious of the musical critics:

> That Finland is thoroughly musical may be inferred from the dozens of choirs sent to the Sordavala Festival from all parts of the country. The peasant voices, in spite of being but slightly trained, or at all events trained very little, sing together wonderfully.

Ernest Young and Renwick each devote a whole chapter to Finnish music; they praise the singers, and give brief accounts of the work of Kajanus, Sibelius, Järnefelt, Merikanto, and others. Renwick mentions the establishment of orchestras in the principal towns, and writes of Finland's 'high rank in the musical world', concluding '[t]he rise of this latest national school of music makes me wonder if there is here a lesson for England'.

The notice taken of music is associated with the recurrent interest in runo singing and in the *Kalevala*. As early as 1800 Edward Daniel Clarke had transcribed a Finnish folk poem, with a translation by Franzén, and John Bowring had published a long article 'Runes of Finland' in 1827. Tweedie has several romantic descriptions of runo singers, with a fine photograph of one group. John Dover Wilson, the first English *lektor* at Helsinki University, described how in 1906 he had attended a meeting of the Finnish Literary Society where 'two bards from the interior were to sing *runos*'; 'though of course I could not follow the Finnish,' he wrote 'I came away with the strong impression that Homer may have listened to just such bards.' There are several descriptions of the Finnish kantele; Tweedie prints a striking photograph of two players. In the 1890s Edward Westermarck and Yrjö Hirn each presented a kantele to the Pitt Rivers Museum in Oxford.

'Sauna', the only Finnish word to be found in an English dictionary, is not recorded in England before Tweedie used it in 1897, but English readers could have known of it for more than century: an engraving in Acerbi's *Travels through Sweden, Finland and Lapland* brought it vividly before British eyes in 1802, the *Edinburgh Review* commenting that 'the Finlandish bath has nothing to recommend it but the naked accuracy of the representation'. The British were excluded from the sauna by their native prudery; nude bathing was regarded as 'a most extraordinary spectacle'. Harry De Windt submitted gracefully in Oulu:

> This was my first experience of a bath *à la Finnoise*, and I am not anxious to renew it, for to stand in *puris naturalibus* and be soaped from head to foot by a buxom lady (even of mature years) is somewhat trying to a novice. But this ceremony was apparently an essential part of the performance, and I therefore made no demur.

The sauna, nonetheless, slowly becomes a memorable part of the British experience in Finland; by the twentieth century taking a sauna was often on the tourist's list. The first, enthusiastic description is by Rae in 1873, who bathed in Lapland just a few weeks before Evans, and probably in the same sauna as the American traveller Bayard Taylor twenty years earlier, but it had no greater enthusiast than the redoubtable Tweedie. 'A

Finnish bath,' she wrote, 'can never be forgotten'. 'I have never heard of a deliberately misconducted sauna' wrote Harry Bell in 1950; today he would simply not understand the English equation of 'sauna' with 'sex club'.

The rise of Helsinki and the decline of Turku is a recurring theme throughout the whole of this period: 'one is the young wife,' wrote Bunbury, 'the other the antiquated dowager'. On 3 September 1830, Captain Charles Frankland awoke early in Helsinki and 'sallied out to look at the city . . . It is the most beautiful and the most interesting new city I ever beheld,' he wrote. Visitors now rarely found Turku either beautiful or interesting, Hill writing even of the 'gloom and desolation'. As the century wore on a more frequent contrast was between Tallinn, which resembled 'old feudal Germany' with its 'curious, high-roofed buildings with old gables and fantastic gargoyles and hanging stories, . . . Gothic and Byzantine churches, . . . battlemented town walls and gates', and Helsinki, 'a grand, new town, with straight, wide, level streets, lofty churches, stately barracks, an imperial palace, [and] a hotel nearly as grand and almost unique in its comforts of board and lodging'. Frank Hall Standish, arriving in 1837, was astonished to discover in Helsinki

> a beautiful modern town, with a theatre and a ball-room, both of which were open yesterday, and to which we were invited . . . half the population flocked to the pier at our arrival, and the military band hailed us with arias from the operas of Rossini, Bellini, and other fashionable composers . . .

During the reign of Nicholas I (1825–55) strict travel restrictions were imposed on Russian citizens, with the intention of keeping revolutionary ideas out of the country. It was relatively easy for Russians to get travel permits to Finland, and the steamers made the journey easy. Helsinki was quick to capital-ise on this, attracting well-to-do Russians anxious to escape the muggy summer atmosphere of St Petersburg. Helsinki's famous park, Kaivopuisto, was developed, with its fine restaurant, Kai-vohuone, and the 'Ullanlinna Sea Spa', opened in 1838.

The transformation not just of Helsinki but of all of Fin-land from what had been perceived by many British travellers as a semi-barbaric backwater to an elegant and unthreatening holiday venue was more or less complete by 1917. The changes are seen in three areas in particular: transport, accommoda-tion, and food.

Transport

The discomforts and perils encountered on the journey between Stockholm and Turku, so often and so graphically described in earlier accounts, now belonged completely to the past. This was now the age of the steamer. John S. Maxwell describes his 1848 journey: he left Stockholm in 'an excellent boat of Swedish build, with English engines', spending the night at an inn in Turku, continuing the next day to Helsinki, then to Tallinn, where he spent six hours ashore before the last leg of the journey to St Petersburg. Eight years later Sturge travelled from Calais by 'rapid railway transit' to Lübeck, intending to go on via Stockholm and Åbo, but found that there was a di-rect steamer to Helsinki the next day. His journey time from England was a little under six days.

'Beyond Hamburg, all is an unknown land,' Whatley had writ-ten in 1839. No longer; the final chapter of De Windt's *Finland As It Is* (1901), 'How to get to Finland', describes three routes:

Route I. *Via* Calais, Berlin, and St. Petersburg. Fare, exclu-sive of sleeping-car (first class) £16-18/10. (60 hours.)
Route II. *Via* Calais, Copenhagen, and Stockholm (first class) £13-1/9. (70 hours).
Via Flushing (first class) £9-5/9. (71 hours).

Via Hook of Holland (first class) £9-3/9. (74 hours.)
Finally there is route No. 3 – by sea direct from Hull . . .
The Finland Steamship Company . . . keeps up an all-
the-year-round service by the Arcturus and Polaris, new
and powerful fifteen-knot steamers fitted throughout
with electric light and with accommodation for seventy
saloon, and thirty second class, passengers. These sister-
ships resemble miniature ocean-liners, with their broad
promenade decks, palatial saloons, and large, airy state-
rooms, all amidships. A ladies' boudoir and comfortable
smoking-room are also provided, so that the most modern
requirements of luxurious sea-travel are fulfilled, while to
ensure safety the vessels are divided into watertight com-
partments. There is a first-class cuisine on board, and
Finnish customs are observed.

These ships – which were perhaps prototypes for Viking and
Silja Lines, which ply the routes between Sweden and Finland
today – sailed every Saturday, and the fare was £5 single and £8
return first class (£3 and £5 second class), with meals charged
daily at 6s and 4s respectively. Midweek passengers could take
the *Astrea* on Wednesdays to Turku *via* Copenhagen.

Steamers transformed travel within Finland as well, with
the opening up of the lake districts of the central and eastern
provinces. After Joseph Marshall in 1768 no British traveller
recorded a visit to Savonlinna for well over a century, but the
castle now became a popular tourist sight. Savonlinna, and
later Kuopio, were used as touring centres, with local journeys
by steamer. 'All those who have travelled on the boats,' writes
Young, 'are unanimous as to the quality of the accommodation, the cheapness of the fares, and the abundance and variety
of the food.' 'Delightful lake steamers,' enthuses MacDougall,
'are found all over Finland, furnished usually with comfortable wicker deck-chairs in which one can laze and revel in the
scenery.' De Windt considered the steamers 'equal in every

respect to those of the Rhine or Danube'. For the British this was an unfamiliar means of transport, and one which inspired detailed and affectionate description.

Whatley had warned that, despite the timetable, captains 'have the most independent notions' of when to leave. Until the end of the century British travellers on both Baltic and lake steamers complained about this brazen disregard of the published timetable. Antonio Gallenga, a *Times* correspondent, fulminated against the 'outrageous way in which a steam navigation company takes upon itself to waste the passengers' time'. Bunbury, travelling from St Petersburg, stopped at Tallinn: 'In reply to the question as to our time of stay here, the captain ambiguously replied, "I must not say that I shall stop longer than two hours."' When Tweedie's steamer from Savonlinna to Punkaharju left early she reiterated incredulously that 'the steamer actually did start twenty minutes before its appointed hour, and no-one then or after made the slightest complaint. Imagine our Flying Scotsman speeding North even one minute before the advertised hour!'

Trains complemented the coastal and lake steamers, and the British discovered many endearing qualities in the Finnish railways. Young was an early enthusiast: 'The cars are excellent,' he wrote 'and the sleeping arrangements are such as are not open to any but the well-to-do in England'.

'Trains in Finland are like the tortoise,' wrote MacDougall; many writers comment on this, but few complain about it. These were, after all, mostly sightseers, not impatient subjects in a hurry to get to Russia. One of the most characteristic scenes, often recorded, is the way in which both trains and boats stopped periodically to stock up with wood.

The interstices of the journeys were still taken by cart. The 'springless cart', the epitome of discomfort, comes in for many agonised descriptions – 'Such jolting!' exclaims Evans, 'we are almost reduced to jellies'; 'we had almost to hold our teeth fast

in our mouths,' writes Rae. Many travellers describe these carts
being driven on dangerous roads, at high speed, by very small
boys: 'they drive so desperately,' wrote Robert Bateman Paul,
'and with such a total inattention to the safety of the springs,
that we were very soon obliged to take the reins into our own
hands'. These boys were obviously ancestors of the modern race
of Finnish rally drivers. Posting still had an important role in
the national transport system since steamers and trains did not
cover all routes. By the end of the period it was perhaps gain-
ing some sort of favour with tourists as being a genuine, even
quaint relic of a vanishing way of life. This is Young in 1914:

> Posting is not recommended for delicate ladies or for
> those who cannot put up with the simplest of food and
> the plainest of accommodation, but young men in search
> of an unconventional holiday, and possessed of the ability
> to laugh at temporary disarrangements of previously well-
> laid plans, would get enough fun and enjoyment to last
> for a long time.

The published accounts are now predominantly of tourists
taking their summer holidays; the train, steamer, and cart could
transport them into the heart of a land so beautiful that some
writers more or less exhausted their superlatives in describing
it. 'If in Finland you are so unhappy as to seek nothing but scenery,' wrote H. W. Nevinson, 'you need hardly move from wherever you may be.' Clive-Bayley had never 'dreamt of anything
more lovely than this country of Ladoga'. Nature was not the
only attraction: small towns which a few years earlier would
have been visited only by explorers now had a distinct summer season; Clive-Bailey was one of several British ladies who
visited Sortavala, which she describes as 'evidently flourishing
and well-to-do . . . The Tourist Club have opened up and laid
out a charming park, where we spent some hours the day after
our arrival.' By the end of the century there were 'essential'

tourist attractions such as Kangasala (near Tampere), the rapids at Imatra, and Punkaharju. In Imatra Gallenga wrote of the 'water-fall . . . awing by its grandeur even eyes who have seen Niagara', but he is rather more impressed by the attractiveness and hospitality of the English Fishing Club. De Windt was told that Punkaharju 'is our show place; you might as well pass through Naples without seeing Pompeii'. Rosalind Travers, by contrast, writes how glad she was to have seen it only out of season and in the rain. By 1908 MacDougall could write that 'travelling has of late years so increased in comfort, that a traveller need only look at the wilderness in a series of wonderful pictures'.

Board and Lodging

Before 1830 a recurrent theme was the appalled reactions of travellers to the 'execrable' conditions at the post-houses between the west coast and Vyborg. '[S]eldom rising to mediocrity,' wrote Clarke at the turn of the century, adding that 'beds are a species of accommodation never found'. Even when they were found travellers often could not bear to sleep in them. Less than forty years later things had changed: Whatley enjoyed 'a very substantial supper' at a post-house where 'beds were clean and comfortable'. Twenty years later Sturge describes 'post-houses, which consist usually of two or three good rooms, attached to a peasant's house, and furnished with a stove, beds, &c, for the use of travellers'. The first 'Society House' (Societetshuset; Seurahuone in Finnish) was erected in Turku in 1811–12, and quickly became the city's most popular resort for travellers. Society Houses were open for business in Vaasa (1821), Pori (1825), Helsinki (1833), Viborg (1833), Hämeenlinna (1840) and Porvoo (1847). These were all impressive buildings in prominent positions. Some of the buildings still stand; the most striking of them, perhaps, overlooking the south harbour in Helsinki, is now the City Hall. They were established primarily as upper-class meeting places, but seemed to cope well with visitors: Rigby, describing a pleasure cruise from Tallinn to Helsinki in in 1839, wrote of 'the Societäts Haus, the only hotel in the town, and a magnificent building', where most of the hundred and eighty passengers found accommodation. Towards the end of the century they were being built also with tourists in mind; in 1901 de Windt wrote:

> Let a stranger be ever so ignorant of the language, he has only, on arrival at a wharf or railway station, to tell the cabman to drive to the 'Societetshuset,' and he will at once be taken to the best hotel in the place.

During the earlier period travellers soon learned that there would be nothing fit to eat on a journey across Finland, and that they would need to take their own provisions with them. Now this was necessary only in Lapland; Evans and Balfour ordered a meal at their 'dirty miserable' inn in Sodankyla, but 'had to fall back on our pemmican when it came!' Pemmican is best known for its use on Scott's expedition to the South Pole. Unprovided travellers had given vivid descriptions of locally sourced food: rancid fish, sour milk, and bread baked once a year. By mid-century complaints have ceased; many of them describe the abundant fresh fish, fruit, and wonderful dairy produce – the milk and cream are praised extravagantly. Rae enjoyed 'an admirable and delicate collection of dishes' in Kokkola, and Tweedie 'luxurious feasts' in Lapinlahti, while at the Hôtel du Nord in Helsinki, Standish seemed to appreciate the Finnish way of doing things: 'although they serve the soup in the middle of dinner, and Alpine strawberries and cream after the fish, I was able to make a hearty repast.'

Women Travellers

In 1849 Whatley had written 'it is generally believed that ladies cannot travel in Scandinavia; nothing can be more erroneous'.

Rigby, the first woman traveller to have written significantly about Finland, would have agreed. She had described in an article in 1845 how women are by their very nature suited to be travel writers, and possess an ability denied to men, one which would now be seen as a species of 'multi-tasking':

> A man either starts on his travels with a particular object in view, or, failing that, drives a hobby of his own the whole way before him; whereas a woman, accustomed by habit, if not created by nature, to diffuse her mind more equally on all that is presented, and less troubled with preconceived ideas as to what is most important to observe, goes picking up materials much more indiscriminately, and where, as in travelling, little things are of great significance, frequently much more to the purpose.

There are six woman travellers presented in this volume, and they demonstrate the truth of Rigby's thesis in many ways. Several travelled occasionally unescorted, and showed many other instances of independence. They describe meetings with Finnish women in terms which few if any of the male writers would have been capable of.

There was a great deal that British women found congenial in Finland. The way in which the women in peasant society shared the men's work both on land and at sea had been noticed, and seen as something of a novelty, by officers during the Russian War: Sulivan notes with surprise and admiration that '[t]he women here are quite as good sailors as their husbands and brothers'. Some fifty years later Young describes a scene in Vyborg:

> The logs are thrown out by the women, stacked by the women, and I should not have been surprised, though I know it is not the case, if I had been told that the trees had been planted, tended, and felled by women, for woman does many curious things in Finland. Women give you your ticket at the railway station, cash your cheque at

the bank, sweep the streets, slaughter cattle, carry bricks, engage in brick-laying, plumbing and plastering, and in many other trades and occupations that we regard as particularly fitted for men. They have their compensation; every woman has a vote, and a number of them have also seats in parliament.

Often women are described as doing 'men's jobs' better than the men: '[t]he booking-office clerks are often girls, and they attend to one's wants with a courtesy and grace that is not conspicuous in the young men,' writes Young. Finland was the first country in Europe to enfranchise women (1906) and to elect them to parliament (1907). British women noted all this with great satisfaction: Travers, packing her bags in England in 1908, announced, 'I'll go to the only civilised country in Europe, the one place where women have got their full rights.' 'Finnish women,' wrote Tweedie in 1913, 'are the most advanced in the world today.'

The political aspect of women's rights was an obvious manifestation, and is discussed by most of the British writers, male and female. They appreciated the way in which sexual equality was not just a campaigning issue, but was broadly taken for granted. 'Women's rights,' wrote Clive-Bayley, had never 'agitated my soul'; she merely noted '[t]here are women as well as men students . . . [t]hey attend lectures together, and are on a perfect footing of equality in every respect'. It was this naturalness and openness which she especially appreciated, and she noticed it more widely in Finnish society:

> There is one feature of Helsingfors life which strikes a foreigner as distinctly good, though curious. I heard of no cases of 'nerves,' or hysteria, or 'revolting daughters.' Parents have perhaps in some instances tried to keep their girls at home, but money is scarce, and occupation is plentiful, and every girl claims her right to make her

own way in the world. There are, it may be, some four or five unmarried ladies without a profession, but they are mostly engaged in charitable works. 'Ennui' apparently does not exist — possibly a reason for the non-appearance of the ills referred to above! There is no line drawn which makes it difficult for a lady of high birth to earn a living. You may bear a title, and yet be a governess, a bank-clerk, or a reporter. You may even be in a shop. You are just as much in society, if you belong to it by birth, as if you sat in your drawing-room all day, doing nothing.

Travers, who had been involved in the Women's Suffrage Movement in England, became closely interested in 'the growth and development of Feminism in Finland', meeting leaders of the Woman's Movement.

Political background; Russification

By the Treaty of Hamina (1809) Finland was ceded by Sweden to Russia; it was not incorporated, but became an autonomous Grand Duchy, keeping its former constitution and legal system, and retaining the Lutheran faith. Alexander I, shortly after, both confirmed and extended 'the framework of laws and institutions' inherited from Sweden. The development and decay of the relationship with Russia later in the century is reflected in British writings, but not, of course, systematically.

Finland had become a nation 'in a political sense', but, writes D. G. Kirby '[w]hether the Finnish people constituted a nation in 1809 is another matter'. As the century progressed, British travellers saw and noted different ways in which the country was progressing towards nationhood, particularly by becoming aware of Finnish as a national language.

Apart from the time of the Russian War, it was only late in the century that the British interest in Finland became political. The actual status granted by Tsar Alexander I in 1809 began to be questioned by Russia in the 1880s; Finland's 'connection with the Empire,' wrote Gallenga in 1882, 'already fraught with much trouble and vexation in the past, may be the cause of still greater danger to them in the future.' By 1890 Finland was being systematically reined in, with traditional rights (such as the separate Finnish postal service) removed. The appointment of General Bobrikov as Governor-General in 1898 and and the 'February Manifesto' delivered by Nicholas II in 1899 were clear indications of 'a new policy towards Finland', ending its autonomy, its independent legislature and its own armed forces. The Tsar refused to receive the Grand Address, with half a million Finnish signatures, or an International Address, collected by Finnish expatriates and signed by 'over 1000 distinguished supporters of the Finnish cause'. The situation was widely reported in British newspapers, notably by Dover Wilson, the Finland correspondent of the *Manchester Guardian*. Finland had many advocates in England, among them Nevinson, a campaigning journalist who actually took the Finnish cause to King Edward VII at Buckingham Palace. *The Finland Bulletin* came out regularly in London from 1900 to 1905, chronicling the steady erosion of Finland's rights. In 1911 the Anglo-Finnish Society 'came into being as one of the consequences of Finland's time of troubles'; there was not a British traveller in the new century who was unaware of Finland's political plight. The Russian bear, tamed in 1856, was roaring again. In 1903 Finnish resistance began to turn to violence, and in the following year Bobrikov was assassinated. Many of the Finnish rights were restored following violent uprisings in Russia in 1905, but repression was soon renewed by the new Russian prime minister, Stolypin.

These political difficulties had little or no effect on tourism, which was being promoted as never before. MacDougall was alone in even mentioning them in this context, dismissing as fanciful tourists' fears that 'they may there be pursued by secret police, or come in for the tail-end of a bomb intended for someone else!' The Finnish Tourist Association had issued its first brochure in English in 1894, trusting that it would be 'the means of bringing the Grand-Duchy of Finland as a tour-ist-resort to the notice of the Anglo Saxon Race'. *Finland – 'The Land of a Thousand Lakes'*, a booklet published in Hull in 1899, detailed 'in a practical way the facilities for Tourists wishing to spend their Summer Holidays in Finland'. These were followed by a succession of opulent travel books in the early years of the century.

It may come as a surprise to a modern reader of a book about foreign travel to find no complaints about being overcharged, taken for a ride, or swindled. Transport, public and private, was noted as costing a fraction of British rates, board and lodg-ing (except in Imatra) often derisively little, and all sorts of pro-duce – cigars, crayfish, knives – not only cheap but of excellent quality. Scott concluded a little advertising article in a Finland Line brochure in 1914: 'Living is cheap, and the hotels are not as a rule expensive. I fear, however, that in order to keep them so, we, who know the charms of Finland, ought to keep the secret to ourselves.'

While all this might suggest that Finland was becoming over-run by British tourists by the early twentieth century, the tour-ists themselves often record how they felt like rare visitants, and were regarded as objects of curiosity. They had to come to terms with the fact that they were at least as interesting to the Finns as the Finns were to them. Throughout her travels Tweedie felt that she was on display: near Lapinlahti the 'na-tives' all 'curtsied or took off their hats', while the visit of the English ladies was reported in the local papers in Savonlinna and in Oulu. The landlord of the post-house in Roveniemi, wrote Hyne 'regarded us much in the light of a travelling cir-cus, and brought us in relays of callers whenever we were on the premises.'

Rev. Robert Bateman Paul

On 28 July 1836 Robert Paul was returning from Moscow, where he had travelled as companion to the son of a friend, when he found himself 'beyond the frontier, and fairly in Finland, that comparatively unknown land, which has been traversed by so few of our countrymen'. Paul, a former Fellow of Exeter College, Oxford, and now a country clergyman, was already known for his books on Aristotle. *Journal of a Tour to Moscow in the Summer of 1836* is his only travel book.

Travelling in their own carriage, they discovered that 'what is called a horse's mouth, the little Finland nags do not possess in the slightest degree'; when Paul tried to pull their post horse back the reins snapped, and the small boy whom he had demoted to passenger because of his dangerous driving, saved the day by calling out to the horse. Realising that it could be managed 'only by uttering certain odd sounds', Paul started practising Finnish horse language as if he were a latter-day Gulliver, and soon achieved such proficiency that 'our driving was rather an amusement than otherwise'.

'I have never travelled in any country, where the foreigner has so little trouble, and is so little imposed upon,' he wrote; the police officer at Vyborg was 'a civil, well-behaved man', and so it continued. They passed Hamina, which 'looked dreary and desolate', and Loviisa and Porvoo, neither 'of much importance', before arriving in Helsinki. The only hitch on the way had been when their horses, driven by the proprietor of one post-house, had jibbed at the first hill:

The Finn, a little dry old man, with a face like an apple that has been withered by the frost, sat with the most provoking indifference, raising and lowering his little arm with the regular motion of an automaton, and sending out of his toothless jaws a sound 'half whistle and half hiss' which the horses treated with the most mortifying contempt.

Paul had to turn the horses himself to get back to the post-house, where they finally agreed to try a different pair.

They travelled, unclerically, on Sunday as they had a boat to catch from Turku; on the way they were pleased to see 'crowds of people going to and returning from church', but not everything was as commendable:

> We saw one or two disgraceful scenes of drunkenness, but as far as we had an opportunity of observing, the vice is less prevalent in Finland than in Russia. However a traveller who merely posts through a country, as we did through this, has no right to give a decided opinion about the moral condition of its inhabitants. I can only say that we *saw* very few drunken men, and were never cheated, as far as we could find out; I therefore think it probable that the Finns are generally more sober and more honest than the Russians.

They saw two lads mowing a field with a rather unusual scythe. One was

> shaving the grass as smooth and almost as short as a gentleman's lawn. How he avoided cutting off his legs, or at least two or three of his toes, I cannot understand, nor was I much inclined to convince myself by actual trial.

In the evening they 'came in sight of Turku':

> On the hills round the town are a number of windmills, which present a singular and not unpleasing appearance. On an eminence in the town stands the Cathedral, and on a rock towering above all the other buildings, is the Observatory, the most nothern in the world . . .

As we could not get beds at the Society house, the only inn in the town, we were lodged at a private house kept by an old lady and her two daughters, fine shewy girls, whom we found gaily dressed for the theatre. However they did not neglect their household duties, for the next morning I found the most lady-like of the two cleaning my boots, and her sister preparing breakfast for the family. They were all kind, simple creatures, and laughed with such hearty good-will at our abortive attempts to speak the language, that we could not resist joining in their mirth, and the house rang with barbarously pronounced Finnish words, and the shouts of merriment which succeeded every failure.

Their hosts' 'little Swedish valet' was sent to find out about their steamer:

he returned, and made the following announcement, with an air of great solemnity, 'Gentlemens, *the damp ship* sail tomorrow morning, at nine.' The craft to which he gave this unprepossessing title, was no other than the steam-packet, (called Damp-schiffe in German,) but the words were ominous; for a damp ship she proved on the voyage, pitching repeatedly bowsprit under, and sending aft a stream of water, some of which found its way into our berths during the night.

They enjoyed a 'very comfortable dinner' at the Society House, and after a good night's sleep arose early and viewed the cathedral, 'plain, but not inelegant'; the observatory, empty and neglected; and 'the University', which 'contains a handsome hall, ornamented with granite pillars and a good library'. The university had burnt with the rest of the city in 1827, so he must be describing Solennitetssalen in Gamla Akademihuset, which was repaired after the fire; the books would have belonged to the Cathedral see and the crown court.

The journey to Stockholm was uneventful. The Russian Consul shared 'some excellent Madeira wine' with them; at dinner they alone drank wine, while the other passengers began and ended the meal with 'snaps', and drank Gothenburg beer.

The Finnish people, Paul wrote 'are by far the most primitive of any that I ever travelled among':

> At some of the post houses it was very amusing to see a little crowd of peasants assemble round the carriage, gazing with wonder at the outlandish appearance of ourselves and our luggage. At one place, I remember, we gave a cigar to an old fellow, who was smoking his wooden pipe close to the carriages: he turned it round and round, and then handed it to each of his of companions, but each returned it with a shake of the head, and the old gentleman would probably either have thrown it away, or carried it home to deposit in his museum as a curious organic remain, had not one of the crowd, who was evidently a travelled man (having probably been as far as Helsingfors in his day) explained with a very complacent and patronizing air the nature of our present; and we left the old man smoking his cigar, and bowing his thanks to us as we drove off.

Thomas Denman Whatley

'Route XLII. – Abo to St. Petersburg' is the unpromising title of Thomas Whatley's account of travelling through southern Finland in the first edition of Murray's *Handbook*. He does indeed give the route, and much practical information, especially regarding the exact regulations governing posting and post horses, but in his descriptions he presents himself more as a daredevil driver than as a careful conductor. Leaving Turku, he and his companion decided to dispense with their driver, 'an urchin apparently ten years of age', and to drive themselves, taking alternate stages. Their sense of adventure was heightened by their having no map, and no way of communicating with the urchin. Their only aid was a piece of paper on which the waiter at their Turku hotel had listed the places which they ought to pass through, and which 'turned out to be almost entirely incorrect'.

They did not clear Turku until late afternoon, and within a few hours a fog came down 'so dense that I really could not see beyond the horses' heads':

> To our great relief, at Keala, the end of the third stage, having just come down a steep hill at a headlong pace, which anywhere but in the North would have made one shudder, and during the whole of which descent the Fin beside me whistled with the most unwearied perseverance, we stopped in front of a clean-looking house, built of trees laid horizontally on each other, and cemented with a mixture of mud and moss. A most good-natured looking man made his appearance, and on his being made to understand that we wished to stay all night, he seemed quite overjoyed, and proceeded forthwith to lock up our

carriage in a large barn, having previously introduced us into a comfortable warm room, where a very substantial supper soon made its appearance. Our attempts at conversation, though not altogether unsuccessful, were preeminently ludicrous. Our worthy host was a real native Fin; he spoke a little Swedish, a little less Russian, with about a dozen words of German, and two or three of English; we luckily found a stranger here who spoke French and Finnish, so that we made ourselves certain that all our directions about being awoke at dawn of day, &c. were understood. Our polyglot discourse was amusingly interrupted by a cuckoo clock . . .

Our beds were clean and comfortable, and the first object I beheld, on awakening, was the grinning face of our host, who, with a damsel of no very prepossessing exterior, had brought us coffee. The grey dawn of day was scarce yet visible for the fog, but our watches told us that it was near five, and with *Spartan virtue* we sprang up, and in less than half an hour we were once more careering wildly though the dense mist. We made a most unsuccessful attempt to procure some breakfast at Lambala about nine o'clock; the abortive effort ended in some intolerable coffee, and bread so hard that I really could not bite it; this hopeful stuff which rejoices in the name of *Knacken Bröd*, or (bread with holes in it) is like a large biscuit full of round holes, and of a very dark brown colour; it is only made once a year, which accounts tolerably well for its consistency.

At Nyby [Uusikylä, near Salo], 'in the midst of an almost boundless forest of fir', they had supper, washed down with 'port-wine, which I may observe for the encouragement of all future travellers in these lands is almost always very good, even at the common post-houses'. The following night, spent at Bolstad, was in contrast to Keala; 'no smiling host to welcome us, but a shoal of dirty, ill-looking, slovenly women'. Their next stop, the last before Helsinki, was at Grahn; they found it equally wretched.

None of the party were by any means remarkable for personal beauty, but the men were decidedly better made and better looking than the softer sex, if, indeed they deserved such an appellation.

Although they were completely soaked by the time they arrived in Helsinki, they were nonetheless required to renew their passports at the police office before they could go to their hotel. Sleeping officials and an impenetrable language barrier added to their discomfort. In Helsinki many of the modern sights were already in place: Whatley describes the Senate House, museum, new church, barracks, hospitals, botanical gardens, and observatory. He was full of admiration for Helsinki, reflecting that 'the rapidity with which it has increased, and become a handsome capital, is perfectly astonishing'.

For the next stage they decided not to drive themselves.

We now determined to trust ourselves to the skill of our new postillion, and certainly a more proper young imp I never beheld: about 12 years at the outside, and but a *shrimp* in size, without shoes or stockings, there was a fierceness in the wild flashing of that urchin's eyes that was quite startling, and his whole procedure was in accordance with his looks. He jerked the reins till the horses reared bolt upright, and then with a yell like a fiend, he started them off full gallop over the rough pavement to Henrisdals, taking us about 15 versts in an hour and a quarter. The night had closed upon us before we reached *Borgo*, where we merely stopped to change horses, being anxious to get on as far as possible this evening, as we were fully resolved that this should be the last night's *rest* or rather *unrest* we would take until we reached the

Russian capital. About eleven the rain had ceased, having previously made its way though every part of the covering of our frail carriage, and we determined to stay for the remainder of the night at the post-house at Illby, which we reached shortly before midnight. All was still as death, but by dint of a little noise we aroused the sleepers, who came out from all directions making a whirring noise, with which they stop their horses, more resembling the noise of a pheasant rising in a thick cover than any thing else to which I can compare it.

The door of the dwelling-house at length opened and out came a good humoured looking Fin, without shoes or stockings, evidently just awoke. I gave him to understand that we wished to stay till morning, to which he replied that we were welcome; and having put our carriage partially under cover he led the way into his house. Here we found the bed he himself had just quitted together with two others, the tenants of which made their escape on our appearance before we had time to speculate either on their age, sex, or character. Our new host set to work most vigorously, carrying away the bedding, and speedily producing new, so that we were soon installed in the nests of these worthy Fins. The man looking as contented and good humoured as if nothing unusual had occurred; in fact they are the most imperturbable people I ever beheld: young and old seem alike, schooled to the same unchanging indifference.

The boy who drove them on from Lovisa was 'one of the smallest specimens of a driver it has ever been my lot to behold', but was 'as steady a coachman as I ever sat behind'. Nonetheless, Whatley reflected that '[n]ervous people have certainly no business to travel in Finland'.

As they approached the Russian frontier 'not only did the traces of cultivation become more scarce, but the population appeared to progress gradually in dirt and ugliness'. Hamina they found heavily fortified, but deserted; 'no sentinel on duty at the gates – the very guard-house was shut up and falling fast to decay'. After 'soup, fish, beefsteaks, and pancakes, not to mention some very good port-wine', they set off in the rain. 'A more miserable evening and night I never travelled in,' he concludes, but the following morning 'arose gloriously' to welcome them to Vyborg.

Elizabeth Rigby (Lady Eastlake)

Elizabeth Rigby was better known in nineteenth-century England than most other British travellers to Finland. The daughter of a physician, she spent more than two years in Heidelberg in the late 1820s. In 1838, after a stay in St Petersburg, she went on a long visit to a married sister in Tallinn, and her extensive travels during the spring and summer of 1839 included an excursion across the Baltic to 'Helsingforst', as she called it. When she returned to England in 1841 her letters, published as *A Residence on the Shores of the Baltic*, proved very popular, and launched her on a writing career, principally in the *Quarterly Review*. In 1849 she married Sir Charles Eastlake, an eminent art historian and collector, the first Keeper of the National Gallery in London, and President of the Royal Academy. As Lady Eastlake she collaborated with him, and after his death in 1865 continued her own writing on art, politics and literature for nearly thirty years.

She became part of 'an intellectual aristocracy of reputable artists, writers and influential figures'; 'one of the articulate and well-connected women in the Victorian art world', writes Julia Sheldon, she 'impinged upon the consciousness of most artists and writers in London society in one way or another'. She gives a dramatic illustration: 'On his deathbed in 1851 the painter J. M. W. Turner was reported to have said "I saw Lady Eastlake".' She has her own place in this history as a travel writer herself, but also for her important article on 'Lady Travellers'.

Her description of a shopping and smuggling expedition by steamer from Tallinn is a new departure in Baltic travel writing. As Barrow had claimed so enthusiastically a few years earlier, travel had now 'become a matter of so much ease' that it was no longer the preserve of adventurous males.

The population of Tallinn in summer was 'swelled with hundreds of bathing guests – chiefly Petersburgians'. An excursion by steamer was part of the summer entertainment of this fashionable resort:

> The reigning topics in the beau monde, after the Empress's illness and the Grand Duchess's marriage, were the *Lust Fahrte* or pleasure-trips to Helsingforst – a city which, although merely a six hours' voyage across the gulf, has been only recently discovered by the Estonians. Two years back a few individuals ventured across, and, being entertained with great kindness by the Finlanders, returned with such panegyrical accounts of the charms of Helsingforst, that multitudes followed their example, and the hospitality of the inhabitants has been put to a severe test. These trips, which take place about once a fortnight, have proved a very successful speculation to the projectors, but a particularly sore subject to the shopkeepers of Reval [Tallinn], who, after paying high duty for their goods, are deserted by their customers for the better and cheaper wares of duty-free Finland. Hence it is that the Russian custom-house here out-Russians itself in every vexatious and annoying precaution for counteracting this evil, and, were the explorers of the new region only men, there could be little doubt of their perfect success, but woman's wit has baffled greater tyrants than they. If it be sweet to drive a bargain, how much more so to smuggle it through seeming impossibilities! – consequently the shopkeepers at home find no greater demand than before these extra regulations were enforced.

The travellers' luggage was inspected and catalogued by the custom-house before they left, and they were charged duty on their return on all items not on the inventory. The list extended to umbrellas, 'an item of great attraction at Helsingforst'. It is amusing to reflect that a century and a half later, such excursions take place in the opposite direction, with shopping cruises from Helsinki to Tallinn, although umbrellas do not feature on the shopping lists of most Finns nowadays.

Rigby's party were the only British passengers among this 'mixture of northern nations and dialects'.

Helsingforst is approached through islands of rocks, some of them only tenanted by fishermen, others massively fortified – especially that called Sweaborg, which is the Cronstadt of this Finnish capital. Nor does the likeness end here, for the town itself, clean and handsomely built, recalls Petersburg upon the first aspect. Tremendous thunder-clouds were gathering over the rocky landscape, and we hurried to the *Societäts Haus*, the only hotel in the town, and a magnificent building, where most of the hundred and eighty found accommodation. Here we were no sooner housed than thunder and lightning burst over the town, but were little heeded in the welcome rattle of knives and forks. The storm subsided into a regular rain, but shopping was not to be neglected – what else did all these good ladies come for? – so we sallied out, buying new umbrellas and Indian-rubber caloshes [*sic*] as we moved along, and laughing at the immediate service these new acquisitions had to perform. And all having much the same errands, and much the same curiosity, we moved from shop to shop, though the streaming and deserted streets, a party of at least thirty, to the great astonishment of the townsfolks. Goods were cheap, but of no great choice; and we could not but admire the military precision of one of these wifeless husbands. Whilst others were debating what first to look at, he came, saw, and chose; – but, unfortunately for his doctrine of promptitude, and more especially for his wife's feelings, they were invariably ugly things.

That evening the theatre advertised a piece in honour of one of our passengers, the lady of a distinguished personage, but we preferred a ball, where we were initiated into the mysteries of a *Suedoise*, a dance with no recommendation but the time it leaves you to improve your partner's acquaintance. The countenances around us were highly uninteresting – light hair and fair complexions plentiful.

On the Sunday the shops were officially shut, but 'had back doors to them, and those wide open', but the English party nonetheless went sightseeing:

We . . . betook ourselves to the rocks, mounting from one sloping mass to another, till Helsingforst, with its numerous islets, lay beneath us, and from innumerable pits in the rocks glanced pools of clear water from the recent rains; while this Northern Adriatic mirrored a sky full and blue as that of a southern clime. Far as the eye could see, no food for man was visible – no corn-field, grass, or verdure of any kind, except that of the dark pine. Weaving and sail-making are the chief occupations and means of traffic of the Finlanders, and their corn they fetch from our fertile Estonian home. Helsingforst has not a population of more than ten thousand, and bears no remains of any former splendour; its oldest houses being shabby erections of wood, which contrast most disadvantageously with those of stone which have started up since its final cession to Russia at the peace of Friedericksham, in 1809 . . .

Our steps soon led us to the Observatory, a building of recent erection, and vying with that of Dorpat in beauty of apparatus; on the hills opposite to which, and upon about the same level, stands a magnificent church, most appropriately surmounting the town, and, like the Isaac's church in Petersburg, still behung with forests of scaffolding. The university and senate's house are also fine modern buildings, and the Botanic Garden, a little rich plot of ground veneered into the grey rocks, bears witness to the existence of flowers, which otherwise these rock-born natives might have deemed mere fabulous treasures.

Dinner was 'a meal of great merriment – above a hundred, including many officers from the garrison, sat down to the sociable table d'hôte'.

After dinner, unappalled by an inky sky, we hired, at a rouble each, a little miniature steam-boat, with a machine scarce bigger than a tea-kettle, which whizzed and fumed us about at the will of two Swedish lads, and landed us at Sveaborg. This island is about five acres in extent, loaded with crown buildings and a population of military, and sacred to the memory of Field Marshal Count Ehrensward, whose monument stands here. Thence we steered for the *Scheeren*, literally the Scissars, a beautiful chasm of sea, between meeting and retreating islands, where trees with *leaves* grow by the water's edge; and where the Helsingforstians in their holiday expeditions land and bear off a leaf with as keen a pleasure as we should the choicest bouquet. But 'pleasure suits itself to all, – the rich can but be pleased.' The rain fell occasionally in torrents around us; but our little puffing bark seemed to bear a charm, or, as a ready Russian officer of the party observed, '*pas un, mais plusieurs*;' and we passed dry on, while some delicious voices on board gave us alternately German and Russian melodies.

Finally, Rigby describes the hilarious lengths to which the ladies went to conceal their contraband goods when they returned to Tallinn; some of the thinner passengers appeared to have doubled in size while in Helsinki! Already the priorities for travellers seem here closer to the twentieth than to the nineteenth century; this chapter surely has a place in the History of Shopping.

George Francklin Atkinson

Atkinson was neither the first nor last of these writers to have travelled in India as well as in Finland; 'Bengal Engineers' is appended to his name on the title-page of *Pictures from the North in Pen and Pencil. Sketched during a Summer Ramble*, published in 1848. The reasons for his change of direction are unexceptionable:

> Returning from the East to a more temperate clime, in search of health, and anxious to visit a portion of Europe comparatively little trodden, I was induced to direct my steps to the North.
>
> The following sketches, and drawn hastily, to render more graphic the account of those scenes they attempt to describe.

Atkinson writes that his descriptions 'are gathered from private letters, penned on the spot for friends at home'; these friends must have possessed extravagant literary taste: of the scores of books in English about Finland that I have read, his has the purplest prose and most extravagant diction, further embellished with frequent quotations from Shakespeare, Milton and Cowper. The pencil sketches, by contrast, are lively and informal.

Atkinson sailed from Ramsgate, and followed the route described in Murray's *Handbook*: via Hamburg to Lübeck, a city which evokes not so much a description as a lamentation, with Biblical echoes: 'Lubeck, charitable Lubeck, so renowned in days of yore: what a falling off is here!' The steamer for St Petersburg left in fact from Travemunde, 'the Ramsgate of Lubeck'. He enjoyed 'a delightfully smooth and agreeable passage' and 'the table was excellent'. Just outside St Petersburg they passed the island of Cronstadt, and upon it and some smaller neighbouring islands which cluster around it, formidable batteries have been erected, one casemated one of three stories shows a triple tier of heavy guns, others are in course of construction, and every possible means of rendering the passage up the river of a hostile fleet impracticable.

It would be only a few years before the British Fleet surveyed Cronstadt and decided that it was, indeed, impregnable.

Most of Atkinson's book describes St Petersburg, where he met aristocrats and royalty, admired the architecture, and was interested and involved in all that he experienced. It is disappointing that he did not devote the same attention to Finland. Instead of the Great Coastal Road, travellers could now enjoy the comfort of a steamer from Cronstadt, stopping off at Tallinn, Helsinki and Turku. As a result, Atkinson's description occupies only one chapter, but it certainly makes up in redundancies of fine writing what it lacks in substance:

> The sea is rippleless, and the small engine works away manfully, gallantly propelling the 'Admiral,' whose name the vessel bears. We have a motley assemblage of travellers; Swedes, Russians, Poles, Finns and Germans in profusion. Our gubernator is an Anglo Finn, born under the Russian flag, and brought up in the English merchant service. He has quite the air of a British sailor, bluff and jolly, a perfect ambulatory refreshment, with a store of anecdotes which he dispenses freely. His risible faculties are most excitable, and a joke sends the 'pearly tears' coursing over his globular cheeks now so resplendent with vermillion, that we momentarily anticipate a fit. He still delights in preserving the custom of his infantine days, by habitually adopting the pinafore when in the exercise of his mandibular energies at the mahogany, as we observe at times similarly performed at continental *table d'hotes,* by the insertion

of the napkin under the chin, supported by the neckcloth, from an exemplary regard to the safety of the habiliments from oleaginous droppings.

The Russian War is further anticipated when the 'Admiral' passes though two divisions of the Russian Baltic Fleet, which Atkinson describes both knowledgeably and disparagingly, adding a surprisingly astute prediction:

Let Russia do her utmost she will never possess a navy formidable but in numbers. A war singly either with England or France would do her immeasurable injury, for her every ship would be soon swept from the seas. She has nothing to fall back upon, either as regards ships or sailors, having no merchant navy, and Finland cannot supply her with a sufficiency, and Constantinople which she has an eye to, without a navy she will never capture by force. More particularly then is it her wisest policy to remain our staunchest ally.

Atkinson introduces Helsinki with a particularly limp compliment: 'a clean-looking town, and famed for its bathing advantages, a sort of Russian Worthing'. His group explored the city as tourists, and visited a small theatre, where they displayed their high spirits by giving an impromptu performance of a scene from *Macbeth* – 'much to our own satisfaction and the astonishment of the attendant janitrix, who evidently considers us to be suitable characters for a temporary residence in Finnish Bedlam'.'

The boat from Tallinn had been full of 'gay deceivers' travelling half-price to Helsinki for the pleasures of a ball; Atkinson and company decided to join them at, presumably, the Society House:

Evening draws on, so we dress and make our way to the Assembly Room, where we find the lovers of the dance footing it away with infinite glee. The same furious waltz as in St. Petersburgh, and the sober methodical quadrille are being performed. As foreigners and Englishmen, we proportionably attract attention, for this track is little beaten by travellers. We are welcomed cordially and urged to dance, but for the present we decline, that we may watch proceedings. There is a very fair sprinkling of beauty, and from the specimens exhibited, Ancient Muscovy must yield the palm to its new relative, Finland.

The voyage along the coast to Turku the next day brings out the best in Atkinson's descriptive writing. Genuinely attracted by the scenes before him, he for once writes in plain English:

The voyage from Helsingfors to Abo is one of the prettiest things conceivable. We pass through an archipelago of islands deliciously green, and rich in wild flowers and plants. Now we pass through a narrow creek, where overhanging boughs brush the sides of the vessel; now entering an extensive lake, the distant foliage sweetly blue; now steaming along as if on a river, with occasional openings, displaying pretty landscapes; and then on to wilder spots—rocks noble in their barrenness, the dark blue waters rippling on their stony sides, whilst over and beyond the lofty mast and snow-white sail of the native boat glides by majestically, recalling to mind –

'The slow canal, the yellow-blossomed vale,
The willow-tufted bank, the gliding sail.'

We are lolling on the paddle-boxes, the morning is fragrant and cool after yesterday's storm, and we revel in the delightful prospect, the ever varying change of form and colour, the rich brown rocks, the luxuriantly green trees fading into purple, the bright blue sky above, the dark blue water beneath, the spray dashing from the bows and glittering in the sun with rainbow hues, all charming to the eye and gratifying to the senses; and of the many pretty scenes we have witnessed, few have pleased us more than this lovely trip through the islands of the Swedish [*sic*] Archipelago.

Atkinson's account fills out our knowledge of the burgeoning steamer activity on the Baltic. It is clear that the Stockholm boat did not have either the comforts or the cuisine enjoyed on the journey from Travemünde; he was anticipating a proper meal in Turku, but it was not to be – nor did he find any consolation in Finnish billiards:

The streets are regular, but the highways would afford pasturage to herds and flocks, the weeds are so luxuriant. A stray cariole enlivens the dreary spot at times. But there is an extensive *société,* to which we are attracted in hopes of discovering therein some more relishing edibles than we have at our manducatory disposal in the steamer. The *salle à manger* we find chequered with tables, where famished individuals are busily engaged, absorbing with astonishing rapidity savoury concoctions of original appearance, the obsequious 'Kelner' displays a document, which imparts the refreshing knowledge that matter for refection is obtainable in endless variety from the cuisinal laboratory.

The Finnish has been liberally and literally rendered into the English tongue for our edification, and we have the choice of ox-steak, calf-steak, calf-cutlet, swine-steak, sheep's-leg, and so on, reminding us of some of the Parisian *restaurants*, where the liqueur "*Chinois à Veaucle vie,*" is translated 'a Chinese in brandy.' Our lot falls upon calf-cutlet, and an unctuous conglomeration appears, redolent of garlick, and smothered in fennel and other species of the grass kind. Our *entremêt* is a *cock-de-bois*, which we innocently imagine might be cock of wood, alias woodcock, but the '*rara avis*' proves to be a species of capon, old as Methuselah, with a parchment hide, and must have lived at the period of the great fire and then and there been roasted. A supply of Finnish beer, a sort of attenuated rhubarb and magnesia tends to gravitate the solidities, but it is funny stuff, and our paymaster disburses the few farthings necessary in liquidation of expenses, and we adjourn to the billiard-room. The Finnish game appears simple; it is similar to trundling twenty-four-pounder-shot into carpet-bags, over a common; the balls prodigious, the pockets yawning caverns, the cloth undulating, like the Brighton Downs, and each cue about as much in a right line as the hind leg of a Covent Garden fruiterer's donkey, spurning tops. It is a difficulty to keep the globes from racing into the craters. We have tried our skill, but not wishing to be smoke-dried, we will leave the meerschaums and the Finns to their devices and enjoy the fragrant air of a lovely evening in its stead.

Travellers had intermittently recorded the overpowering effects of Finnish pipe smoke from the time of Joseph Marshall, in the mid-eighteenth century.

They slept on the boat, and next morning continued their journey: 'The steam is up, the small boy vociferates "all right," with a genuine guttural *r*, and we bear away for Stockholm.'

S. S. Hill

One of the first of the professional travellers who were systematically adding new countries to their portfolio, Hill had
already published books about Peru and Mexico, Egypt and
Syria, and the Sandwich and Society Islands. His *Travels on the
Shores of the Baltic* describes a journey begun in 1847, but it
was not published until 1854 when the outbreak of the Russian
War made Baltic news topical.

Hill disclaims any ambition '[t]o convey anything more than
the impressions of a summer tourist', but in the chapter devoted
to Finland even this modest aim is rarely achieved. Reading the
dull slabs of Hill's prose ('The hills of Finland are not of any
considerable elevation . . .') prompts some belated condonation
of Atkinson's verbal excesses. Hill gives informative accounts
of Denmark, Sweden and Russia, but Finland, as so often, gets
squeezed out. In Turku he booked in at 'the best hotel that the
place afforded', and presumably his hotel in Helsinki was of a
comparable standard. In each town he had a day or more to
explore.

Hill does not in this volume display many of the skills now
expected of a travel writer, but puts together whatever information he is able to pick up: the Åland islands

> are said . . . to have a scanty native population of foreign
> origin, who cultivate rye, but live chiefly on fish. They ap-
> pear to have pasture for only a few head of cattle; but our
> captain, who was a Finn, informed us that in their stunted
> and spare fir forest were found abundance of wild boars.

He certainly appreciates the scenery, but does not waste any
words on it: 'I do not know a short passage that might exhibit

scenery of more interest, than that between Sweden and Finland.'

His impressions of Turku, like those of several other travellers of this era, are mainly melancholy ones of departed glory (in 'the ancient senate-house' 'all . . . was gloom and desolation'). He was struck by at least one feature not elsewhere remarked on: 'the gay colouring of the buildings, the walls of which are painted white or straw colour, and the roofs light green, which appears to be a mode purely Russian'. Otherwise his observations are routine and perfunctory:

> The streets of the town are broad and tolerably uniform, but they exhibit little to arrest the attention of the stranger; we therefore proceeded to the inspection of such of the public edifices as attracted our notice.

Hill's final words on Turku are well in tune with the mood of change and decay:

> The once fair town was at the same time seen beneath us, harmonising in her decay with the desert wastes around. And, as we stood gazing from the windows of the deserted Observatory, we perceived the ill-omened birds, the eagle and the kite, both floating in circles over the tenantless buildings of the half-deserted city, as if it were already her funeral hour.

Helsinki evokes a very different mood, one of light, colour and life:

> On the morning after landing, we set out at an early hour to make a little survey of the town. This new seat of the provincial government of Finland, presents a remarkable instance of energy and progress. Thirty years ago it was a mere fishing village; but on account of the advantages of its position, it was chosen for the seat of the government of the province; and, already, it possesses all

the public buildings and institutions which usually characterise and embellish the capital of a great province.

On the last stage of the voyage, after Tallinn,

we passed the spot where the naval action between the Swedes and the Russians was fought in the year 1789 or 1790. It was marked upon a chart which was spread for the passengers' inspection, by a cross. Our captain was a Finn, whose ancestors were at the time of this battle common subjects with the Swedes; and, although he had hitherto appeared to us sufficiently phlegmatic by nature or habit, now, as we passed the site of this memorable triumph of his country, he seemed to be seized with all the generous enthusiasm of national sentiment in the stirring times of war: and, as we glided peacefully over the waters which once bore the contending fleets, he pointed out to us, upon the sea, the exact spot, as he believed, where the ships floated at the time of the action, with as much rapture as if he saw before him the phantoms of the hostile vessels still engaging.

Despite his rather inert travelling habits, Hill had somehow formed very positive impressions of the Finnish people, in addition to his recognition, already mentioned, of 'the genius of the Finns for music and poetry'. He concludes, rather pompously, that 'they have attained a degree of civilisation beyond that usually found in countries so disadvantageously situated for improvement and progress'.

Selina Bunbury

Hill was a travel writer, Bunbury a miscellaneous author who published nearly a hundred books, comprising historical novels, autobiography, and evangelical tracts, as well as travel. She sometimes turned her diaries into novels rather than into travel books; *Evelyn, or A Journey from Stockholm to Paris* (1849) is one example.

Born in Ireland, she had a recurrent interest in Sweden, and certainly knew Swedish. Her *Life in Sweden* (1853) is a very readable travel book, describing her involvement with fellow travellers, hotel staff, and various hosts and hostesses. She published two books with substantial Finnish episodes, describing visits shortly before and then immediately after the Russian War. Bunbury seems to live a great deal in the past, and her most distinctive writing is in the romantic mode.

A Summer in Northern Europe records a journey made in 1853, but was not published unitl 1856; her impressions of Åland are therefore coloured by her knowledge that its peacefulness was about to be destroyed:

> A supreme stillness reigns over a vast unanimated space; even in summer time, no living sound is heard save the flapping wing of a heavy water bird, or its melancholy cry; and in winter when the air is more still, when no water gurgles, no wave murmurs, . . . – it is a silence that may be felt.
>
> How little did I think as I pencilled down such thoughts while passing to the Gulf of Finland that silence such as I described was soon to be broken by the roar of British guns.

Bunbury's romantic picture of the enchantments of the north seems to have roots deep in her past; her childhood dream of Uppsala university and cathedral got a rude shattering when she actually saw them, and the same experience was in wait for her in Turku:

> 'There is Åbo!' and we jump to our feet for a first sight.
>
> There is the old castle on the hill, and the building now called the Observatory, and a little village of my favourite red wooden houses. All is quite Swedish.
>
> It is strange that coming here should at once seem to place me back in my very childhood. 'Åbo, in Finland, where there is a University,' were the first words passed through my mind, as I saw the view before us. They were the words of the geography, and wonderfully curious had been the notions I had formed of Åbo, where there was a University.
>
> . . . at the moment of approaching Åbo, my childish notions concerning it were uppermost in my mind. A place of deep learning, full of professors dressed in furs, and with skins as dry, hard, and brown as the covers of their old volumes; a place buried both in snow and learning, where, as there was but very little sun-light, I conjectured the old astronomers might be studying the heavens both day and night, and where the people were always praying or chanting in a great grand cathedral.

The reality was a sad disappointment: 'Åbo is a fallen place. Its university is gone, its observatory idle; the wide streets are very silent.' Her imagination found consolation only in contemplating the 'wild romance' of the story of Gustavus Vasa.

The sea passage to Helsinki provided further consolation, 'full of charm to an imaginative mind and fancy', and the city itself was an attractive contrast: 'Helsingfors is quite another place from Åbo: one is the young wife, the other the antiquated dowager.' Yet here too Bunbury turned to her imagination, as she romanticised the city scenes, picturing them in winter:

> Here are Russians, Finns, Swedes, a sprinkling of English, Scotch, and perhaps Irish, all as merry as possible. The fine military uniforms, and the furry dress of the Finn peasant, the handsome sledge, with its decorated horses and tingling bells, and the sledge of burthen; the brisk little Finn horses and the quick galloping Russian. And then at evening there are the lights glancing, twinkling, and flashing along as the covered sledges glide off with lightly-dressed ladies to the balls.

Bunbury's whimsical vein was not exhausted by this vision; her imagined picture of the 'real Finns' is imagination bordering on the ludicrous:

> Nests of lakes and immense fir forests cover the districts where the real Finns are found; a hardy and wild race, despising the comforts and in profound ignorance of the business of civilised life, their character seems to correspond with that of the nature around them. They take in their country the position that the natives or aborigines of a subjugated country generally do, and have borne the imputation of all the crime or misdeeds that have been committed throughout the length of the land.

These comments reveal Bunbury's limitations, and clearly belong to someone who had kept upper-class Swedish-speaking company in Finland.

From Helsinki she went by boat via Hamina to Vyborg, returning by carriage after a stay of only two hours. It is revealing that she was conversant with *Travelling Sketches* from fifty years earlier by the artist Sir Robert Ker Porter, like her a romantic fantasist; she was reminded of him as she travelled, as he had, on the Coastal Road east from Vyborg:

The description and sentiments of that most pleasing writer, Sir H. K. [*sic*] Porter, who used to please me in happy childhood, here recurred to my memory. How little did I then think that I should be, not only in the same scenes, but should see them under somewhat similar circumstances. He travelled this way just before Russia invaded Finland, and when a war between Russia and England was pending.

Like Porter she sensed the calm before the storm – 'little did I think that so soon Finland was to have her coasts battered by British ships of war'. This was not the only affinity; part of her quotation from Porter shows perhaps why he and not Murray was her chosen reading: 'It is the theatre in which a romance writer would place his supernatural visitants.'

Bunbury does, at times, profit from her imagination; the following account of a Finnish forest has no parallel in English writing about Finland:

> Here is a great forest I want to explore, and there is a nest of lakes I want to get to, and through the driving mist I can only dimly see fir, and lake, and granite rocks, and great boulders here and there – and say to myself this is Finland.
>
> There is a strange peculiarity in these immense forests which is not without charm to me. Dreary as it undoubtedly is to travel on a straight line of road, through one for a vast number of miles when all view at either side is precluded, there are in many of them scenes that produce a strong effect on the imagination.
>
> The solemn silence may be for hours unbroken by the slightest sound. It happened once that by the upsetting of a carriage, I was left alone in one until the driver had ridden back to procure another, and during that time my only fear was that the silence to which I *listened* should be broken; the fall of a leaf would have terrified me.

Strange sights meet one in such places where nature reigns in the gloomiest and most solitary aspect; the solemn firs, indeed, scarcely seem to own that reign, but rather to exist in despite of it.

She seems here to anticipate the mood of Sibelius, especially of the quatrain which he supplied to his publisher to clarify the meaning of *Tapiola*:

> Widespread they stand, the Northland's dusky forests,
> Ancient, mysterious, brooding savage dreams;
> Within them dwells the Forest's mighty God,
> And wood-sprites in the gloom weave magic secrets.

THE RUSSIAN WAR

When Matthew Kirk was appointed as British Ambassador to Finland in 2002, he was told by a friend that he would soon be busy with the Crimean War anniversary. When Kirk diplomatically pointed out that Finland was a thousand miles north of the Crimea he was told that, notwithstanding, 'it is in what is now Finland that the Crimean War was won'.

The complex causes of the Crimean War went back many decades, and have no place in this present study, but it is worth noting that what is now called the Crimean War was at the time known in Britain as the Russian War. When war was declared on Russia on 28 March 1854, the British fleet was already on the way north; the Baltic campaign was neither an afterthought nor a sideshow. In the course of two summers the war brought large numbers of British sailors and marines to Finland. Some of them did not return; they are buried in cemeteries as far apart as Kokkola, Åland and Helsinki.

The Baltic became a theatre of war for three main reasons: to keep the Russian Baltic fleet out of action, either by destroying it or by blockading it in port; to damage Russia's trade by destroying ships and obstructing routes; and to force Russia to divide its military forces between two fronts, thus weakening its strength in the Crimea. Perhaps as many as 30,000 men were diverted from the Crimea. There was another motive: Lord Palmerston was a member of the Cabinet, having been War Secretary and Foreign Secretary earlier in his career, and had his own agenda. 'In a memorandum to the cabinet,' writes Orlando Figes, 'he outlined an ambitious plan for the dismemberment of the Russian Empire and the redrawing of the European map: Finland and the Åland Islands would be transferred

53

from Russia to Sweden . . .' He interpreted Russia's annexation of Finland in 1809 as part of its larger plan to secure the Baltic and move its sphere of influence, if not its territory, westwards. The war was an opportunity to reverse this.

The Baltic dimension of the Crimean War is little known now in Britain. It lacks the glamour with which the contemporary events in the Crimea have been embellished: no fall of Sebastapol, no Charge of the Light Brigade, and, of course, no Florence Nightingale. Yet in 1854 and 1855 the names of Bomarsund and Sveaborg, as well as of Cronstadt, were made subjects of popular patriotic concern, and events in Finland were debated, perhaps for the first time, in Parliament at Westminster. The Baltic campaign marked an important chapter in the history of the British Navy; the fleet which set off on 10 March after being reviewed by Queen Victoria off Spithead was witnessed by a huge crowd. The *Illustrated London News* described it as 'the noblest fleet that ever left the shores of this country', and the scene at Spithead as 'magnificent beyond description – almost beyond conception'. It was 'the most advanced fleet in the world'. Naval historians give a rather different picture – of the unsuitability of deep-draft steamers among the Baltic islands and shallows, crewed, in Ponting's words, by 'a motley collection of volunteers and reservists drafted unwillingly'. Napier was appointed commander, principally because of his seniority – he was sixty-eight. He was known to be 'ambitious, arrogant and conceited', was a heavy drinker, and had 'long shown signs of instability'. His reputation as the Nelson of his day had been achieved during the age of sail, but he was now commanding a fleet of steamboats. Both his personality and his strategies loom large in all accounts of the 1854 campaign.

For once Britain was allied with France, its traditional enemy; the Baltic campaign was a joint Anglo-French expedition. For Finland, too, the war marked a new epoch. As Marjatta Bell has observed, 'Finnish history is riddled with wars, but attacks from the sea had been rare, and attacks from the west almost unheard of'. For the inhabitants of Finland it was both a novel and a frightening experience.

No war had ever been so fully or so immediately reported, with British press correspondents accompanying the fleet. Steamships could be in the Baltic in three days, and aided also by the electric telegraph, the War Office could monitor events quite closely. The *Illustrated London News*, making extensive use of war artists, gave the nineteenth-century equivalent of television coverage; although the time lag was often two weeks, the illustrations made events seem more immediate. Naturally, as with all serials, the readers wanted some action in every episode.

A brief outline of the war gives a necessary background to the first-person accounts which follow.

1854

The British Fleet, after remaining some time off Gotland, arrived in the Åland islands to await the arrival of the French. Since the archipelago 'could not be safely navigated without a native pilot' and Sweden declined to provide help any of any sort, Sulivan, the Fleet's hydrographer, set to work surveying. The size of the ships made the narrow passages between the islands of the archipelago particularly dangerous. While he was thus engaged, a detachment of the fleet sailed east for a preliminary survey of the Helsinki and St Petersburg defences, and another went north under Admiral Plumridge (who had already destroyed farmers' vessels in Åland) to comb ports in Ostrobothnia for war material; this series of raids gave several towns on the Finnish west coast their first significant experience of the British.

Meanwhile, the first raid was at Ekenäs (Tammisaari), on the south coast, on 20 May, led by Captain Yelverton. Two British steamships, *Arrogant* and *Hecla*, with local fishermen acting as pilots, navigated through the dense archipelago towards the

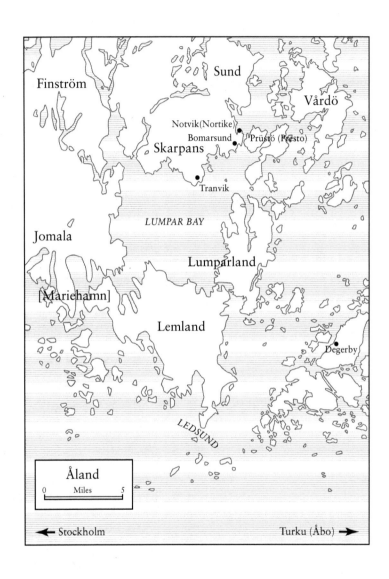

Finström

Sund

Vårdö

Notvik(Nortike)
Bomarsund   Prüstö (Prästö)
Skarpans

Tranvik

LUMPAR BAY

Jomala

Lumparland

[Mariehamn]

Lemland

Degerby

Åland

0   Miles   5

← Stockholm   Turku (Åbo) →

LEDSUND

town, but found unexpectedly heavy cannon fire from defensive batteries on Vitsand, north of Hanko. A party of marines managed to land, and captured a Russian cannon as a trophy (it was later presented to Queen Victoria, and put on display at Osborne). The British suffered three fatalities, one of whom had been shot and lost overboard, but was found by 'local fishermen, who buried him in an unmarked grave on the island of Kalvenholmen.' A Finnish barque, *Augusta,* loaded with a cargo of salt, was boldly taken from its moorings, much to the astonishment of the local inhabitants, and was taken back to Sheerness and sold. Sulivan quotes Yelverton's version of events:

> Ekness [Ekenäs] was at his mercy, and they saw women and children flying from it and collecting outside, many well-dressed ladies among them, and the people removing their things. I said I wished he had sent a flag-of-truce in to say they had nothing to fear, as we should not fire at a defenceless town; and he wishes he had done something of the kind.

Meanwhile, in the Gulf of Bothnia, Plumridge promulgated his intentions in a Notice, distributed ahead of the landing at Oulu, and possibly at other towns.

Notice

The English Admiral will not molest or injure private persons or their property.

He only intends to destroy the castles and Defences, shipping and Property of the Emperor of Russia.

So long as the Inhabitants continue peaceably within their houses, they will be protected, but should they offer assistance to the Russian Troops, they will be treated as ennemies.

The English Admiral desires that Women and Children should be sent out of the Town.

Hanway Plumridge
Rear Admiral

H.B.M.S.
Leopard at Uleåborg
the 1 June 1854

Plumridge was held responsible for these raids, though it seems that it was was his subordinates who exceeded their brief; he was harshly criticised, both in Finland and in England, for his destructive tactics, and was nicknamed in Finland 'Brandamiralen' and 'amiral Plundering' (Fire Admiral and Admiral Pillager). An Englishwoman living in St Petersburg wrote that mothers would frighten their children by saying that 'the English admiral was coming'.

The first Bothnian raid was on Raahe on 30 May, led by Captain Gifford, whose own words, 'to take, burn or destroy', have often been used to describe the British tactics. His journal, writes Greenhill, 'becomes almost a gleeful catalogue of the wanton destruction of property, ships, timber and pine tar, and the buildings in which the stores were kept'. News of this first attack got back to England quickly, and led to public outrage and questions in Parliament.

The British moved north to Oulu, where, forewarned, the residents had taken steps to protect their shipping. Gifford 'threatened a deputation under a flag of truce that he would bombard the church if he was met with any resistance'. Gifford wrote: 'the Russians had scuttled all the shipping afloat, but our men burnt them as well as a number of buildings'. With large stores of timber, spars, tar and pitch, estimated as worth half a million, '[t]he fire . . . could be seen for many miles around.' The firing was indiscriminate, and only a fortuitous change of wind saved the whole town from destruction. The only British fatality was a seaman, Thomas Dennis, who had found some vodka in a storehouse; his charred remains were discovered later by a search party.

The publicity given to these raids led to other towns, such as Jakobstad and Kristiinakaupunki, also taking evasive action, by hiding or scuttling ships, while in Tornio threatened material was shifted over the Swedish border. Meanwhile, Kokkola was preparing a more proactive welcome. The British officers (under the flag of truce) were denied entry; one of the nine gunboats subsequently sent to attack the town was fired on, and ran aground when retreating (it is still in Kokkola, and can be seen there in the 'English Park'). The British withdrew within the hour; there were seventeen dead, many wounded, and eleven prisoners taken. Nine of the dead were taken ashore and buried in the Maria cemetery, and the others were, presumably, buried at sea. This 'ill-starred expedition', as Napier called it, brought the campaign of destruction to an end, and Plumridge returned to Åland. Napier considered it a political disaster as well:

> Very little, with the exception of a few barrels of pitch found at Brahestead, was the property of the Russian Government. It was the private property of shipbuilders and others, and no small portion was English property! upon which money had been advanced, as is customary in the English market. Apart from this, the materials destroyed were the property of the Fins, who had not offended us, and with whom it was politic to maintain a good understanding, this great object being frustrated by a wanton destruction.

Three major Russian forts spanned their Baltic dominion, all protecting harbours: Cronstadt, sheltering St Petersburg; Suomenlinna (Sveaborg), outside Helsinki; and Bomarsund in the Åland islands, marking the western extent of the empire. The Russian fleet remained at anchor within the first two. Bomarsund, a symbol of Russian expansionism, but neither completed nor fully operational, was the easiest target. An attack, with limited forces, on 21 June, had no success, and is memorable chiefly for the bravery of a ship's mate, Charles David Lucas, who was awarded the first Victoria Cross. The Allied Fleet assembled at Åland, leaving a few ships to watch Cronstadt and Suomenlinna, and prepared for a full-scale attack on Bomarsund. This attack, under Napier's command, began six weeks later; an immense force of British and French warships and troops encircled the fortress, and after fierce artillery fighting the Russians surrendered on 16 August. A number of British casualties were buried on the surrounding islands; probably one of them was Lord Wrotterry, a lieutenant in the Royal Engineers – there is a wooden cross bearing his name in the Åland Museum. The captured fortress was blown up on 2 September, to prevent Russia from reoccupying it. The ruins remain, a peaceful and picturesque relic of this forgotten war. Soon after this both fleets prepared to leave, with hundreds of prisoners, captured at Bomarsund, being taken to England and France (see Appendix 4).

Napier appears to have agreed with Shakespeare's Leonato that '[a] victory is twice itself, when the achiever brings home full numbers'. This approach would not do for the *The Times*, which pilloried him for his ineffective leadership, and his failure to deliver triumphant victories at Suomenlinna or Cronstadt. The Admiralty, swayed by public opinion, questioned Napier's assessments. His spiky and disrespectful manners had not endeared him to authority, and he was replaced the following year by Rear-Admiral Dundas, a more diplomatic and manageable commander. Napier spent the rest of his life justifying himself.

1855

The fleet sailed at the end of March, and by mid-April the blockade was in place again in the Baltic. Activity was now mainly in the Gulf of Finland although the blockade was extended as far as Tornio, and there was a handful of relatively uneventful landings at west-coast towns.

Dundas knew what was expected of him: a successful attack on Suomenlinna, if not on Cronstadt. More than two months were spent reconnoitring both fortresses, but the first action was seen in May when British and French ships captured and destroyed several vessels outside Hanko, on the southernmost tip of the Finnish mainland. This led to one of the major incidents of the war, 'the Hanko massacre'. Attempting to return to shore seven prisoners taken at sea (one of them a ten-year-old boy), and to buy provisions, Captain Fanshawe, although showing 'the flag of truce', was fired on by a Russian unit. Eventually five British sailors lost their lives, as did the Finnish captain of one of the captured ships, and British prisoners were taken. This became, in a small way, a counterpart to the Kokkola affair, with the press now casting the Russians as the villains. '[S]o atrocious an act,' wrote Fanshawe, 'resounded through Europe.'

Further east Captain Yelverton and a French commander reconnoitred the mouth of the Kymenjoki, which was guarded by the fort of Ruotsinsalmi on the island of Kotka. This, together with two outlying fortresses, was destroyed on 20 June. Next on the list, on 5 July, was the fort on Svartholm, outside Loviisa, along with the barracks and government stores. Two weeks later it was the turn of Hamina, where Yelverton's division severely damaged the newly constructed batteries. A few days later Kotka was revisited; this time the bridge from the island to the mainland was destroyed, the marines were landed, and all the military stores were burned.

Suomenlinna had not been forgotten. A preliminary reconnoitre in June had been unsuccessful, and a sailor had been killed by a cannon ball. The bombardment proper began on 6 August and continued for several days. The allied ships had superior fire power, and were themselves out of range of the Russian guns, but the British mortars could not withstand the heavy demands of continuous firing. The fortifications were damaged, but, it turned out, not materially; there were about seventy Russian fatalities. 'The Russians,' wrote G. F. Dodd, 'claimed a repulse which was duly celebrated'.

On 13 August the fleet departed for the anchorage off

Naissaar (Nargen), an Estonian town north-west of Tallinn. 'When the guns fell silent,' writes Greenhill 'the people of Helsinki were convinced that a landing was to be made, and it was then that panic spread.' Within hours the city was deserted; it took a few days for the scattered residents to realise that they could return to the town in peace and quiet.

Dodd, a contemporary historian of the war, summed up:

> Thus ended the second Baltic campaign, which bore an unsatisfactory resemblance to the first in being marked by only one important operation. The vast fleet of the Allies in 1854 had effected nothing worth recording in the pages of naval history except the capture of Bomarsund; the still more extensive and powerful fleet of 1855 had nothing of importance to record save the bombardment of Sveaborg. A few forts were battered, many ranges of government buildings and stores were burnt, and numerous small trading-vessels captured; but it will remain as an instructive memento of the mode in which this war was carried on, that the most powerful fleets the world had ever seen performed two notable achievements only, in two years, and that even one of these was neither a victory nor a capture, but only a partial destruction.

Dundas produced, though to a very limited extent, what the British public wanted, and what Napier had failed to provide. He would certainly have continued in command in 1856 had peace not been concluded by the Treaty of Paris. Had hostilities continued, the Baltic would, in the opinion of a modern historian, have been the 'decisive theatre' of the war.

The Nature of the War

It is difficult to isolate the purely Finnish aspects of the Russian War. Finland's status as a Grand Duchy was not properly understood in England, and few commentators, and perhaps even fewer of the naval hierarchy, distinguished Finns from Russians: George Giffard, the Captain of Plumridge's flagship *Leopard*, certainly did not. Contemporary histories, as well as memoirs of commanders who had had a part in the war, commonly refer to either 'the enemy' or 'the Russians' (sometimes 'Rooshins'). Officers who went ashore used Swedish-language interpreters, so must have realised that they were not dealing with Russians; instructions from the War Office, reiterated by Napier, required officers to take care not to damage the possessions of 'the civilian population', and to confine themselves to seizing or destroying actual or potential war material. The distinction was undoubtedly difficult to observe, and this may, to some extent, explain some of the unfortunate events in Ostrobothnia.

The political situation was complex and must have been been confusing, since most of the Russian ports were actually in Finland – stretching from Vyborg to Tornio. In fact, most of the merchant ships sailing under the Russian flag were Finnish, and many of the maritime towns of Finland were both ports and shipyards. Many ships, some still only partly built, were destroyed, but some were taken as war-booty, sailed back to England and sold on the open market. The first and one of the finest of these was the *Fröja*, belonging to a wealthy Turku merchant, C. M. Dahlström, which was loaded with salt. It was captured off Beachy Head and towed to Portsmouth, its arrival reported in *The Times* and pictured on the front page of the *Illustrated London News*. The daring exploit at Ekenäs led to the first capture from Finnish waters.

Implementing the 'take, burn or destroy' order, not surprisingly, made enemies of the Finns. Plumridge's tour of destruction in Ostrobothnia, in Admiral Paget's words, 'has engendered a hatred of us on the part of the Finlanders, which will make them fight us *con amore*'. This opinion was recorded by Bunbury and by Sturge in Finland shortly after the war. After Plumridge returned to Åland more particular care was taken not to alienate the local inhabitants. Napier, well aware of these dangers, wrote to Vice-Admiral Parceval on 22 July:

> I have given positive orders to allow nobody to go on shore, and I hope the inhabitants will not be annoyed in any way – hitherto they have not. If you approve of what I have done, perhaps you will take the same steps; if men once get on shore, there will be no preventing mischief.

The damage which had been done in Ostrobothnia could not be undone, but these orders were, with a few exceptions, observed for the remainder of the war.

'This little island aggregation [Åland] becomes at last the scene of a war in which neither its interest nor its patriotism is involved,' wrote Hamley. Dodd agreed, considering it a grave injustice that the Finnish population should have been involved at all in the clash of the Great Powers:

> The hardy Finlanders of the north know little and care less about Turks and Crimeans; yet were their homes and sea-side chattels certain to be placed in peril by the results of a quarrel which in the first instance affected the south of Europe only.

Some of the British commanders seemed to sense that Finland was in certain respects an occupied country, and that the war was only against an occupying force. The headquarters for Yelverton's detachment were on 'Hogland' (Gogland, or Suusaari, an island 35km south of Kotka), where 'the people were Finns,' Fanshawe wrote, 'and therefore had no keen sympathy for the Russians or animosity to our people'. The local population ashore in coastal villages and towns, and aboard on coasters, was understandably terrified by the appearance of foreign ships, and the British often had to go to some trouble to reassure and even comfort them. Sulivan, for example, stopped a Finnish coaster to collect information:

To their perfect astonishment I gave them a bottle of rum and a good lot of biscuit, two things they are fond of, and sent them back to their ship. They had been sure that they would be sent to England and put in prison.

Many anecdotes illustrate both the concern which the British showed for the native population – as opposed to the Russian militia stationed in Finland – and the care taken by the Finns, on their part, to distance themselves from Russian military activities.

With few recorded exceptions the British appear to have followed the orders which Shakespeare's Henry V gave in France: 'nothing compelled from the villages, nothing taken but paid for'. Often they paid generously for their provisions – principally milk, eggs and meat – obtained when they went ashore. Hirn describes the frequent practice of these supplies being taken out to British and French ships, apparently under duress, but being discreetly paid for when the empties were returned. Discretion developed into the charade of farmers and fishermen going out with supplies of food with the deliberate intention of having them requisitioned by pretended force. They needed to keep up the appearance of being victims and not collaborators, as Paget wrote:

> . . . later it became a sort of understood arrangement that they were to have the appearance of endeavouring to escape, for woe betide them if they were reported by the Cossak videttes [sentries] on the hills to be trafficking with us.

Several of the accounts which follow, especially Sulivan's, describe little incidents which show how widespread this fraternisation was.

There were many nameless, unremembered acts of kindness on both sides. Hirn recounts several stories about the friendly communications between the Ostrobothnian townsfolk and the naval officers: for example, a gentleman from Vaasa, who had been invited aboard one of the ships, left his pipe behind; he got it back some days later with good wishes of a British officer, with the hope that it would prove to be a pipe of peace. Among the British officers Sulivan did more than placate the people he met on shore; he would invite the ladies back on board for wine and biscuits. Fanshawe wrote that Yelverton's 'charm of manner won all hearts, so that the Hogland ladies were delighted with him'.

> Yelverton asked whether he might hope to entertain them at a dance on board the *Arrogant*. 'It would be delightful,' they thought. 'But we are at war; how can we come and be entertained by the enemy?' 'Oh,' said Yelverton, 'we'll manage that. I'll take you all prisoners;' and the entertainment duly came off.

Don describes Finnish women 'crouched in terror' in a captured boat; they were 'hoisted aboard and given a glass of sherry' before joining a dance on the quarterdeck. Back on Åland, after the destruction of the fortress at Bomarsund, the stores of corn and meal were distributed among the local inhabitants.

Kind and humane behaviour was not the prerogative of the British: the prisoners taken at Kokkola were well-treated; the able-bodied, according to some accounts, were even 'invited to a ball, where they reportedly danced with the ladies'. Eleven were then taken to St Petersburg; one died en route, while the casualties were well cared for in hospital before being moved on five weeks later, and eventually being exchanged for Russian prisoners. Dodd gives details:

> The invalids were abundantly supplied by the inhabitants with coffee, tea, bread, butter, seed-cake, beef, fish, rice, and potatoes; and when the poor fellows found the black rye-bread distasteful, one of the officers caused white bread to be made for them daily at his own expense.

General Wendt, the commandant, came or sent to them every day, and furnished supplies of wine, pipes, and tobacco. When the men had somewhat recovered, they were supplied each with a new blue cloth suit, new shoes, woollen socks, and a cap. Those who died of their wounds were buried in the church-yard – the funerals being attended by the officers and principal inhabitants.

Remarkably, this most striking instance of fussy, unadventurous British eating habits comes not from some genteel middle-class lady traveller, but from men who could steel themselves for battle, injury, danger of death, and captivity – but not for rye bread! After 'the Hango massacre' Lieutenant Geneste wrote to Fanshawe:

[s]ince our arrival at Eckness [Ekenäs] we have received every attention and kindness from the Russian general and officers that our position would admit of. The wounded men have been treated with the greatest care and consideration.

Even when the unprompted British dislike of the Russian enemy is discounted, descriptions of the war reveal a recurrent trend of admiration of the Finns: there was more to them than simply not being Russian. This was especially noted in the Åland archipelago: Hamley, describing the prisoners taken at Bomarsund, wrote that '[t]he few Finns among them showed, in manner and aspect, like beings of a superior race'. Finns were praised particularly as sailors, and as a literate Christian people.

Several features give the war in the Baltic particular interest. Firstly there was the jingoism, with the English press fueling anti-Russian feeling; *The Times*, in particular, wanted to see results. Napier took a realistic view of what was practicable, and was blamed for not producing striking victories. Russia, knowing the power of the allied forces, never allowed its fleet out of port in either Suomenlinna or Cronstadt. Napier was ironically aware of his failure to satisfy the popular expectations, writing, 'Well might Admiral Berkeley say, "There was not enough bloodshed to please the people of England."' 'It was a good thing to take Bomarsund,' he wrote elsewhere; 'It pleased the people of England, but there was not bloodshed enough for them.' English readers who remember the Falklands War of 1982 will recognise the phenomenon of the tabloid newspapers' bloodthirsty jingoism.

An idea still persisted in the 1850s that war was a species of game. Sir James Graham, the First Lord of the Admiralty, writing to Napier, complained of the Russians 'skulking within the harbour', and he resented the Swedes' refusal to join in. It was, he wrote, 'a disgrace to Russia that she dares not show a ship in her own waters'. They wouldn't come out to play! Since the British ships were, as a result of this, engaged in very little action in the Baltic, the sailors passed the time, on occasion, with games of their own, especially with amateur dramatics, and by playing cricket on the islands. The rocky terrain must have presented challenging batting conditions. Captain Paget noted of one of the rare naval engagements that 'It was very good fun', and one certainly reads much more about 'fun' than about the cholera which killed many of the British and French troops.

Not only was the war at times described as a game; there were even spectators. Several rich amateur sailors headed north from Britain in their pleasure yachts 'to see the fun'. The Baltic campaign seems to have been regarded by them as a sporting engagement; the rich and idle would get a group together, as they might today to go to a World Cup competition in a distant part of the world. A Cambridge don, Rev. Robert Edgar Hughes, published a detailed account of his own two voyages, which have provided valuable material for this volume. Several advertisements, such as the following, appeared in the London newspapers during the summer:

SEAT OF WAR. – TRIP TO THE BALTIC. – The Advertiser, being desirous of visiting the scene of operations in the Baltic, is anxious to meet with some gentlemen who would join in hiring a screw-steamer to proceed thither and attend the motions of the fleet. Any gentleman anxious to join in the expedition may obtain further information by applying by letter addressed to . . .

Two generations earlier such gentlemen might have joined the list of hardy adventurers described in *Not So Barren or Uncultivated*, who faced discomfort and danger during their often intrepid journeys without maps. Now they took it easy: Lord Newborough's steam yacht *Vesta*, for example carried a female cook and housemaid. Many of them 'joined in' the naval activities around the Åland Islands and in the eastern Baltic, even being invited aboard warships. The hospitality was reciprocated, with British officers being entertained on board some of the yachts:

> Lord Lichfield brought his yacht *Gondola* up to the Gulf to see what was going on, rather as if to a regatta, and he took captain George Elliot of the *James Watt*, Lord Clarence Paget and Harry Keppel for a trip.

Mr Campbell's schooner *Esmeralda* was fitted with a distilling apparatus which supplied other ships with pure water, a valuable asset when cholera was rife. There was also a Scottish baronet, Sir Robert Arbuthnot, in his yacht *Mairs,* and Hughes mentions yet another English yacht, *Pandora*, as present after the bombardment of Suomenlinna. It did not end here, as Don records:

> We had lately been joined by several pleasure yachts from England, and also by traders from various ports. One enterprising Dundee skipper flew from his little barque a huge flag labelled 'Provisions.'

Another Englishman viewed Bomarsund from a Stockholm ferry, specially diverted to provide a sight-seeing trip.

A description of Bomarsund in the summer of of 1854 reads like the society column in *The Times*. As far as its name is known in England today, though, it is for those two pillars of English life, cricket and beer. The village of Bomarsund, in Northumberland, grew up around a coal pit, opened in 1854 and named, presumably in a wave of patriotism, after the recent British victory. Now it has a cricket team which has won the national village championship, and a very successful brewery, two of whose ales are named *Bomar* and *Castle*.

Captain Bartholomew James Sulivan

Such fame as Captain Sulivan has today comes not from his two summers with the Baltic fleet, but from the years which he spent as Lieutenant on the *Beagle* during its voyage of scientific discovery (1831–6), memorialised by Charles Darwin's *The Voyage of the Beagle*; he and Darwin formed a lifelong friendship. Sulivan was a hydrographer, but having neither wealth nor political influence he could not get promotion; at the outbreak of war 'he was appointed to the *Lightning*, a small and feeble steamer, for surveying duties in the Baltic, and more especially in the gulfs of Finland and Bothnia'.

Despite his modest rank, Sulivan had a good deal of influence over the strategy at Bomarsund; he had surveyed the channels, so was in a good position to suggest routes, and 'the way in which these places might be attacked'. His tactful manner of suggesting strategy to Napier is a model of how to advise a superior. A year later his plan for the bombardment of Suomenlinna proved to be 'a masterpiece of naval power projection'. Sulivan's letters give the picture of a modest, humane, sensitive Christian gentleman, whose affection for the Finns is much more striking any hatred of the Russians:

> The more I see of them, the more I am interested in the people. It is a pleasure to be able to establish such a feeling with them when they were taught to look upon us as enemies, who would treat them ill and plunder them. I hope to induce the admiral to order that no more of their vessels shall be burnt or their property injured.

He describes several island landings; on the first occasion, he wrote, 'we came on a fine large village [Degerby], where in a moment there were men, women, and children running in every direction'; he 'made friends' with 'one old man, much too feeble to run'. Seeing that there was no danger, the villagers slowly returned, and Sulivan made friends all round. Only then did he discover that

> one of my friends was the collector, and in fact a government officer, and it became a question of whether I ought not to seize him and the custom-house; but after the way I had made friends with him, I could not think of it without giving him reason to think that I had broken faith, so I would not molest him. Some of the women brought out baskets of eggs, of which I bought about two hundred at one halfpenny each, dividing them afterwards with *Driver* and our officers. After staying about two hours, we parted the best of friends, they promising to let the other islanders know we should not injure them or their property. We got some milk from women at the other village on our return, and promised to send back their nice white pails, which we did, and I put a little coffee and sugar in them.

Every detail of this anecdote shows what Sulivan's son describes as his 'simple and manly piety': '[t]o rich and poor, old and young, he was the same earnest, helpful friend and companion'.

On a subsequent visit to Degerby, his handling of an officious police officer shows some of the the genuine difficulties faced by a conscientious officer in wartime; one may admire Sulivan's firm but fair management of this situation, and notice too his willingness to take off his jacket and lend his men a hand:

> On my way to shore with Evans in the gig, I told the ship's crew that if they saw me pat a man very affectionately on the back to seize his arms behind him and take him to the boat. On landing, all the people were indoors but the collector, who came gravely forward bowing, till he came

close and recognised me, when his countenance changed most wonderfully. He began shaking hands very energetically. I saw a lot of faces peeping out of one room. Soon all my lady friends rushed out of the door. They had not recognised me through the window until they saw the collector shake hands with me. Even the collector's old wife, whom you remember had been 'packing up to run away' when I first landed, ran out and shook my hand with both hers, as if she recollected my not burning the custom-house down; and the nicest-looking young lady, the married one with the baby, ran in and brought out a most beautiful nosegay of roses of all kinds, which she gave me.

I then complained to them that all the villagers were acting as our enemies, in spite of all that I said when I was last here, as they were cutting away the buoys we were putting on the rocks; and I said that if they did not prevent it, I should have to burn all the boats of the nearest village, and, if that did not stop it, the village itself. They said it was the police officer made the people do it, threatening if they refused to send them off to the fort.

Shortly after a gentleman in a green uniform came, and told me he had charge of the place, and I saw he must be the very man. He certainly was a bold one. I soon after said I must have some sheep, etc, and as the people could not sell them I would take them and give the money. The gentleman in green said he would not allow it, and they should not take our money. I went up close to him and said

'Then you mean to act as our enemy.' (I had an interpreter.)

'I cannot allow them to take the money. I have charge here, and it is my duty to prevent it.'

'Then,' I said, 'I must treat you as an enemy,' tapping him on the back at the same time. In an instant his arms were pinned, and he found himself in the embraces of three men, who walked off to the boat. The ladies screamed; the old Mrs. Collector got hold of my hand, went down on her knees, and cried terribly, saying that he had a wife and seven children, the youngest only a year old. I told her that I had just the same, but it would not prevent a Russian officer from taking me prisoner; and as this man avowed himself a Russian officer and acted against us, though he did his duty only, I was obliged to do mine and take him prisoner. Some of the younger ones screamed, one tall fine young woman went off nearly faint, and there was such a scene, but more with fright at the thing than care for him. I believe they thought they all were to be carried off. Soon his poor wife came down in terrible distress, and his eldest daughter begged me very hard to let him go, and almost tried my feelings too much; but all I could promise was, I would take him to the admiral, and I would ask for him to be allowed to go to Bomarsund, where his family might join him, provided he promised not to return here, but that would rest entirely with the admiral.

His wife went off with him; and I, with two men, walked to our old village, a mile inland, where the people had said they could not sell us lambs; but now they heard the police officer was gone, they were ready to sell anything. Evans and more men soon joined, and we took back several sheep, and nice lambs at three shillings and sixpence each, milk, and cream; and as we could not carry all, I took off my coat and backed a fine lamb.

When I came back I invited the ladies off, and all but the old one accepted, and brought off the poor man's eldest daughter. The poor people on shore had been crowding round me begging me not to let him come back again. The ladies certainly did not seem to think that I had done very wrong, or they would not so readily come off. The husband of the nice-looking one stood on the jetty. I begged him to come, but he said he could not. I said I would keep all the ladies prisoners, and his wife too. He said he was quite willing to trust her with me.

They remained an hour, had some wine, biscuits, figs, etc., admired your [i.e., Mrs. Sulivan's] likeness, took a number of tracts, were rather surprised that the figure of England in *Punch* praying for the success of the war should be kneeling before a cross, and asked if the figure were not that of a Catholic. I assured them that we were Protestants, and I gave the younger mother a Swedish testament for her little daughter, when she could read, and then we parted the best of friends, though it was sad to see the poor wife and children taking leave. I think no one ever before captured a prisoner in an enemy's country, and at the same time had a party of six ladies on board to lunch.

There is a charming sequel to this story:

I had a letter to deliver at Degerby to his wife from the prisoner I took, and had orders to bring his clothes down, he being kept in *Duke of Wellington*; so we all landed, had a walk to the village out in the country, got some cream and milk, called on all our lady friends, got lots of roses from the gardens, had a very kind reception even from the prisoner's wife, and, knowing that from the blockade they were deprived of all their common necessaries, I was in the act of sending on shore some coffee, sugar, and a few bottles of wine, when a boat came alongside, put a large basket of green peas and a wooden milk-bucket of raspberries in the cutter, said they were for the captain, and pulled away before an answer could be given.

Sulivan's humanity and tact are again seen in the following episode on Älgö, in the Ekenäs archipelago. Off Hanko two 'deserters' in a punt came on board, and acted as guides, pointing out the islands where sheep and cattle might be bought; Sulivan was ordered to go with them on 'a foraging expedition':

> We went up the channel to Elgo Island, and I soon found these men knew nothing about the place, and that on the island where they wanted me to go there were two Russian telegraph stations. So at last I sent them to see what they could get in their own punt, telling them to tell the people that they should be paid for everything they liked to sell. I then went in the gig with six men and Evans (all of course well armed), to see what I could pick up myself, and we soon came to an island, where in a little cove I saw several cows. I thought I saw someone; so I landed and went in alone, thinking that would show they need not fear; but I could find nothing but cows, and no sign of dwellings.
>
> Feeling sure that the people would not have left their cows behind if they had fled, we pulled round the island until we came to some sheep and lambs on a point, and shortly after a pretty cove among islands, where were several boats and nets and four or five cottages. As we pulled in I waved a white handkerchief, and soon we saw some heads peeping through a window, and as I landed one young woman walked down and met me, evidently in great alarm, and she looked dreadfully frightened as I shook hands with her; then two more came out, equally frightened. (I had a good interpreter with me.)
>
> On going into the house, it was a most painful scene! One poor old woman got up in a corner, put up her hands in an agony of terror, and cried bitterly. On a bed in a corner, huddled up, were three young women, all crying, and in all there were about eight or nine, including one girl of about twelve. It took some time quite to reassure them. They said they had been told we should murder them all if

we came, and destroy all their property. The men had had all been taken to work at the new batteries where *Arrogant* and *Hecla* had been [Hanko]: and, when the women saw me pulling in on the opposite side, they ran away, and all from the four houses collected in this one room for safety.

They were in the act of heating a large brick oven to bake a batch of rye bread, enough to last a fortnight. The loaves are flat, about a foot in diameter, and have a hole in the middle, through which they are strung on a stick. The women soon went on raking out the fire and putting the loaves in, and I got some potatoes to roast in the ashes. They had a bullock and some sheep they would sell; so I sent off for the purser of the flag-ship, and a boat and the butcher from *Basilisk*. The women were all clean, modest-looking people, though very poor, and they wore comfortable dresses, some in English materials, and some in home-made. They could read, but had only a Prayer Book and an English Psalter. Freshwater, my coxswain, just reminded me of the Swedish tracts, and that made me ask if they had a Bible, but they had only the Psalter, so while they were killing the bullock, I went off and got a large Swedish Bible, and some tracts.

We gave them £3 10s. for their little bullock, but the sheep were too poor. We also bought same salt and fresh fish from them, and I bought one of their little wooden spoons, to their great amusement. I brought them also some tea, sugar, and biscuit; and when we left it was in very different circumstances than when we came. When I gave the old woman the Bible, she got hold of my hand and kissed it, and then all the others did the same. I thought they were going to give me other kisses, they got round me so. When I went off, I sent back some coffee in the punt, and they sent back some delicious cream, and we enjoyed a first-rate cup of tea with it.

Everywhere he went Sulivan showed his Christianity in action. He was not alone among the British commanders in having religious material on board; the tracts he distributed were presumably in Swedish. He seems to have been following the model of John Paterson, the indefatigable missionary in Finland early in the century.

Sulivan has an eye for the ladies, noting how attractive they are, and describing carefully their appearance, dress, and behaviour – mindful, of course, of what will interest his wife:

> A few evenings ago a small sloop was stealing along the channels [near Degerö] . . . We found her full of hay, and the crew consisted of husband, wife, and son, and a boy about ten. We soon quieted the poor woman's fears by releasing the vessel. I was surprised to see in such a little vessel such a nice clean cabin, and a woman doing such work, yet neatly dressed, with a regular fashionable lady's monkey-jacket over-all, and very clean. She was very fair and clear-skinned, with auburn hair like many English women.

He was impressed with the amount of practical and physical work that women performed, especially when, as in the episode above, they were left to do everything because the menfolk had been drafted. In another observation, from Åland, Sulivan admired something that he would not have seen in England:

> The wife of the farmer was away in their vessel, of which he is half owner, going to Stockholm with two cows to sell, to get money to buy what they required. The women here are quite as good sailors as their husbands and brothers. We find little boats carrying a press of sail, and in a nasty sea, with perhaps only two or three women in them, and always part of the crews women: they seem born to it. In the summer they are fishing, milking, shearing sheep, and perhaps going in a boat to the cows

morning and evening, as they put them on all the smaller islands to eat up the pasture. Sometimes we meet a small boat with two or three people in it, and a cow standing as quietly as possible, though looking too large for the boat to hold in safety.

Sulivan must surely have been the most attractive English officer in the Baltic during the war. After the bombardment of Suomenlinna and the threat to Helsinki he wrote, 'I would rather have had a share in saving that place, and the ruin and misery its destruction would have caused, than the share of credit I received for Sveaborg.'

Colonel Charles Hamley

Hamley's reflections on the despoliation of the Åland Islands are recorded in the Introduction; his Russian War memoirs appeared in *Blackwood's Magazine* in 1855. 'The pictures of our camp life,' he wrote, 'had none of the shadows which fell so darkly on our brethren in the Crimea.' In fact they have a whiff of the Boy Scout about them; Baden-Powell himself would not have felt out of place on the Åland which Hamley pictures during a day in the life of 'the English soldier':

> The supplies are abundant. The parties sent for water return ever and anon with a purchase, and are greeted with a cheer. His larder exhibits a miscellaneous collection. Here there is a calf or pig hanging by the legs from a tree; here a black lamb, goat, or goose, tethered near the tents. There are pots and pans everywhere, holding the oddest things, cooked in the oddest way. Everywhere there was the smell of tobacco.

Hamley is a most attractive writer, one who can make even military details readable. In the passage below he conveys vividly the juxtaposition of the military camp and the traditional peasant life; as he puts it, '[i]n one picture, what a contrast of the elements of peace and war!' the scene is 'Tranvik, a village and bay about four miles south of Bomarsund':

> As the day broke on the morn of the 8th, the advanced-guard of marines landed on the narrow beach, made their way through the rocky thicket, and gained the open ground beyond without meeting a foe. The mist lifting heavily and slowly, showed stacks, palings, patches of meadow, and other signs of habitation near us. Presently a

bit of a steeple, the side of a windmill, a mass of red roofs, and large looming homesteads, gave us the vague outline of a village, dimmed and mazed by the folds of mist. As our skirmishers passed through the scattered houses, feeling for the enemy, the peasants were just waking up to their labours, and evinced no sign of fear or surprise, no apprehension of violence or plunder. The women came to the doors, the pigs wallowed, and the fowls strutted most temptingly and trustfully before us.

The road wound now round an indent of the sea, and there forts Nortike and Presto arose before us, looming grey, grim, and sullen. No shot was fired; and we passed on to make our first halt beside a plantation. The men sat down in groups to munch their biscuit and bacon, and smoke their pipes under a hedge, shady and green enough for the days of merry England. Suddenly there was a sound of wheels. "Field-pieces!" said an alarmist. The sentries erected their muskets fiercely, and the men stood to their arms, when, lo! round a turn of the wood came a pretty pony-carriage driven by a lady, a priest sitting beside her. Our interrogation was imperfect, but their story seemed to run thus: She was a widow; her husband had been killed some time before by one of our shells; she had suffered enough from war, and wished to seek a city of refuge in one of the neighbouring villages. The priest was bent on some errand of mercy or pastoral duty. Their story was accepted; a passport was given them, and they went on their way rejoicing. Even a little Finnish handmaiden, who came in a little cart behind with some household stuff, and had remained fixed in a state of strong despair from the time she first cast eyes on the soldiers, brightened up as she passed our posts, and smiled and kissed her hands. Such was our share of the adventure.

For the possibly tragic sequel to the story, see Appendix 2.

William Gerard Don, MD

Don was just short of twenty and not yet qualified when, because of the sudden demands occasioned by the war, he embarked as ship's doctor on *The Duke of Wellington*, the flagship of the British Fleet. This was the start of a distinguished career, leading finally to his appointment as Deputy Surgeon General in 1885. His *Reminiscences of the Baltic Fleet of 1855* was printed at the suggestion of friends nearly forty years later, but not published.

On 14 June most of the Allied Fleet headed down the Gulf towards Cronstadt, anchoring off Seiskari. Don provides the only British account of this remote little Finnish island, only twenty-five miles from Cronstadt, and ceded by Finland after the Second World War. He found the move a pleasant change from the confines of the ship:

> On the 16th a large number of British and French officers landed for a ramble, and made straight for the chief village in the centre of the island. It was intensely hot in the thick woods, but presently we came to a delightful cool meadow, brilliant with flowers, and buzzing with bees and other insects. The village close by was much larger, and the houses greatly superior to any on Nargen, but looked equally forlorn and deserted; we were told no less than 300 men and boys, from 8 to 50 years of age, had been drafted away under the conscription; and consequently only old men, women, and children were left. Some of the girls were pretty, but the young women decidedly plain, and the old veritable hags.
>
> I gave a little, flaxen-haired maiden some bits of ship

biscuit, for which she innocently kissed my hand. They repudiated being Russians, and called themselves, with much emphasis, 'Finsk' – that is Fins.

The furniture of the houses usually comprised a few stools, some small tables fitted with deep drawers, two or more large boxes, which also served as bedsteads, and a plate rack. Near the door was the usual plastered stove, containing a bread oven, and having a few cooking utensils atop. Spruce beer, which they offered us, was the gala drink, but it had a turpentine smell and flavour. A large number of sledge dogs and domestic cats were about, as well as a few cows and pigs; and the poultry, perhaps for fear of the Fleet foragers, were shut up as at Nargen, but they were much in evidence through crowing and cackling.

The chief building was the church, built of dressed wood, and having a small tower or steeple. It was full of pictures, representing Christ, the Crucifixion, the Baptist, Virgin and Russian saints. The altar was enveloped in gold-embroidered, shabby, black velvet, and on a wall adjoining hung the incongruous barbaric outfit of the priests, consisting of sundry seedy vestments, two enormous cocked hats, a wreath of ribbons, and a couple of swords. The uses of these paraphernalia puzzled us. Bibles and prayer books in Russian, were scattered about; and at the door hung a poor box containing a few brass copeks, to which we added some silver of a better coinage. We behaved with becoming decency in the church, and the only constructive sacrilege was climbing the steeple and ringing the fine toned bell.

Rev. Robert Edgar Hughes

A fellow of Magdalene College, Cambridge, Hughes was one of the half-dozen or so wealthy British adventurers who decided to take their yachts to the Baltic in 1854 to see what the British fleet was up to. He enjoyed his jaunt so much that he repeated it the following summer, and on his return published the log of his voyages, *Two Summer Cruises with the Baltic Fleet in 1854–55*, which went into a second edition the following year.

Travelling such a distance in a small sailing yacht was an unusually adventurous way to spend a Long Vacation:

> She is a very small cutter-yacht, about as long as a moderate-sized drawing-room, and scarcely so wide as a four-post bed: to judge from her low sides, her large sails, and her narrow deck, it could scarcely be supposed that she could trust herself at sea, or venture to do battle with a gale of wind; and, indeed, I should not now venture to put in print the adventures of such a very small and insignificant member of the Royal Thames Fleet, were it not that our cruize took us among scenes and circumstances which do not commonly come within the scope of a yacht voyage.

Despite predictions that he would be drowned, and being warned that he would be 'caught by the Rooshians and knouted to death', Hughes and his brother, with a small crew, set off on the *Pet* on 14 July and reached Gotland on 1 August, spending some time on shore there before heading towards Bomarsund. 'The Swedish seamen,' he wrote 'are excellent, fine, sturdy fellows, very like English; but, I must confess it, cleaner and better-clad.' The beautiful daughters of a Gotland merchant came in for even more extravagant praise. A few days later Hughes was among the ships of the French and British fleets, which 'after the dreary solitude of the Baltic, formed a most exciting scene'. Hughes describes it with the enthusiasm of a patriotic schoolboy:

But there was little prospect here of sleep or repose: boat after boat came alongside to convey a welcome and to ask for news, and soon the band of a line-of-battle ship burst out with the stirring strains of *Partant pour la Syrie;* another and another took it up, and the lonely waters of Led Sound, which had probably never rippled to other music than the droning tones of an Åland fisherman, or the shriller melodies of native maidens as they rowed their cargoes of fruit to the market of Bomaren, were now taught to vibrate to the notes of *God save the Queen.*

The next day Hughes was offered a tow by the *Cuckoo,* to arrive at Bomarsund on the eve of battle. For him it was an unforgettable scene, and a romantic experience which he tried to evoke with some fine writing:

I have had many a pleasant day's sailing in my life, but this little cruize in Lumpar Bay surpassed them all; the bright sun, the pleasant breeze, the noble fleet, French and English, with their bright colours and ringing music, the enemy's batteries, the troops landing, their gay uniforms glistening here and there among the dark foliage of the forest, while from time to time a gun from the batteries would roar out a sullen curse of defiance, and send its red-hot offspring muttering and moaning high overhead to seek a peaceful bed in the dark depths of Lumpar Bay.

Hughes does not appear to have been regarded as a nuisance, and was flattered to be accepted by the naval fraternity. He felt, nonetheless, that the sailors were not quite a match for those he had so admired in Sweden: 'brutal oaths and foul unmanly words' seemed to touch a raw clerical nerve.

He went on land frequently, and recorded various cameos of island life, for example when the heavy guns were being hauled into position:

> The natives had all turned out to see the fun, and the foremost of the group was a tall, slim girl, who had seen some seventeen summers, her neck and white shoulders, almost to the waist, uncovered, except by her long fair hair, which hung at full length around her, and which she was most industriously combing with the utmost unconcern. At a little distance the group formed a strange and pretty picture.

One particular excursion ashore echoes the accounts of several travellers of the earlier epoch, especially of their aversion to piimä (sour milk), and to the bed-bugs which were a traditional summer torment of Finland. They pulled up at a nearby homestead, and as they went ashore 'a mild-looking man appeared signalising friendship vigorously', and they 'advanced into his dwelling':

> Having regaled me with schnaps and sour milk, which I smuggled past my lips somehow, he proceeded to recall his affrighted womankind, who came flapping in with their broad naked feet, and immediately proceeded to pass from a state of alarm and dismay into one of the utmost kindness and familiarity. One was an elderly lady, rather dark in complexion, and very leathery about the gills; she was followed by another old dame, who very evidently was a lady of the cow-keeping persuasion; she resembled the first very strongly, but was more odorous. Next came three demoiselles – bare-footed, flat-ribbed, red-legged, giggling young ladies, with coarse features, but beautiful fair hair, which they wore long and dishevelled about

their shoulders. But for a nervous twitchy way they had of continually calling upon their fair fingers to perform the functions of a comb, this hair would have been very charming.

These young persons received my advances with native innocence, occasionally bursting into sputtering laughs, and whispering and tickling each other in a corner.

While this was going on I reconnoitred the apartment, wishing to know how a respectable Åland farmer lives.

It was a spacious room, adorned here and there with rough carving on the beams and doorposts. Three tiers of beds, resembling the bunks in a ship, formed one side of the apartment. Here it seemed from the number of these couches the whole generation, man, woman, and child, must have reposed; an arrangement indicating certainly an accommodating and sociable disposition.

After the surrender of Bomarsund the *Pet* landed, Hughes went ashore, and he and his brother each helped himself to a 'prize', a 'beautiful percussion musket'. He gives a number of details of the state of the Russian soldiery, with such powerful and chauvinistic disgust as does not bear reprinting, concluding 'Such is the race that has swallowed up lands and nations in quick succession, and now threatens to overwhelm the fairer lands and the nobler races of Sweden, Norway, and Denmark.'

After the battle there was a water party, with Hughes and several of the other sightseeing yachts joining the British and French fleets for their jollifications:

For us it was quite a holiday campaign, the ships dressed in their colours, and with their bands playing, floated securely in a roadstead as safe as Barnpool. Gigs dashed rapidly from ship to ship, and smart little pleasure-boats, manned by officers, rowed merrily about. Four English yachts, 'Esmeralda,' 'Mavis,' 'Foam,' and last and least, the 'Pet,' had borne their owners to this unfrequented retreat. The 'Sparrow Hawk' cutter, and two or three traders, supplied French brandy and Dublin porter to all thirsty souls. Officers on leave from Ledsund, and gentlemen from the yachts, bivouacked and picknicked within hail of the Russian forts, and scarcely one horrid sight of death or suffering on our side disturbed the bright pageantry of war.

Hughes became so addicted to the 'bright pageantry of war' that the following spring he 'found it impossible to resist the temptation to undertake another Baltic cruise'. He had already shown in the previous summer that, like Sulivan, he had an eye for pretty girls. One of his first descriptions, after entering Finnish waters is a touching and picturesque little scene on an expedition to one of the islands near Naissaar:

> A few Finnish peasants, chiefly women, remained upon the Isle of Nargon, which is treated as common property by the allies. Picnic and cricket parties were frequent, and the lonely rocks were made to ring with the sound of French and English laughter.

> On one of these expeditions, I saw a pretty sight. Under the shade of a tree a little native girl, with large, surprised blue eyes, and long, fair, unbraided hair, was sitting mending a net, and beside her a young ship boy of the 'Geyser' lay full length, his eyes bent upon her in silent admiration.

> The two children had evidently struck up a little love affair, and the handsome sunburnt English boy, in the beautiful dress of the British fleet, the fair Finnish child, the tall outlandish pine over head, formed a charming group. Poor boy: *Pacem duello miscuit; ah miser!* He was speedily called away to cool the captain's champagne; and I would wager that whenever he hears the well-known strains of 'The girl I left behind me,' the image of a dark Russian

pine, a broken net, and two large, surprised blue eyes, will ever be one of his best and most innocent recollections.

It is well-attested that 'all the nice girls love a sailor', and therefore hard to believe that there were not more such attachments formed, perhaps not as innocently as this one, during the war, but this is the only Anglo-Finnish romance that I have come across in this, or indeed in any other era.

Although several of the naval officers involved in the war wrote memoirs of their experiences, or had their letters and journals used by biographers, their accounts are mainly professional and technical, and contain few experiences of Finland. It is Hughes who provides the fullest and most readable account of a raid on a Finnish port; he was not content merely to observe. The *Magicienne* and the *Cossack* came into Naissaar, and Hughes and party were invited to join the latter 'to beat up a Russian position on the island of Kotka'. On board, Hughes observed a marine persuading the ship's doctor to pass him as fit; away he went, 'delighted at the prospect of possibly shooting, or abetting to shoot, a Rooshian or two before supper time'. There had been very little military activity during either year of the war, so the British marines welcomed the prospect of any sort of action, as did Hughes:

> Leaving this [the dismantled fort on Ruotsinsalmi] on the starboard hand, we saw the beautiful gilded cupola of Kotka church towering high over the trees, and soon afterwards we entered the narrow passage which leads up to the position. Here the drum beat to quarters, and it was fine to see the delight and spirit with which the men welcomed that for which our authorities have so profound a hatred – active service. The men crowded round their guns in a high state of eager fun; the captains of the guns, the best men of the ship, with their handsome faces and

sinewy arms all bronzed by the sun and wind, at the rear of their guns with the lanyards in their fists; the old gunner prowling about to 'consecrate' (*Anglicé concentrate*) the guns; the officers, less sanguine than the men, evidently in a state of despondency and alarm for fear lest, after all, there should be no enemy to encounter.

'Too true,' writes Hughes; the Russians 'had decamped and left the island, the town, the barracks, two old women, one pig, and several geese at the mercy of the enemy'.

Soon after the marines had landed, a bright tongue of flame darted out from among the pines, a cloud of smoke followed, then a roar, and a murky glare, and the whole barrack, a huge building concealed behind the woods, was in a blaze . . .

In the evening, a boat from one of the ships landed to complete the destruction of the bridge. No sooner were the men ashore, than a flotilla of geese, belonging to the garrison, was seen recreating themselves in a shallow pool. Away we all went, sailors and marines, hand over head, head over heels, rough and tumble, into the water, out of the water, now up, now down, after the geese. Never was such a cackling heard at Kotka; never such roars of laughter. We soon had the whole flock, except the patriarchal gander and the partner of his bosom, who paddled, with dismal cackles, away to the deep.

Afterwards, we went up into the deserted village. The houses, with their windows and doors loosely barricaded, as the peasants had left them in their flight; the great government buildings entirely stripped and empty; the two unhappy old crones left behind, with other unprofitable articles; the smouldering ruins of the burning barracks; the traces in the better houses of comfort, or little home luxuries − a pretty fuchsia in a flower-pot, a little bird-cage with the door open, just as some poor girl had snatched away her pet bird and left the cage in her haste; all these things told their little tale of the tears and the terrors which war brings with it.

In the second edition Hughes adds the following detail:

I picked up a little silver locket containing a miniature picture of the Virgin and Child upon porcelain; it was a very pretty memento of Kotka Isle.

To resume:

The barracks, as usual among Russians, were handsome outside, but mean, sordid, cheap, and dirty within. Large stores of wood were piled in front of these buildings, which promised us a fine blaze so soon as the time for our fireworks should arrive.

At night, a party of marines was landed, and a boat or two rowed guard to protect the bridge. The wind had changed in the evening, and was blowing fresh; the embers of a large government house in the village had blazed up with the breeze, the flame had spread to a large farmyard, and from thence to other houses, and half the village was in a blaze . . .

After this little diversion [a pig; see Appendix 3] our work of destruction began. We burst down the barrack doors, broke them up, and, piling them in the still uninjured part of the building, set fire to them, and soon had a royal blaze; then we got some dry furze, stacked it up among the wood stores, and fired the whole, till the island and the fiords around it glittered and roared with the fire.

There are discrepancies in Hughes's account which he does not correct or clarify in the second edition – guarding the bridge after it had been destroyed, and the fate of 'the two crones' who had been left behind. He possibly muddled the latter story with one which he might have heard about during the earlier attack on Kotka:

> There was little found in the fortress by the British. However, during the burning of the buildings, an old lady, Maria Purpur, was found in her bed. She refused to move, causing a dilemma for the sailors, who had been ordered not to harm civilians. Thus, they took her, in her bed, to a nearby church and then proceeded to burn the fortress building. The Orthodox Church in Kotka commemorates Maria Purpur with a statue, as it was believed that she saved the church from also being burnt. However, it is unlikely that the church would have been burnt, as Yelverton was particularly diligent in ensuring that buildings with no government connections were spared.

Having travelled so far, Hughes was not going to miss out on the bombardment of Suomenlinna. He gives a detailed account of the ships, the guns, and the strategy of the attack, but nothing is as engaging – nor engaged him as much – as his adventures on Kotka island.

The Christian virtues are more clearly manifested in Sulivan, the captain, than in Hughes, the clergyman. Bunbury refers to him as a 'clerical seaman and amateur warrior', while Greenhill and Gifford write with disgust of his joining in a sheep-stealing raid on one of the islands, and describe him as 'a bloodthirsty young gentleman who emerges as one of the least pleasant characters of the whole campaign'.

Lord Dufferin

Another of the amateur followers of the Fleet who published an account of his voyage was Lord Dufferin, or, to give him his full title, Frederick Hamilton-Temple-Blackwood, 1st Marquess of Dufferin and Ava. One of the most distinguished British travellers to Finland ever to publish an account, he was a courtier, a best-selling writer of travel books – they included the North Atlantic and Iceland – and a noted diplomat. He became, successively, Governor General of Canada, Ambassador to Russia, to the Ottoman Empire, and finally, in 1884, Viceroy of India. Thirty years earlier he had been in the Baltic.

Dufferin travelled in his yacht with a small party, including Lord Arthur Russell, and arrived at Bomarsund just in time to witness the assault. His article 'Bomarsund 1854, from the deck of the Foam' came out in the *Cornhill Magazine* more than forty years later, largely transcribed from his journal. As soon as he arrived in Åland the whole party went aboard Napier's flagship, *The Duke of Wellington,* where 'almost all the captains of the English fleet were assembled'. Here his lordship, in the words of Alfred Lyall, his biographer, 'found his congenial element':

> The whole scene was very exciting and interesting. The splendid fleet, full of motion, music, piping, and hoarse boatswains' voices. Barges skimming about in all directions, with their captains' flags flying astern; while every now and then 'boom' went the report of some huge gun from a seventy-four practising her men at the target. Unfortunately she was also practising her rifles, and as now and then some crooked-eyed fellow tried his hand, whiz

went the ball past our noses . . . A beautiful sunset, which
I saw from the stern gallery, sitting on a sofa beside the old
admiral [Napier].

'Like many imaginative men . . .,' Lyall wrote, 'he was evidently anxious to try the effect of inoculation with the war-
fever, to test himself in situations that string up human energies
to their highest tone, to witness the reality of what every one
reads about, and to feel the sensation of being actually under
fire.' He was, with Napier's permission, aboard the *Penelope*
when, advancing to draw the fire, in order to ascertain the
range of the Russian battery, it was lured onto the rocks within
range of the Russian guns. Despite the circumstantial detail,
Dufferin's description of this experience gives a matchless picture of an unflappable English temperament, keeping his head
when some of those around him were, literally, losing theirs:

Having . . . accomplished his appointed task, Captain
Caffin put his helm over, with the intention of sheering
off'; but at this very moment crash we went on the top
of a sunken rock, and there stuck. In vain the engines
were reversed, and every effort made to set the vessel free.
Rejoicing in the success of their ruse, for they had pur-
posely lured us into our present position, the Russians in
the main fort began to make a target of the unfortunate
Penelope. It was a little time, however, before they got
our range, but I confess that at first I could not help duck-
ing each time a cannon ball hurtled overhead. At last,
bang went a round shot through both our paddle boxes.
Having heard that it was a prudent measure to put one's
head into the first hole made by cannon shot in a vessel's side, though disdaining to practice the expedient, I
determined to watch whether it would have been successful. A minute or two afterwards there came another shot
within two or three feet of the first, and immediately after

a third, which knocked the previous two holes into one, a circumstance which satisfied me that the above theory did not hold water.

After it became evident that we were stuck hard and fast, measures were taken to lighten the ship. Shot and shell were brought up from below and hove overboard, and, this having no effect preparations were made for doing the same with the guns. All this while – for these operations occupied some time – the aim of the enemy was continually getting more and more accurate. Being myself unoccupied, while everybody else was busily engaged in discharging his allotted duty, I had ample opportunity for observing what was going on, for counting every fresh impact of the Russian shot, for speculating on what the end of the affair was to be, and for analysing my own sensations. I do not say that these were altogether pleasant, but still I was conscious of a certain satisfaction at finding that I had no feeling of nervousness, in spite of seeing one or two horrible sights as various casualties occurred in my neighbourhood. One man was struck across the face by a heavy splinter, which buried itself in his brain. Another had the top of his skull taken off as clean as if it had been done with a knife, while a third poor fellow was cut right in two. Once, indeed, I had a narrow escape, for, as I was pacing the deck, I stopped opposite the wide embrasure for the big gun, saying to myself that a logician would take up his position on this very spot, as the chances of being knocked over by a cannon ball were no greater here than in any part of the ship, while there would be an absolute immunity from splinters, which cause even more destruction than the shot itself. At the very moment that this thought was glancing through my mind, bang there comes a round shot right through the port, striking the deck within half a foot of my toes, and covering me with sawdust. But the most singular accident of all was one which happened to an unfortunate French officer who had come with a message, and was standing in a boat on the offside of the *Penelope*. A cannon ball came clean through two lower deck ports and took off his head. What pleased me most, however, during the whole business, was the gallant behaviour of a little midshipman, a mere child, thirteen or fourteen years of age. About the time when the fire became pretty hot, I happened to come across him, and, as he seemed to be as much out of a job as myself, I touched my cap and took the liberty of observing that it was a fine day, to which he politely replied that it was. Encouraged by his urbanity, I ventured to ask him how long he had been at sea, to which he answered, 'I have only left my mamma six weeks, but I ain't going to cry upon Her Majesty's quarterdeck,' a remark which, I think, as worth recording as many a one made by more illustrious heroes. Soon after this, however, a man was killed close to him, and the poor little fellow fainted, and was taken below.

As the situation became more serious, a certain angry feeling began to prevail - at all events, among the crew, if not the officers - at the Admiral not sending a big ship to draw the fire of the fort from its present victim; but soon afterwards Captain Hall (a very gallant officer known in the Navy as 'Nemesis Hall'), in command of the *Hecla*, another paddle steamer, came in to tow us off. But it looked as though this resource was to prove as useless as our own efforts, for the *Penelope* still refused to move. At this juncture Captain Caffin, with wonderful but most unwelcome consideration, expressed his desire that Stanley Graham and I should transfer ourselves to a boat, and remove from under fire. My instinct was to demur to his suggestion, for I naturally desired to see the affair through; but, as I did not feel justified in adding to the commander's anxieties at so critical a moment, I obeyed his orders, on condition that he would afterwards write us a note to say that it was at his especial request that we were deserting his ship. Stanley Graham [third son of First Lord of the Admiralty], who, though scarcely yet convalescent from a bad fever, had shown the greatest coolness during these trying hours, was especially anxious that this should be done, in view of his professional reputation. Having, however, got into the boat, as good luck would have it, through some misapprehension on the part of the coxswain, instead of being conveyed to a distance from the field of action, we were simply transferred to the *Hecla*, which was merely 'out of the frying-pan into the fire', for the Russian fort was becoming even more attentive to the rescuing ship than to her original target. However, to make a long story short, the *Penelope*, having got rid of all her shot and guns and of some of her ballast, after a sojourn of four hours on the reef, was at last got afloat, and, amid the cheers of her own crew and of her rescuers, was triumphantly towed back to her former tranquil berth. This happy consummation having been arrived at, Captain Hall kindly asked me down to luncheon, and I have scarcely ever enjoyed a meal more.

We do not learn if Dufferin got from the Captain a note to clear him of any suspicion of cowardice; Caffin must surely have had greater priorities. After experiencing 'the sensation of being actually under fire' a good luncheon is, of course, especially welcome.

A true Renaissance man, Dufferin was a poet as well as a soldier:

The next day was a lovely sunshiny morning; the air was loaded with the wholesome smell of the pine woods which clothed the valleys; and as we passed upward through the heathery, rock-strewn slopes, wild flowers, butterflies, the hum of bees, and the odour of the sweet-scented shrubs, encompassed us with a sense of peace and beauty which contrasted strangely with the violence of the drama in which we were about to engage.

Dufferin still had not had enough: fortified by his lunch, perhaps, he 'joined a party to visit the trenches of the French army'. The violent drama in which he engaged himself included 'shot, shell, and grape whizzing every now and then over our heads':

finally, seeing a white flag hoisted on the fort, they walked straight up to the gate, were sharply ordered back by a Russian officer, who cried to them that the place had not yet surrendered, and regained cover under a satisfactory shower of balls and bullets.

When it was over Dufferin went ashore and managed to persuade the commandant to allow him to take as souvenirs 'two beautiful field-pieces'. He returned to Scotland, and 'landed triumphantly at Dunrobin' with them, and with a young walrus, acquired on the voyage. Back home he was planning to set off for the Crimea, to see the other theatre of war, but was prevented by illness.

Selina Bunbury

Peace was proclaimed; but as we moved slowly up the clear flowing Neva, we could not forget that war had only just ceased its horrid din, for, independently of all other causes of recollection, there were with us a band of Russian prisoners whom we were escorting home to St. Petersburg.

The first volume of Bunbury's *Russia after the War* sees her arriving in Russia in 1856 for an extended visit. From the 1830s it had became increasingly common to make excursions from St Petersburg into Finland; in summer especially it was seen as a peaceful refuge from the oppressive and sultry atmosphere of the 'swamp-built city'. Bunbury was determined to get away from the stifling city atmosphere, and had a particular reason for wanting to head west:

We are going to Finland, and my object and intention are to get into Sveaborg. People stare at me, and say briefly that I cannot do that, but I am sure I can do it.

She had to jump though a number of hoops contrived by the police before she could set off; having to wait until a police official had woken up from his nap delayed her a week. At Tallinn '[i]t was Saturday, and all our gay folks were out on a pleasure trip to Helsingfors to spend the Sunday and return with this same steamer early on Monday'. As far as the Baltic went, Helsinki was clearly the place for a night out:

At Reval we changed almost wholly our society; we were now six hours from Helsingfors, and the change that took place in the lady part of passengers was a brilliant

one; the effects of a night at sea and the homely appearance of persons who who were travellers merely, were no
longer discernible on our deck; we had no longer voyagers
with fur or wadded mantles and enormously stout pillows;
the dresses were of the lightest and gayest description; the
ladies were for the most part young, but whether so or not
their air and dress transformed our previously business-
like looking steamer into something more like a party-of-
pleasure boat. The captain seemed to enjoy the change; he
looked round him, grinned, walked with his hands in his
pockets, and looked up to the sky, out to windward, and
grinned again.

He was grinning because he knew that a storm was brewing. It
duly brewed, and badly spoilt the party mood, but as the boat
came past the 'silent guns' of 'the small fortified islands' into
the smooth waters of Helsinki harbour the spirits of the visitors
revived.

Three summers earlier Bunbury had had little to say of Helsinki, and had preferred to imagine its charms in winter; now
she was completely won over, comparing 'antique Reval with
active modern Helsingfors'. She attended both the Lutheran
and Orthodox churches, but for all her piety did not feel comfortable with either: 'It is fastidious certainly, but I have found
it almost equally hard to associate my devotions with those of
the Swedes while sitting, or with those of the Russians while
standing.' There was plenty of space to observe and assess the
congregation in the former church, 'that great conspicuous
building on the granite hill':

> The greater number of the congregation were the plain-
> er class of women, shopkeepers' wives and daughters,
> wearing the graceful and rich black silk handkerchief over
> their heads. A party of Finnish soldiers, with their ser-
> geant, seemed to find the monotonous singing of the first

long psalm devotion enough for them; as soon as it closed they quietly rose and filed off.

In the Orthodox church, by contrast, there was a crush.

At the university she received a little lesson about the way things are in Finland:

> I wanted to see the old books and manuscripts that had been brought to the new capital of Finland after the fire at Åbo; but the chief librarian was absent; and when I asked the subordinate where they were, he gave me a very extensive direction; he gravely answered, 'God knows.' I told this to a lady, who informed me that the same reference was almost universally given in Finland to enquirers on all sorts of subjects.

Religion and scholarship were not the only attractions: there was also the spa and the bathing place. Kaivopuisto overlooked Suomenlinna, and offered 'a pleasure house as well as a bath-house; there is a *restaurant*, and music and walks in the gardens, and dancing in the house.' This was a fashionable resort, especially for Russian tourists; the park refreshed 'the weary, languid spirits that escape from grand St Petersburg'.

The spa was the scene of the most interesting encounter which she recorded in Finland:

> In the evening we went there for a bath; there was something in the countenance of the woman who gave the tickets that excited attention. It was the expression of a thoughtful, resigned, habitual, sadness of mind – the countenance of one who had taken a view of life from its shaded side, and kept looking at that side only.
>
> She was a Fin of the lower classes; but I heard afterwards she was a native and original poetess, and that her productions were numerous. She showed us where a shell or a bomb, during the bombardment of Sveaborg,

had fallen on the roof and shattered the whole side of her wooden tenement. The inhabitants quitted it and retired into the town.

'And it was the English who fired it!' we said as if reproachfully.

'Ah!' she answered in a gentle tone, 'it might also have been the French.'

One might desire to meet such delicacy of feeling towards a foreigner more commonly than we do in England.

There was, indeed, only one matter relating to the recent war that Finlanders, especially mercantile ones, spoke of to us with scarcely repressed indignation – it was of the mode of warfare carried out at one period of it in the Gulf of Bothnia, and of the destruction there of private property.

One of the first merchants here actually had tears in his eyes while speaking of this. 'I so liked England,' said this good-hearted Swede, for though subjects of Russia they are still Swedes by nature – 'I was proud in England; I had spent some years of my youth there, and had always wished every one to like England as I did. I was humiliated as if it were my own nation that did the wrong, for such conduct was indeed like that of the pirates of old times.'

It was at the bathing place that she met a lady whom she calls 'Mamsell Malvina', who used her feminine wiles to bluff their way onto Suomenlinna; Bunbury's only interest in going there seems to have been that it was forbidden. At least this was enterprising; both her visits to Finland were otherwise distinctly unadventurous. One excursion was a visit to 'a pretty and romantically situated wooded villa' on an island just outside Helsinki:

Here from the point of this high mass of granite, rising above most of the great trees, the son of our host stood or sat witnessing the fire that was apparently devouring Sveaborg; he says it was a splendid sight . . .

The return over the water at night, when the glowing sun had withdrawn its heat, but left its light and its ruddy hue in the clear sky, was one of those moments which stamp a picture on the memory; which add another fragment to the mental kaleidoscope into which in times of dreariness we can look and see that life has not always been dressed for us in sad-coloured garments, but that with a good share of its toils and trials God has given us that love his own works in the glory of nature which keeps the heart still young and the spirit unbroken.

This mixture of sub-Wordsworthian and evangelical response to Finnish nature is not matched by any other British traveller, which is just as well, since her feelings seem to be beyond the reach of grammar.

'The next day,' Bunbury records, 'we started in a comfortable open carriage, with post horses, on an excursion to the interior of Finland.' This promises at last something like exploration, but all that she records is a picnic, no more than a couple of hours drive out of Helsinki:

In the woods we gathered the delicious wild strawberries so plentifully sold in Helsingfors, and the blueberries that make the preserve used here and in Sweden as a sauce with meat.

Our young people spread the cloth on a flat rock, and set out a tasteful repast adorned with the freshest flowers; and sitting round that rock in the forest, we did not envy the luxuries enjoyed by the summer residents of St Petersburg.

The evening after our return to the lively little capital, we went to the gardens of the Bad-hus, where there was a sort of assembly room and a *restaurant*.

The account of this 'excursion' is a foretaste of what summer holidays in Finland were now going to mean for the British.

She returned to St Petersburg, with 'the pleasantest Fin in the world for a captain', stopping at Hamina on the way. On her earlier trip Bunbury had been disappointed not to find her fairy-tale university in Finland; three years later she had come down to earth, and found there many innocent, comfortable and genuine pleasures.

Joseph Sturge

A surprising sequel to the Russian War was the arrival in Finland of Joseph Sturge, the founder of the British and Foreign Anti-Slavery Society, on a fact-finding mission. He was a Quaker, and a noted pacifist; no stranger to such journeys, he had travelled to the West Indies and twice to the United States on humanitarian assignments. He is known to historians as one of the 'moral radicals who left their stamp on the emergent Liberal Party in mid-nineteenth-century England'.

In January 1854 Sturge had been a member of the deputation from the Society of Friends which visited Tsar Nicholas I in an attempt to avert the impending Crimean War. Now that the war was over, he was acting in response to the feelings expressed in England about the destruction of 'the property of unarmed citizens' by British marines in Finnish coastal towns. Sturge's biographer, Henry Richard, describes, in his own distinctive idiom, how Sturge was affected:

> The wail of the unfortunate sufferers reduced thus to extremity of distress by British hands, and by acts which were in violation of even the cruel 'laws of war,' floated across the seas, penetrated into the quiet retreat of Edgbaston, and struck on the ear of one whose heart was sensitively attuned to 'the still sad music of humanity.' Mr. Sturge could find no rest without making an effort for their relief; and in order to do this in the most effectual manner, he determined to go in person and explore the true state of the case on the spot.

Sturge's short account of his journey to Finland was privately printed after his return to England. More detail is found in letters printed by Richard, where he describes the expedition (taken with a fellow Quaker, Thomas Harvey) as a sacrificial duty: only 'the strong power of Christian benevolence supplied an adequate impulse' to risk the dangers of travelling in the interior of Finland! They arrived at Helsinki, 'our little steamer freighted with peace and goodwill', on 15 September 1856, and stayed at the 'Society House'.

Our only letter of introduction here was to a gentleman who is now from home. No one there could speak English when we called, but a gentleman was sent for who could, who had been travelling through Finland with the Governor-General this summer. Though we did not tell him the object of our mission, he gave up the afternoon to us, assisted us in getting what Russian money was wanted and getting a new passport, which we found was needful. We found that the only posting here is by one rough two-wheeled vehicle, and that we are about 150 miles from the point we want to reach. We therefore bought a comfortable carriage in which we can sleep at night, for about £20., which this gentleman used in travelling with the Governor-General. There are not more than one or two persons in the whole of this place of about 16,000 inhabitants that can speak English well, but we have engaged a sailor, who understands tolerably English, and Swedish, and the Finland language, to go with us to Tamerfors, where we hope to be on 4th day evening if we get off from here at eleven to-morrow and travel all night. The gentleman's name, who has so much assisted us, is Frederick Lerche, and without telling him exactly the object of our visit, we have ascertained enough to confirm my previous impressions and to strengthen my belief that our coming is well timed. This harbour is one of the finest I have ever seen. The fortress of Sweaborg, which was destroyed by the English and French fleets, has been but partially rebuilt, but the destruction of other buildings is not so great as I expected to see, and no houses were destroyed here.

Despite travelling almost non-stop on their jouney to Tampere and then on to Turku, Sturge was very observant, and gives an intelligent account of what he saw; his is the first British description of this route:

Many of the houses are sufficiently spacious and comfortable, but the approaches are deep in mire and dirt. Cattle of small size, ponies, sheep, and long-legged long-snouted swine seem abundant. Houses of a superior class, still of wood and generally of one story, but well finished and painted, occasionally occur; being the residences of priests, official persons, or affluent peasants. The quaint churches with their steep gables, and with the belfry or spire a detached building, also strike the eye of the stranger. We passed a few estates in a higher state of cultivation, and with mansions usually commanding views of some noble prospect of rock, lake, and forest scenery.

Below the 'peasants,' (a term here implying ownership of land,) there is a class cultivating land on a labour-rent, or subsisting on casual employment. Hence, though there are evidences of a plentiful supply of the necessities and even the comforts of life, in a somewhat rude and primitive style, there is a part of the population whose pallid looks, dirty persons, and inadequate clothing, tell a tale of privation, corroborating a remark made by F. Uhden, that half the infant population of Finland dies before attaining the age of ten years. On these journies we passed and met great numbers of country carts, going to the nearest town with wood, hay, dairy and other produce, or returning empty or laden with town merchandise. On the road to Abo we met at intervals twenty or thirty carts, each conveying three bales of cotton to the cotton mill at

Tamerfors, a two-week journey there and back, with the same man and horse.

In Tampere they visited 'Ferdinand Uhden, well known as a Christian philanthropist', who told them of the 'strong revulsion of feeling' against the English for their conduct during the war. They continued to Turku, on bad roads and with unsatisfactory horses:

> Though the day was mostly wet, we could but enjoy the splendid scenery on the lakes. They are studded with islands, clothed with beautiful timber, so placed and planted by nature that it would have been almost impossible to have done it with more effect had they been arranged by the most skilful landscape gardener.

> Abo: Sept. 19.
> We are here at a comfortable hotel, called also the Society House; and after getting a few hours' rest in bed, and a good breakfast, we both, I think, feel as well as when we left home. We have just been to call upon Enrick Julin, to whom Ferdinand Uhden had already written to inform him of the object of our journey, and one of our letters from Newcastle was also addressed. As far as we can judge, it would have been almost impossible to have found a man more suited to give us advice and counsel. He does not speak English, but he has a son about twenty-five or thirty who does, and who interpreted in this case for us, and who appeared to enter into all his father's views and feelings; indeed it is a privilege to see such apparent noble qualities in two generations of the same family. He (the son) is going to start with us as far as Nystad and Raumo at five o'clock to-morrow morning, and we shall probably not be back here until third day morning, but it will probably not be needful for us to go farther north.

At Uusikaupunki they spent two hours questioning 'some who were sent for to give proof of the way our soldiers had robbed them of their little property', before setting off for Rauma, where the next day they 'saw and examined several cases in which the British had plundered the poor people'.

Sturge's *Visit to Finland* gives details of the evidence he took of the offences committed in these two towns, and on the islands near them. He describes attacks on Uusikaupunkki on 23 June by the *Harrier*, and on Rauma on 1 July by the *Driver*, which are barely mentioned by chroniclers of the war. This is part of a statement taken from 'G. W. Ramsell, merchant':

> Although Captain Storey always paid for such provisions as he had obtained from Nystad, yet on the neighbouring islands, the sheep and cattle were sometimes hunted up and seized without payment, and in some cases the sailors ransacked the houses, taking away clothing and other things, besides wantonly destroying property, including many small vessels and fishing nets. He should think that twenty or thirty boats were destroyed between Nystad and Raumo.

Some of the victim statements which Sturge recorded were, Richard writes, 'very painful and affecting':

> One case was particularly touching – that of a poor widow of very interesting appearance, who wept much while she gave her statement, which was that the British had destroyed her husband's little vessel, and also their cargo of wood which was on shore, which included not only the whole of their own small property of about £50, but that of some friends who had helped them to build the vessel. Her husband died two or three months ago, of what would be called a broken heart, and left her with a child of four years of age, not only without support, but

she would have to go through the bankruptcy court. This was fully confirmed by others.

Sturge's feelings were patriotic as well as humanitarian. He found that on several occasion he was being confronted with the wounded perplexity of the Finnish people he spoke with:

> Need it be said that it was evident the reputation of our country had suffered deeply in the estimation of those simple, honest-hearted people, through the lawless proceedings of our navy? Formerly, no country stood so high in the esteem and affection of the Finn; but now, as one of the poor fishermen said to us, 'they can't think of the English as before.'

One of Sturge's sources of information in Turku was 'a gentleman temporarily resident there, who had been one of the interpreters on board the British fleet during the war'.' 'In his opinion, the losses and sufferings of the inhabitants of the Åland isles had been the most severe.' It is clear from this evidence that all British commanders did not conduct themselves as honourably as Captain Sulivan.

A committee was formed in Turku 'to investigate into the losses sustained during the late war, from the soldiers and sailors of Great Britain, by the inhabitants of Finland who were chiefly supported by their own labour and that of their families'. After Sturge returned to England another committee opened a subscription, which raised £9,000 to be used by the Finland committee. The scope of the fund was extended not just 'to reimburse some of the poorest of those that had been despoiled' but also to relieve victims of the famine suffered in Finland the following year. Sturge's Finnish mission is remembered in a poem by a fellow-Quaker, the American John Greenleaf Whittier.

Edward Rae

The ease of steamer travel bred, perhaps inevitably, a generation of unenterprising British visitors: there is not much travel writing about Finland in the mid-to-late nineteenth-century. In *The Land of the North Wind* (1875) Edward Rae writes that 'travel, like everything else, is beginning to grow commonplace'; his own book records, inimitably, experiences which are far from commonplace. A wealthy Liverpool stockbroker, he could have toured the world like a plutocrat, but he was an adventurer, a man who had ambitions which went far beyond finding 'the best hotel that the place afforded'.

'We live in difficult times,' Rae writes in his Introductory Remarks, 'and young men of initiative are put to their wits' ends for novelties.' His first idea was to sail up the Gulf of Bothnia, and follow the river Muonio northwards, but realising that 'the journey up-stream would be so slow and toilsome in the midsummer heat, and aggravated by mosquitoes', he adopted another route. A voyage to the Norwegian Arctic coast, followed by a journey southwards through Lapland to the Gulf of Bothnia would be, he considered, a genuine novelty – as, indeed, was his next journey, travelling among the Samoyedes in Siberia.

Rae and his companion left Hull on 2 July 1873 by steamer for Trondheim, and continued north by coastal steamer to Altenfiord. From there they headed south by horse and boat to Kautokeino, entering Finland at Kaaresuvanto, near Enontekis, then following the Mounionjoki and Tornionjoki downstream to Tornio, and visiting the Finnish coastal towns as far south as Vaasa. In addition to their portmanteaus they took with them 'stout hampers, as the best means of carrying our food and necessaries'; they would rarely be exceeding walking pace, and so could not depend upon finding regular provisions.

Rae is distinctively different from any other British traveller to Finland: he adopts the slightly self-mocking and ponderously comic tone which was immortalised a few years later by Jerome K. Jerome in *Three Men in a Boat* (1889). Jerome himself could hardly have come up with a more striking name for Rae's travelling companion: Henry Pilkington Brandreth, who Rae refers to usually as 'the Doctor', describing him as 'a gentleman of energy, endurance, and unexceptionable appetite'. On the journey they made to the White Sea Peninsula a few years later Rae arranged a cricket match against an all-Lapland XI, captained by 'the Doctor', and bowled out Lapland for 0 in their second innings.

The route to Muonio had presented few problems except mosquitoes; these inspired him to a burst of Byronic verse:

> The mosquitoes came down like a cloud on the sea,
> Their trumpets all sounding in hideous glee:
> To their wives and their daughters a summoning note,
> On the fair Englishman's succulent flesh as they gloat.

In Norway he had engaged a couple of guides, whom he named 'Brick' and 'Somerset', the former having 'about as much sense of humour as a crayfish'.

> We rambled happily along, picking berries and flowers, and reindeer moss: then we rode again, and so got over the fifteen miles that lay between Eaouda Muodki and Suajarvi. The stage was a short one, and Somerset and Brick, demoralised by enervating repose at Kauto-keino, were indisposed to do more than saunter along. Consequently we had the pleasure of seeing a glorious double midnight rainbow: and the jovial genial old Sun himself was our midnight torch. We disestablished a Lapp maiden in the hut of Suajarvi before we could sequestrate her apartment, but she left three little Lapp brothers and sis-

ters in a deep childlike sleep in one corner, all unconscious of the presence of the ferocious white men . . .

Beyond the farm huts, in front of our quarters, was such a draw-well, so deep, so clear, so cold, that our fingers were numbed in washing, and the Doctor's nose took quite a colour. The tall graceful old Lapp-Finnish method of raising the water was in use. A long, tapering, curving spar, like a Nile-boat's yard, and weighted at one end, balanced itself across an upright pole twenty feet in height, and the pitcher or bucket was suspended from the slender extremity.

They were disappointed that the cloudberries – 'a kind of dwarf amber-coloured mulberry' – were not yet ripe, and were frustrated in their attempts to acquire a sheep-bell, but at Kaaresuvanto they 'obtained many little bells, which shall find their way to our private belfry'.

We landed amid general satisfaction in Karesvando [Kaaresuvanto], and were marshalled to a cleanly unpretending house, in which was a room, in which was the most portentous stove we had ever cast eye upon. Full one-third of the area of the chamber did this massive erection occupy – a great frowning whitewashed mountain of stone, with a hot and deadly entrance for the fuel. We pitied any frost that might find its way in here in the genial Christmastide, and could not at all realise snow remaining upon the ground within a dozen yards of it . . .

The next morning they parted from 'Brick and Somerset, who came to despatch us upon our watery journey down to the Gulf of Bothnia'.

We began to forget the discomforts of the fjelds and forests in the delightful occupation of gliding down the swift clear noble stream, past its pines and birches, rocks and shallows, eddies and rapids. Every half-hour or so brought us to a rapid – sometimes a succession of rapids – down which our boat would shoot like a swallow in pursuit of a dragon-fly: our steersman, with all his faculties sharpened, guiding us with a paddle – the other boatmen tugging lustily at their oars to keep steerage way on the boat. In the winter months the Muonio is frozen to the depth of eight or ten feet, and in all places of lesser depth, down to the ground. It is strange to imagine this river so full of life and strength, icebound, silent, and immoveable. The fishes must be put to the greatest inconvenience, as no fish can look forward cheerfully to being frozen.

It was a delicious feeling to skim past the banks and the grey waterbeaten rocks at the rate of fifteen miles an hour, the stream tearing and bubbling along beside us: and the quick gliding in the eddying water below the falls was almost as delightful. Our steersman and his merry men were perhaps unamusing, but we learned to speak a few words of Finnish from them, words to which we were able to add afterwards, and we think of them gratefully . . .

We walked up the path leading from the landing-place to the homestead of Muoniovara, resolved to spare neither Herr Forsström nor his able-bodied household the necessity of administering to our clamorous appetites. We stepped blithely up to the wooden platform surmounting the half-dozen steps, characteristic of all houses in this country, and rapped unhesitatingly at the door of the large wooden building. A cleanly half-awake maiden, wrapping a shawl about her, came to the door, and at once asked us to come in and make ourselves comfortable. We arrived in a bright clean room, overlooking the landing-place and the small lake, and the fine sweeping river, and the sloping fields and woods, and finally the pretty village of Muonioniska beyond the river, and farther still the soft purple hills of Russian Lapland, brightened by the morning sun. In twenty minutes not only the handmaid, but Mrs. and Miss Forsström were up, and busying themselves with providing chocolate, cream, eggs, tongue, sweet bread and biscuits. We have a tender recollection of luxuriating upon these, until we felt it was quite time to crown the slumbers we had availed ourselves of in the boat, by a dive into the soft white beds the maiden had prepared.

After a sweet night's sleep, they 'made a memorable breakfast, ending with cranberries and whipped cream', and 'had a long chat with jolly old Mr. Forsström and his well-informed intelligent son'.

It was at Muonio that Rae was introduced to the sauna. He was the first – but the first of many – Englishmen actually to take a sauna and describe the experience.

> I asked for a warm bath to rehabilitate me after the forced uncleanliness of the Fjelds, and Mr. Forsström suggested a Finnish vapour-bath. The Doctor preferred a swim in the river, so [I was] left with young Forsström, while they made my bath ready. In about an hour and a half they came to say that I had better wrap myself up in my capuchon and very little else, and run across to the bathhouse. It was a wooden house, perhaps twenty feet in length by fifteen in width, supported on piles, with a few steps leading to the door. One small window admitted all the light, and in one corner of the floor was a pile of heated stones. The temperature was high, but dry and comfortable. Two or three benches, and pails of cold water and towels, completed the arrangements. I was directed to leave everything at the door of the hut, and in a few minutes the bathing attendant, a decent hard-featured woman, came in without the slightest embarrassment or false delicacy, and bathed me much as if I had been in a

Turkish bath. By-and-by she told me to mount by a wooden ladder to a small raised platform, when she threw a pailful of cold water upon the heated stones, and the hot steam came round me in clouds. I was directed to switch my limbs and shoulders with a bunch of birch-twigs, until the gentle perspiration came upon my forehead and face. Then I sat with my feet in a bucket of delicious cool water, while the bathing-mistress poured soft water over my head and shoulders: then I was soaped and drenched again until I felt as clean as an ivory statue. Then came the drying, and the delightful gradual cooling, and I skipped across to the house exhilarated and clean. I have now a great respect for the Finlanders' bath: and a respect, too, for their straightforward frankness and primitive absence of reserve, which is the truest delicacy after all.

They had prepared for their journey down the rapids by visiting a certain Mr Abraham to secure him as guide and pilot ('Mr. Âbraham, we presume? He said mildly that he was.') Descending the rapids was exhilarating, with Mr Abraham confidently in charge:

> We glided away from Muonioniska in all the glory of the Arctic evening sun. The broad swift river, with its fringe of silvery birch-trees, was a sheet of gold, and in the stern of our boat was Abraham's form standing out against the sky. In twenty minutes we heard the roar of the fall – a dull hoarse sound – and Abraham's eyes grew brighter, and he examined keenly the washboards which had been nailed all round, above the gunwale of the boat.
>
> In a few minutes more we were among them – the whirling, boiling breakers – one handsome clear-eyed boatman pulling in front of us, the Doctor and I in waterproofs and skins sitting abreast in the middle of the boat: behind us another boatman pulling quickly, and in the stern the fine

figure of Abraham, stooping eagerly forward now, and his
eye flashing like a hawk's. It was a wonderful sensation:
how the torn and broken rocks flew past, how the furious beaten waters swept round and over them! How they
howled and roared along with us! How the men pulled,
at a glance from Abraham, and how they watched for
his eye! Above the rocks on either bank were pine-trees,
clear and beautiful against the sky, but we were going too
swiftly to see much of them. Our boat flew like a hunted
sea-bird, never touching a rock or stone, guided by the
unfailing hands of Abraham and his famous crew. It was
a curious feeling: one of such absolute and happy confidence in men that we saw for the first time a few hours
ago: but it was delightful to see the perfect way in which
they controlled the boat.

Downstream, at 'the pretty little settlement' of Areavaara
they ate at the home of 'a good-natured kindly woman, who
bustled about to make us comfortable' and refused to take any
payment. Abraham and his men were succeeded by three boatmen of very different aspect and ability: 'The first man has a
shaggy wild imbecile expression: the second is the most dismal
soul that we ever saw in our lives: while the Driveller systematically misleads us'. On the Kengis cataract he nearly misled
them to death:

> . . . the Driveller is a ghastly object to look at – his face
> like a corpse, and his lips pale green: the boat is half full
> now, we are sitting in water up to our waists, but down we
> go, tumbling and swerving to escape the rocks – and the
> great violent stream bears us like a sinking eggshell, past
> grinning gaps and roaring foaming cascades, till we gain
> a jutting bank of rock, and can look back upon Kengis
> rapid with emotions of less satisfaction than those with
> which we viewed the previous cataract.

Before the end of the century taking a tar-boat down the Oulu-joki from Kajaani had become a feature of the Finnish summer tour; Rae's experiences are those of an authentic traveller.

At Pello, 'an important-looking place', Rae felt that the land of the north wind was now behind them: 'Pello was more in the world than any place we had come to yet'.

Well north of Tornio, at Matarengi (on the Swedish side of the river from Ylitornio) they paid off the boatmen, and enjoyed 'a capital dinner' at the inn. They travelled now by springless cart (a 'karyol'). After 'good coffee' at the first station

> The Doctor drove to the next stage, where two pretty clean little girls became our pilots: one perhaps seven, and her sister eight years old. It was droll to see their pretty child faces in their hoods, looking back from their karyol as we sang some favourite song in chorus, and to hear them laugh merrily.

'It was in lovely sunshine that we drove into the long-anticipated goal, Haparanda', Rae writes, and the welcome sight of an inn: 'comfortable and clean, with the pleasantest, best-looking, and plumpest of landladies, and the most admirable and abundant food'.

They booked berths on 'the steamer Aâwasaksa, sailing a few days afterwards for Uleåborg and the coast of Finland'. This gave them leisure to explore: to see the old church at Tornio with its 'isolated old belfry with a covering like an armadillo', and to take a jaunt on the river to Kemi, where they had been assured that there was 'gold to be found on its banks' and 'an ancient stone church, in the vaults of which lay the ancient embalmed bodies of five hundred ancient bishops'. 'We had a bright fair little Finn as our charioteer, who laughed and taught us Finnish all the way to Luukos, our only station.' On the way they crossed the Raudanjoki

> in a flat-bottomed boat, impelled by a family of about

nine individuals, from the mother who steers, to a little boy who wields an oar about twenty-seven times as long as himself.

Finally in Tornio, after misdirections and misunderstandings, they were befriended by 'a bounding lunatic' who undertook to show them the bishops. They saw just one:

> We lifted, he and I, a part of the floor-planking, and found a wooden sarcophagus which held the mummy of one of the bishops. Poor old bishop! when the lunatic lifted the white linen shroud which covered him, his rigid, shrunken, parchment-like old body lay as bare as when he came into the world many long centuries ago.

The lunatic 'apologised for the impossibility of showing us the four hundred and ninety-nine other old bishops, as they were laid safely away down in the crypt, out of his reach'. Needless to say, they did not find any gold either.

From Haparanda – in fact from Sangis – it was a short sea journey to Oulu; on 'a bright and lovely Sunday morning' they 'moved up the Oulu river and attached the steamer to the wooden quay, half a mile below Uleåborg'.

> We sailed in the little steamer up past quays, with timber stacked upon them, and pretty wooden houses among green trees: we saw a series of three fine wooden bridges spanning the mouths of the Oûlu, and moored finally at the entrance of a little canal.

A church service was 'simple and impressive'; afterwards

> we went to find a photograph of Uleåborg – then a bokhandler, to ask for an old Bible and a Finnish grammar, securing an old psalm book and an assurance that Brâhestad, our next port of call, was the place of all others

for a grammar. Afterwards we had an admirable Finnish dinner, and passed the remainder of the day in idling round the streets.

There is something Finlandish, picturesque, and at the same time pretty, about Uleåborg – the part towards the Oulu is very much so. The houses are wooden – some very old-fashioned, and there are many pretty green little enclosures, with seats for idlers, dotted about in the town.

They had determined to use Finnish whenever they could, and their attempts to procure a Finnish Grammar provide a recurrent comic theme as they travel through Ostrobothnia. Many earlier travellers had heaped abuse on the Finnish language. Not Mr Rae:

> The Finnish tongue I think is the finest I have ever listened to. I have never been so struck with a language: to hear these illiterate boatmen talk to one another in sounds that rivalled the most beautiful in the ancient Greek, made us jealous, and very ambitious to speak it with them. No weak mincing words, nor coarse gutturals: more dignified than the delicate French: more manly and strong than the soft Spanish.

The steamer called at the major towns as it went south, and at each place, excepting Jakobstad, the travellers went ashore to see the sights, to try to buy their Finnish Grammar, and on occasion to eat. At Raahe they 'came into the thriving well-built little place with some surprise':

> We sought a bokhandler's to ask for an old Bible and a Finnish grammar – securing a psalm book, and an assurance that Gamle Karleby, our next port of call, was the place of all others for a grammar. Opportunities for perfecting ourselves in Finnish seemed to be postponing themselves as time went on, but we thought we could

worry the Finnish passengers with success enough to prevent the time from being thrown away.

We sailed down the coast of Ostrobothnia, and came to Kokkola or Gamle Karleby, where, as our custom was, we got a boat and went on shore. We were pulled up a pretty river, with decayed rickety old warehouses here and there among the gardens upon its banks – melancholy evidences of present decline and not distant fall. We were accompanied by a Finnish gentleman . . .

This good Finlander told us that in Gamle Karleby a respectable middle-class family of four persons might live upon twenty-five pounds a year. Everything was cheap here – bread, meat, fruit, milk, coffee, fowls, eggs, fish, and lodging. The Doctor and I, by a common impulse, resolved to go straightway to the principal inn and partake of the handsomest dinner that gold could procure. Give us, we said to the landlady, the richest and most extravagant dinner that the resources of Finland can produce. The poor landlady, almost doubting her senses, asked what we would like. So that the meal is sumptuous, we replied with magnificence of manner, we limit you in nothing – go unrestricted and provide the banquet.

We were in half an hour invited to fall upon an admirable and delicate collection of dishes, which we should not easily have met with in far more pretending places than Old Karleby.

They were surprised that the small amount of Finnish which they had picked up was more than many of their Swedish-speaking travelling companions knew, but they met on board too a group of 'Finomânes', 'strong in admiration for their own fine language'. Throughout this part of their journey Rae reflects with amusement on the refusal of the 'Finlanders' to use – or even to recognise – the Finnish place names.

Vaasa from the sea looked so imposing that they hardly

thought that they could venture on shore in their travelling clothes, so they put on gloves, linen cuffs and high white collars. With white handkerchiefs in their breast pockets, Rae writes, 'we thought we might pass in a crowd':

> The houses are really large and imposing, but everything is exceedingly new: new streets, new trees, new gardens, new pavements, and a new church, fearful and dreadful in form. Each fourth house – I don't think I am exaggerating much – was a vodka establishment, and red-eyed swollen vodka drinkers staggered along in every street. This was our first interview with vice since we had come aboard.
>
> We went into a bookseller's and asked for a Finnish and English grammar. They were very sorry – in Uleåborg there were plenty. This we denied: then they fell back upon Bråhestad [Raahe], from Bråhestad to Gamle Karleby, from Old Karleby to Åbo. We said in our bitterness that we did not believe there was such a thing as a Finnish grammar.

Vaasa was, literally, Rae's last port of call in Finland. From there they took a steamer to Stockholm, sailing in the evening. 'When I looked out of our state-room window in the morning,' he wrote, 'we were out on the open waters of the Bothnian Sea, and had lost all sight of Finland.'

Arthur J. Evans

Evans is best known today as the archaeologist who excavated Knossos. He had been appointed keeper of the Ashmolean Museum at Oxford in 1884, ten years before his first visit to Crete, mainly on the strength of his archaeological writings about the Balkans. He has been called 'the second founder' of the Museum, having brought together different collections of the university under one roof. His visit to Finland is, I believe, virtually unknown.

His house master at Harrow School had written about him to the Principal of Brasenose College: 'You will find him a boy of powerful original mind I think, if any questions in your matriculation examination should take him off the beaten track.' The was not only a metaphor, since Evans had already travelled extensively, as far as Turkey and Romania. During the Long Vacation in 1873 he spent about a month travelling in Finnish Lapland with a school friend, Francis Maitland Balfour, brother of the future prime minister Arthur Balfour, and 'regarded by his colleagues as one of the greatest biologists of his day'; he was killed climbing Mont Blanc at the age of thirty-one. It was, in short, a remarkable pair of undergraduates who set off for Finland in August 1873.

Evans sent his journal home in several instalments to his step-mother, with covering letters (one package took just ten days from Tornio). The journal reveals him as curious and adventurous as well as knowledgeable; his narrative and descriptions contain numerous geological, botanical, anthropological and linguistic notes. He supplements his descriptions with marginal sketches, and must in addition have had a sketch-book, since the Pitt Rivers Museum has a collection of drawings from this expedition, meticulously detailing places, buildings, boats, people, and artefacts.

They travelled by sea from Hull to Gothenburg. Sweden, as they saw it from the train, was 'a Land of Cream, wild strawberries, blue eyes, & flaxen hair', but Stockholm was disappointing: '[a]ll expectations excited by the title – Venice of the North – have been dashed'. There is, he writes, 'hardly an attempt at good architecture'. They headed north by coastal steamer, stopping at several towns; 'the country almost defies description for its loneliness'. Near Piteå

> [we] had our first experience of Finns – a tall drunken man of that race made a futile attempt to board us while in the Skellefteå Fiord – he however fell off the gangway into the water & had to be fished up again by the Captain, & on landing made a second attempt and was knocked down by the Captain. The Finns have a very bad character for drunkenness here, tho' the Swedes needn't talk!

The little wooden town of Luleå enchanted them, and the whole voyage was so pleasant that they were sorry when it was time to disembark at Haparanda.

There they discovered that they could 'get to a place called Sodankylä, in the heart of Finnish Lapland, by road, & the first part to Roveniemi by post, so we will hire our bearers at Sodankylä'. They decided to '*do* for ourselves', to save the bother and expense of hiring an interpreter. They were reassured to be told that the Finns 'don't laugh at you if you can't speak their language correctly'.

In Tornio they had their 'first experience of the hospitality of the country':

> We were invited by the Crown something or other, evidently *the* Official of the place, Herr Hermansen, to his house where he & his son, who luckily spoke French & acted as interpreter [lived], & a Ritter [Knight], Wilhelm

Aeurez, insisted on hearing all our plans, and giving us every possible help – the Ritter was about the very best man in the whole country to have hit upon for advice, as he is a member of the Royal Survey, & has spent 10 years drawing a map of Finland – & he was able to put down new places on my map & made out the most careful itinerary to the 'fells' for us – add to this that we were plentifully supplied with coffee &c &c, & that the son made out a list of useful Finnish phrases for us. I gave the father a portrait of Prince Alfred with which I think he was much pleased.

Travelling by road to Rovaniemi was not nearly as easy as Evans had anticipated; at one point he got separated from Balfour, one cart was 'the most cranky vehicle I ever saw', and another jolted so much that they were 'almost reduced to jellies'. But worse was to come after Roveniemi, when they left 'what these people are pleased to call the high road' for a by-road; at one place they had to perform a 'Blondin-like feat' of crossing a wide stream using two long pine trunks. The path towards Sodankylä was beset with difficulties, and made treacherous by heavy rain.

Torvinen – August 21 Thursday

We started off once more this morning on foot & again found no difficulty in getting bearers. Our way lay through the most impassible country we have come to yet – a succession of hopeless mosses [bogs] over which we had to be guided at every step to avoid sinking altogether through the treacherous skin of roots & scanty vegetation, & every here & there came to watery places through which you had to wade knee-deep. In the woods we started some capercailgie [grouse] & we have also seen some blue hares, but the track today, as yesterday, was extremely lonely. For two days the only habitations we have seen were the two we stopped at, & we have met only one human being. There were however plenty of berries to pick, especially two kinds of bilberry (called severally mustika by the Finns), & certainly the mosquitoes added a piquancy to the scenery! There is one very delightful plant that grows every where about these swamps, like a rosemary with sunset coloured stalks & tiers of spiky leaves, the aroma from which is delicious & can only be compared to concentrated essences of evening pinewoods – called cinerica here. When we got here the people saluted the bearers in the usual fashion out here by gently putting the arm round the waist which is then reciprocated. During much of our walk, as the whole of last night, it rained, and considering all the difficulties which beset us, it is astonishing that one of our bearers, a girl, should be able to do the whole distance, about 11 English miles, in 3½ hours, with a heavy weight on her back, when every step was a struggle. These people have wonderful powers of endurance.

They learned from a local that no Englishman had been seen in Sodankylä in recent memory:

> when he heard the route by which we had come here, across country and not by the Kinniträsk, which is the *road* way, he could hardly believe it at first & burst out into uncontrollable fits of laughter. Afterwards he told everyone he met this.

Evans writes with more sarcasm than anger about the royal surveyor in Tornio, who seems to have lied in every breath: 'our old friend . . . seems to have in particular an extensive reputation out here!'

> Our merry friend goodnaturedly insisted on accompanying us to help us get some few supplies which we were in need of; shot, paper, oil, &c, & it is wonderful what

resources this unpromising place developed under his skil-
ful guidance. They culminated in two bottles of sparkling
beer (they got it from Uleåborg) to which he treated us –
Oh what luxury!

The interior of the Finnish cottage we saw was very
comfortable; clocks on the walls, & fiddles, (they are a
very musical race), lots of handsome pipes, and curiously
worked tobacco pouches; in the windows roses, cactus,
stocks & heartsease. Having supplied our wants, we invited the Ländman, or 'Nimismies' as the Finns call him [po-
lice chief], to partake of English tea, & with the excellent
soup we have with us, Captain's biscuits, tea, and Scotch
whiskey to wind up with (eked out with good native butter and cream) & made his heart glad. I further gave him
a good English hunting knife, which I think pleased him
very much. He tells us that we are now in a country of
tame reindeer – and that when we get to the fells we may
expect to see wild reindeer and bears.

Both the hospitality and resources of Sodankylä impressed the
travellers, and they especially admired the shop, 'where you
can get anything from bread to books'.

Continuing north, they followed the river Kitinen to
'Kaarelkoski', where Part Two of Evans's Journal opens:

We have succeeded in getting boats up the river to here,
propelled in the usual miraculous manner [i.e., being
poled] up a series of rapids; in one of them we got our
broadside to the torrent, & nearly upset; in another, the
roar of which could be heard a mile away & more, we had
to get out & the men had absolutely to drag the boat up
through the foaming water & over the rocks. These boats
from their raised beaks are well adapted for these rivers
as the water in the ascending rapids cannot reach over
the bulwarks as it otherwise would, & the oars are very

good for rowing in the shallowest water, (the river, though broad as the Thames at London Bridge, being rarely deeper than 2 or 3 feet.) The blades are shaped exactly like bronze spearheads.

The shores of the Kittininjoki are . . . lined with primeval forest, and as evening drew on, and when the whole surface shone like silver, the contrast between the water & the shadowy firs, & golden sunset, was glorious.

Kaarelkoski, the little group of wooden sheds at which we have got shelter for the night, is the most primitive place we have yet come to. We sleep on the floor of the tiny dairy, the rest of the furniture being 46 pans of milk in every stage from freshness to cheesiness. Coffee is served us in a kettle but for eatables we are thrown entirely on our own resources. Under the roof of our hut they have kindly put up little platforms and pigeon holes of bark and wood for the martens to build in.

Bill for lodging, milk, butter, coffee &c was 1s 9d for all of us.

Continuing north they 'took many walks along the shore and through the forest, keeping up with the boat'. At their next stop Evans found the accommodation 'delightfully primitive', while further on he was surprised by the comparative prosperity:

they are really very well off, with seven or eight cows, barley, rye & potatoes, & any amount of large salmon for the trouble of getting them, wood and bark to make all their little necessaries & for fuel unlimited. Indeed here at Kungar as at Niemella the host is well enough off to afford a few extraneous luxuries such as coffee, sugar, composite candles, a few teacups, several guns, pewter spoons & glasses & such like things, which in much less out of the way parts are often absent.

He wrote that '[a]fter seeing any of the half-civilised races of eastern Europe', he was surprised to find how self-sufficient these remote farmers were.

Leaving the river Kitinen they headed for Ivalo, passing through gold-rush territory; a letter written there is headed 'the Gold Diggings'. They met prospectors 'who have been in California and Australia & who speak English'; from them he learned enough to describe knowledgeably both the process and the economics of gold washing. There was coffee and schnaps to be drunk here, in a mining colony of about 350. One of the miners, Ludvig Knoblock, offered to accompany them on the next part of their expedition, to 'the nearest Lapp station':

> We have invited him to supper. What a supper! We have not had such luxuries since we left the steamer – six different kinds of preserved fish, all really good, potatoes from 6 miles off, our Capercailzie, port wine, pastry and cloudberry compôte – what an oasis of civilisation!

Evans describes the prospects from the mountain tops with something of an artist's eye:

> The view from the summit of the peak which is called Pietarinlautuoivi [Pietarlauttanen] Peter's table head gives a splendid panorama of the Fells. Low conical peaks; barren rocks; trees few & stunted compared with the forests of the lowlands. From here we made our way over the broad undulating table land of the range we were on, called as a whole 'Hammastunturi' – the tooth mountain & I saw two tame reindeer for the first time. We passed here and there bogs covered with Cloudberry, mostly over, & the leaves the colour of a Virginia creeper. This berry will keep for a year after being simply boiled. As we neared the edge of the plateau, the lake of Hammasjärvi, on whose bank the Lapp station we were bound for is situated, appeared below, backed by range after range of low mountains whose blue & slate coloured shadow kept shifting & changing as

fleecy clouds swept between them & the sky. We had to walk a long way through the forests & swamps that line the edges of this large lake before we saw the Lapp huts & were finally ferried across the Lake by a real Lapp & a little woman with a cap shaped like a Doges Crown.

Evans was delighted with his excursion to the Lapp settlement, and describes it rather as if it were a visit to a costume museum:

> what a relief after the dull costumes of the Finns, to come upon a people who evidently love ornament and colour. Our hostess was prevailed on to dress up in her go-to-meeting clothes for me to photograph her – it was positively overwhelming. I thought I had seen brilliant costumes in Servia, but nothing approaching this! scarlet the prevailing hue, orange, blue, green, purple, in bands, crosses, tartans, elaborate embroidery – and her cap! No longer the Doge's Crown, but Minerva's helmet, exquisitely graceful, but far too bright for Pallas. This dress is worn by the Lapps about here when attending church on special high days and holidays.

Evans describes the hut meticulously, and appends a careful drawing, remarking that 'inside there is some semblance to the plan of a Lapp hut given by Scheffer two centuries ago'.

Their guide had to return, so it was a Lapp woman who guided them to another, even more remote Lapp settlement:

> We were received by two Lapp men, one in blue and yellow coat, the other in dirty brown, the 'grand irreclaimable savage' with hair which apparently never has been cut, streaming over his shoulders, & a mouth big enough to swallow a loaf.

On 1 September they set off for Inari ('Enare') with 'the grand irreclaimable – I beg his pardon, Johanninpoika Marataja . . . acting as our guide'. Their first destination was 'the hut of a fisher Lapp overlooking a beautiful creek of lake Enare'. Inari had not previously been described in English. It is well known today because of Philip Pullman's creation of Serafina Pekkala, a witch queen from a tribe near Lake Inari in *His Dark Materials*.

After this, the Lapp interlude was over and they were 'again in Finnish civilisation'.

> Our host, whom it will be better to speak of as 'the miss-ing link', ferried us across the creek, and guided us through pinewoods strewed with immense boulders, till, as it was getting dark, we came in sight of the wooden church & huts of Enare, and a little further on a quaintly – but for these parts fashionably – dressed little man met us, who turned out to be the Pastor, who insisted on taking us in and 'var so göd'ed' us into discussing a bottle of sherry, while he got his handmaid to prepare the most sumptuous repast we have had in this country! & had a clean room prepared for us to sleep in. We then found that all the other huts we had seen were untenanted, being only used as temporary habitations by the Lapps, chiefly when they come to church once a fortnight; truly, as he expressed it, he has to do Apostles work. The 'missing link' is his near-est parishioner, four miles off, and he has also the charge of the parish of Usjoki [Utsjoki] on the Norwegian fron-tier four days off, on foot, mostly over difficult ground – this he visits six times a year, four times in winter, when travelling here is easier, and twice in summer.

They enjoyed 'more superabundant hospitality' next morn-ing, with duck, pike and potatoes – 'very fine for Finland'! Ex-ploring an old cave they decided to do some excavating and surprisingly came upon a Bronze Age pendant: 'Surely it is the most northern bronze age relic ever found!' (It is identified by the Ashmolean as a twelfth-century silver hair ring, and is currently (2012) on loan to the Inari Museum.) Returning from Inari, and heading south-west up the Ivalojoki ('the river gold'), they met 'a delightful little family' and their 'little girl of 3 in a Lapp cap & blue tunic with the usual blue stripes about it & a little boy of 5 who recited his ABC for our edification'. This girl is the subject of one of Evans's most attractive drawings.

On 6 September, three days later:

> At Kultala, securing guides, provisions &c for our route to Muoniska [Muonio] through country wilder and more uninhabited than any we have seen. Our friend the Australian, Bjorkman by name, a very sensible pleasant man, came in the morning to show us the gold he had got with 7 men in the last two days – 97 grammes – about £14 – very good. Indeed, he thinks this place richer in gold than any he has seen in Australia & believes that in another valley near still more gold would be found, & he is the most knowing man in the place in such matters . . .
>
> We have bidden one last & final farewell to every English scruple. We have taken a *Finnish bath*. There is a wooden hut built on purpose. The water was boiled in a large caldron on the rocks outside, then it was put into a large wooden bath decorated with crosses at the corners, like Oxford frames. On the other side was a raised kind of hearth on which were placed stones previously heated in a fire. Then water was poured on these until the whole place was like the inside of a boiler, & then you undressed, & then – I can't put off the shocking confession any longer! *She* bade you ascend the platform at the end of the hut & beat you – in the costume of Adam before the Fall – with leafy birch rods steeped in hot water, every now and then almost blowing off the the roof of the hut by pouring more water on the hot stones, & then turning you over and whipping you on the other side & having by

this time reduced you to a state of abject submission & the consistency of a boiled chicken, she puts you into the bath & scrubs you from top to toe, after which she scaled you with a towel, & must needs dress you and serve you up. Outside once more the fresh air gradually revives you – you, it is well to make this shocking narration as impersonal as possible! & you feel ready to walk a hundred miles. The proper thing is to wind up with a plunge in the river, but the weather tho' fine is too cold for that now.

'[W]ith Autumn falling upon us with shocking rapidity' it was time to head for home, but first to say farewells:

We had a general gathering of all our Ivalo friends to dinner. They liked English soup and English biscuits, but when it came to English tea I heard whispers of 'Skreglig stark'.

From this point the journal entries are shorter. The travellers struggled across a dangerous muddy plain, and failed in their only attempt to come to terms with a reindeer:

the saddle wasn't good, we could not balance the knapsacks properly, and the reindeer kept twisting about and butting at the Lapp who led him so that the luggage kept falling off his back. After several trials we had to give him up as a bad job and send him home by his driver.

On the positive side they saw 'a fine Aurora. A broad band of light arching like a rainbow across the Northern sky'. They left the Ivalojoki at Peltovourna, ('the first village we have seen in five days'):

From here we took a boat down the Onasjoki and went down some rather startling rapids, much swollen by the continued rain. To add to this pleasurable excitement, one of our bearers who poled at our bows was utterly incapable, and at the very worst part of one rapid, just as we were dodging almost broadside to the current to make for an opening between two rocks, at all times a rather difficult manoeuvre, he lost his pole, & hastily catching up another, lost that too, & we should infallibly have been upset, had not our little Lapp jumped, with great presence of mind, on to a rock where the water was not too deep for him to get a firm footing, & caught hold of the boat; an upset just then would have been rather a ticklish experiment! Some hours down the river brought us to Kyroe [Kyrö] a Finnish Kestikivari [inn] where we slept, but we are so far from civilisation that we cannot get corn rye bread, but have happily secured fresh salmon. Here I got a Lapp reindeer spoon with most characteristic zigzag ornaments.

On 13 September they 'set out to cross the Pallastunturi range to Muonionkoski, about 30 miles, the rain still pouring'. There, *chez* Forström, they felt that that they were back in civilisation: 'Fancy seeing a real bed once more! & real sheets!' This was where Rae had taken his sauna only weeks before. They now followed the same route as Rae; their rapid journey following the river Tornio down to the Gulf of Bothnia is recorded in just a few pages of the journal. After the primitive world of wild Lapland, Sweden seemed to them tame and uninteresting. The travellers arrived back in England on 7 October, Evans 'wearing a reindeer-skin coat so offensive to his step-mother that she wrote "I can't think how he can bear himself".'

The Pitt Rivers museum has many relics of Evans's expedition, notably a full Lapp winter costume, on display, and also many spoons carved from reindeer antlers, a powder horn, and numerous drawings and photographs.

Annie Margaret Clive-Bayley

Bunbury's travels were uneventful to the point of being predictable, but by the 1890s we find women genuinely exploring Finland, at times without any male company. In succession Miss Clive-Bayley, Mrs Alec Tweedie, Mrs Sylvia MacDougall and Miss Rosalind Travers published full-length accounts of their travels in Finland. Clive-Bayley's *Vignettes from Finland: or, Twelve Months in Strawberry Land* (1895) is the first of these.

Yrjö Hirn, Professor of Aesthetics at Helsinki University, gave MacCallam Scott a dramatic account of the impact upon Finland of this independent female traveller:

> She was an elderly lady, he said, about sixty years of age, and she came direct from India to Finland. She had read something about Finland which strongly appealed to her, and she had a great desire to see the country for herself. She remained there for a year and wrote her book. In the worst days of the Bobrikoff régime, Professor Hirn was a member of a small committee whose object was to keep British public opinion informed as to the nature of Russia's action in Finland. One day they had a visit from a pleasant, elderly lady, who gave her name as Miss Clive-Bayley. She was very indignant at the Russian oppression, and she seriously proposed to them that, if they would supply her with the necessary explosives, she would herself travel to the East of Finland, and blow up the railway bridges which connected the country with Russia. Then they could get on with the revolution.

This is a good story, but investigation does not bear out either the facts or the implications. The first pages of *Vignettes from*

Finland describe her journey from England on the *Urania*, leaving Hull on 12 July 1893. She may well have been pleasant, but was forty-one, hardly elderly, and certainly not sixty. Born at Nagpur in India, she was the daughter of Sir Edward Clive Bayley, who spent his professional life in the Bengal Civil Service. She had returned to Britain with her family, and perhaps remained when her parents returned to India, since she had been presented at court when she was nineteen.

Nothing in her book hints at any personal revolutionary ambitions, but there are numerous comments, from the moment the *Urania* docked in Turku, which make clear where her sympathies lay. During her tour of the town she notes that 'the names of the streets were indicated in Russian, Swedish and Finnish, a precaution quite necessary, as there are Russians who scorn to know the languages of the conquered country'.

Her first act in Finland was to summon a drosky by telephone. The British in the 1890s considered the telephone one of Finland's marvels: steamer and rail timetables could be checked, hotels reserved, and delays notified, even in distant Karelia.

After a quick tour of Turku she made the three-hour train journey to Urjala, where she was to stay as the guest of the daughter of the du Furuhjelm family at Hongola manor, south of Tampere. Here she began a serious study of Finland, discovering and assessing a lot of information about the country. Her book has a long chapter about farming on the estate, showing her informed awareness of the economic and social implications of agricultural development. She appears to have an excellent practical grasp of the operations of the steam dairy, and of the economics of distribution. Her account of her year in Finland is full of both facts and reflections about agriculture, land tenure, politics, local government, the church, and education. She is a forerunner of the ideological travellers, who in the 1920s and 1930s came to Finland to find out about its advanced institutions.

She was helped in this by her travel-companion, the daughter of the house, Annie Fredrika du Furuhjelm, whom she had met and befriended in London earlier in the decade. She was in her mid-thirties, already becoming a figure in the international women's movement, and was later eleced to Parliament. Although Clive-Bayley denies any special interest in the Women's Rights movement, writing that it had never 'agitated my soul', she was certainly influenced by her companion. Her life after returning to England was involved with nursery education (as a member of the Froebel Society, which promoted the kindergarten system), and with her weaving school, which was associated with the Society for Promoting the Employment of Women. One purpose of her visit was to find out about weaving and handicraft, which were were dying out in England, but still thriving in Finland. Everywhere she goes in Finland she notices clothing, for example 'the wonderful variety and splendour of of the aprons worn by all classes'.

Her first view of Finland, from the train to Urjala, is typically observant – fencing, livestock and drainage are what she notices, as much as scenic beauty. Here, as elsewhere, she appears overwhelmed by the profusion of wild flowers. Her account is also notable for its collection of Finnish sayings. She rarely misses an opportunity to underline her observations with a local proverb: 'a crane in a tree soon breaks its leg', or 'God did not create hurry'.

She made three major excursions. The first, by carriage, postcart and boat, was to Tampere, Ruovesi, Wirrat and Ahteri, returning to Urjala by train.

> Our first trip took us north-east, with lengthening days at each northward step. Tammerfors, the 'Manchester of Finland,' was curious and interesting in its way. We dined above a rushing rapid (*fors*, in Swedish, means 'rapid'), and we fed on the products of Finnish waters, trout, salmon, strömming (a kind of sprat), fresh-water crab, and on

the wild duck, then in season. We had our tea later in the garden of the restaurant, where the water rushed and tumbled close beneath our feet . . .

The old man who showed us over the garden [asked] if it was really true that we had a woman king in England? 'Woi, Woi!' was all he found to say to express his amazement, but subsequently he seemed much relieved to hear that she had three sons living.

The ladies, persuaded that they should adventure beyond the cultivated environs of Tampere, decided to head north and 'to let our course follow the windings of convenience, and the somewhat uncertain arrangements of local boats'. Thus it was that they arrived at Ruovesi, where, after attending the morning service, they watched the church boats departing, a scene 'not to be easily forgotten'. There were also brief brushes with Runeberg:

Here we were, in the house in which Runeberg used to dwell as a tutor. There is the birch-tree, with a ladder up to it, into which he used to scramble when he wanted to write. But up it we were not allowed to go, as it is too rickety for use. The house was let to the local doctor, and he and his wife gave us coffee. A room – kind of 'front parlour' – was arranged in much the same style as you would expect to find in such a room in England, combined with polished floors, crowds of growing plants, and some rather artistically-copied photographs in neutral tint washes.

Later in the afternoon the pastor took us across the water, again sailing his own boat, to a little grove called 'Runeberg's Spring.' Here we drank some very pure water, where the poet used also to drink, cups, according to the custom of the country, being improvised out of birch-bark.

The most adventurous part of the expedition is recorded in the chapter entitled 'To the Wilderness'. After a day's travel heading north in a 'little springless cart' they spent a night at Kaivos, where they found both the fish and their pillows so 'odoriferous' that they went without food and sleep. Next morning the boat took them to a farm, where they could get no refreshment but milk, because that week a little steamer had twice brought parties of sightseers who had 'eaten everything that was eatable'. From the farm there was an hour's walk to Helvetinjärvi – 'Hell Lake':

> The sun was really hot, and the midges, for the only time that summer, were troublesome, and tired after our bad night, and somewhat hungry, we started for the forest walk. It was not easy going, but there was so much beauty round us, and we saw so many tempting things to gather, that the way seemed shorter than it was in reality. In one place the torrent rushed foaming white over its own black waters, and is appropriately termed 'Hell stream,' from the region it is supposed to drain. But the winding path through deep meadow grass, and across slippery granite excrescences, and empty but muddy stream-beds, led us to our goal.
>
> Then we went on to the lake; the most weird, isolated and melancholy tarn imaginable. Overhead at first the sky was blue, but the waters beneath us were of horror-striking blackness. High granite cliffs shut us out from the world, cliffs which there was no chance of scaling, as they shot up, sheer and precipitous, to the clouds that gathered black with coming storm.
>
> The boatman was determined to give us the whole benefit of its horrors, and a full view of 'Hell's' mouth. At the far end of the lake we got out, but after scrambling some way up the narrow gorge, my limbs refused to drag me, and my friend did not go much farther. Our guide did not approve. We had not seen the boiling, angry stream, and he thought us faint-hearted tourists. But so tired and

oppressed were we, that neither of us could speak, and I fell asleep ere we reached land.

If ever a place were haunted, that lake must be such a spot, for the feeling of desertion and unutterable depression was almost unbearable.

Helvetinjärvi was already on the itinerary for 'tourists'; in 1982 it became a National Park.

Rather than endure the smells of Kaivos again, they decided to post north to Virrat, and return to Tampere by train from Ähtäri. On the way '[q]uite unexpectedly we came upon a lake known as Toriseva, a strip of water as weird and strange as that of Helvetinjarvi'. This chapter is entitled 'Beyond the Wilderness', but today they could have enjoyed following the official nature trail, and could have learned from the website that '[t]he scenic Torisevan Kahvimaja café, open in the summer season, looks over the rugged view'.

The second excursion was to South Karelia, travelling by train via Riihimäki, 'where we were glad to get some hot tea'. There they were joined by two English ladies, who were to be their companions for the tour. They made something of a sensation speaking English together at the inn and 'the passengers, who were also waiting for their train, were much amused'.

1893 seems to have been an unusually cold summer in Finland; 'the potatoes and oats had been lost to a hard frost in July'. The cold becomes a tediously recurrent topic. What Clive-Bailey does appreciate is the peace which Karelia offers:

> if a weary, overworked Briton wants beauty, rest, and perfect comfort combined with change, let him try this lovely spot, well-named Rauha, 'the abode of peace,' and stay there for a while. Five marks (= 4s.) a day is the charge for board and lodging, not, of course, including wine.

She seems, paradoxically, too rushed to enjoy this peace herself, worrying endlessly about steamer and train times.

There is virtually no description of Savonlinna, 'where there was much to be seen and but little time to see it'; they saw the castle but 'we had but a few minutes to spend in this historic place'. They were always concerned about mealtimes, and anxious not to miss their tea; the telephone seems to have made their travels more rather than less fraught. The weather did not interfere with the experience of Imatra; Clive-Bayley found it 'too grand for description', and the scene 'too beautiful for words, could they have been spoken', but Imatra already had a reputation as a tourist trap, where visitors were 'fleeced unmercifully'. Other beauty spots were spoiled by the weather; at Punkaharju, where '[e]verything is kept in park-like order', the 'charms' could be only imagined.

For more than a hundred years travellers had been describing the posting arrangements in Finland, but only rarely do we read anything informative about the posting stations, their proprietors, or their ordinary living conditions. The little we do read is often abusive, with travellers preferring to sleep in their own carriages. 'We were anxious to see something of the people,' Clive-Bayley writes, so at a post-house near Sortavala, while their tea was being prepared

> we strayed into the Pirthi [pirtti], or dwelling-room, where a tiny hammock suspended from the rafters held the youngest member of the family, a lovely, two-year-old child. Her fair, clear skin, and sun-bleached hair shone white against the yellow tints of the canvas or sacking among which she lay. Her legs and arms were uncovered, and had an artist strayed that way, the limbs, firm and round, and curved in full and perfect beauty, would have caught his delighted eye. Close by the door hung, suspended from a beam, a double-mouthed crock, of which we presently saw the use; for, with a slight touch, forth flowed the water in oriental fashion, over our hands, as we washed them.

Presently, the Isanta [isäntä], or master, came in from the field, and after an elaborate toilet and change of linen, sat down to potatoes, milk, and rye-biscuit, with the rest of his family. Our driver was present too, and the boy, 'Antti' – of course. Is there any house in Karelia without its 'Antti'?

The remainder of the group was formed by four women, the Emanta [emäntä], or farmer's wife, and two daughters, and the mother-in-law of Anna Maria's and Antti's mother. The latter was in the fields, and the two grandmothers looked as if there had just been a difference of opinion, when we first came in. However, Anna Maria possessed herself of a sixpenny silk handkerchief, which I had bought at a London sale for some such purpose, but which I had tied round my neck that day to keep off the sun. Her joyous crowing woke the family to life and interest, and Anna Maria was not the least delighted member of the family, when she discovered thus early in life that she possessed what all Finnish women so greatly prize – a red silk kerchief for head-gear. It was finally hung up on the rafters, which, as usual, were treated as wardrobes, bread stores, and general receptacles for fishing, gardening, and other implements.

Although Clive-Bayley rather likes to think that she is an explorer of the wilderness, she is in fact rather more at home with the comforts of Sortavala: '[t]he Tourist Club have opened up and laid out a charming park, where we spent some hours the day after our arrival'. These comforts, together with warmer weather, improved her mood. She 'was delighted with the work' which she saw at the weaving-school, as well. Looking back on her travels so far, she concluded:

never before had either of us dreamt of anything more lovely than this country of Ladoga, where the hills cradle the many bays and islets of the mighty lake. Lonely and isolated the fertile region may be, though alas! year by year, the railway advances, and the shrill whistle of the steamer invades still further the stillness of the inland waters.

Here, not for the only time, we meet the paradox of tourists who deplore the means which made their own visits possible.

Clive-Bayley's repeated attempts to hear runo singing came to nothing:

> We asked about Runo singers, and he [the driver] replied that we had left one behind us in his village who could sing all the songs that ever were, but it would have been no good to ask him to sing that day, for he could not have sung 'while the books were open,' *i.e.* in church-time.

Later, near Ristijärvi, they met another potential singer:

> But when we asked for a song, the man's face grew rapt in expression, and he slowly shook his head, and said that he could not sing in cold blood; he must be inspired, an answer which, it is said, is the sober truth.

She did, however, later in the year, manage to visit and take tea with the legendary oral poet Larin Paraske.

The visit to the Valamo monastery, on an island in Lake Ladoga, was a mixture of spiritual response and worries about lunch. They set off in 'cold, dreary mist', but

> the sun appeared, and we found every one was rushing on deck; and as we joined the stampede we saw, peering among the mass of rich foliage, blue domes, and golden minarets, bright glimpses of red walls, and white stone work — a scene half oriental in its mosque-like architecture, half tropical in the luxuriant wealth of vegetation.

The scene she describes is principally of huge numbers of assorted pilgrims being efficiently catered for.

From Valamo they boarded a large pilgrim boat to the adjacent island; 'the pilgrims simply swarmed in'.

> My friend and I watched the crowds with interest. Some pilgrims were scribbling hastily at the last moment the names of those for whom they desired to pray. The proper tariff for such prayers was printed, and hung up in the hall of the guest-house. Many had their prayers ready written, and our beautiful guide received a sheaf of these papers every time he appeared. Presently we went inside the chapel, and bought photographs and remembrances, listened to the hurried reading of these prayers, and to the music, in which our merry urchin of the boat was one of the chief singers.

She mused on the spiritual life, recording the 'sighs and groans of the worshippers', but was musing also on the inedible buckwheat porridge, and on having to make her own arrangements because she 'could not stand' the public washroom. Nonetheless '[w]e were almost sorry our plans took us south to Petersburg, for we had greatly enjoyed our stay in this quaint and curious place'.

Clive-Bayley spent the winter in Helsinki, a stay long enough to make her observations more measured and less impressionistic than those of travellers who were merely passing through:

> Social entertainments in Helsingfors consist chiefly of coffee-drinking about 12 o'clock, and small dinners at 4 o'clock. Calls of ceremony are made between 12 and 3, but friendly or intimate visiting may take place after 5.30 till 7. Society has three broad divisions: a Russian circle, of which I saw nothing, except at a few public places, and from what I observed there I do not fancy that the cultivated Russian of continental society is to be found in this capital. Secondly, Svekoman, or Swedish society, which contains many families belonging to the old *régime*, those

who, when the Russian governor in old past times did entertain, formed a sort of upper circle. Among such families there still lingers a delicate polish and suavity of manner, which is not handed down in the more Radical portion of this section of the community. Frank, bright, and with a touch of genuine kindliness, society as at present constituted has the '*bonne camaradie*' of a republic, rather than the polish of a court. Lastly, there comes the Finnish society, delightful in its hearty kindliness, its generous appreciation, its literary energy, enthusiasm, and determination. In fact, in education, commerce, and literature, the Finnish capital is the most go-ahead little place imaginable.

Her account of the city is as observant and informed as her earlier description of the farm at Urjala. She notes that '[t]he very servants are well informed, and the air breathes education', describes and admires the school system, and gives a long description of the principal paintings in the Athenuem.

The third journey, in June 1894, again took her eastwards, via Sortavala to Joensuu:

> There we spent June 24th – S. John's Day. Bonfires raised on huge poles, flame all through the night over East Finland, and men, sober all the rest of the year, keep the Baptist's festival with deep libations.

From Joensuu 'we drove through another glorious summer night to Kuopio, where I was eager to visit Mina Canthe, the great play-writer of Finland'. She bought some Finnish cloth in the shop, and Mrs Canthe 'kindly gave me the MS' of 'her most famous work'. This episode rather abruptly concludes the book.

Clive-Bailey describes the liberated position of women in Finland but does not regard it as a cause for particular celebration. That would be done by other British ladies: within a year of the publication of *Vignettes from Finland* Mrs Tweedie had landed.

Ethel Brilliana (Mrs Alec) Tweedie

Ethel Brilliana Tweedie arrived in Finland in June 1896, sailing direct from Hull on the *Urania,* for a stay of ten weeks. Her account of this trip, *Through Finland in Carts* (1897) proved very popular, and went through several editions. There is nothing in it, writes Anka Ryall, 'suggesting that the tour was anything but a delightful, unconventional, and educational holiday trip', but Tweedie's personal circumstances were in fact desperate: her husband had just died a bankrupt, leaving her and their two young children destitute. 'Pulling myself together,' she later wrote, 'I went to Finland to write a book.' Her education had included time at a German school, where she met a Finnish girl who, as a guest in England, 'had often done her best to persuade' her to visit Finland; they left soon after her husband's funeral.

Tweedie's life had been comfortable and prosperous before her husband's financial ruin; a photograph (introduced as the frontispiece in the revised edition) shows a woman dressed in the height of Victorian fashion, with ostrich feathers in her hat. She had already published *A Girl's Ride in Iceland* and *A Winter Jaunt to Norway*, and the success of *Through Finland in Carts* launched her on 'a profitable writing career', which included further travel books. She was a New Woman, earning her own bread: her journeys, she wrote, 'have almost all been made alone', sometimes in the saddle. She wrote in the Preface to the second edition of her Iceland book (1894) that it had 'unwittingly originated an angry controversy by raising the question "Should women ride astride?"'

She travelled with her sister, Olga, and 'Frau von Lilly'; this was not the school friend, but Léonie Aminoff, twin sister of

Sylvia MacDougall (whose own *Summer Tour* was published in 1908) and who 'was connected with some of the oldest families in Finland, and great and wonderful was the hospitality we – my sister and I – received upon her native shores'. These three formed the basis of the party (strangely, nothing is heard of the school friend from Germany); they were joined by various Finnish companions for different stages; often there were six of them, but they were 'a very merry party of forty or fifty' in Vyborg. All the 'delightful friends' Tweedie mentions were Swedish-speaking.

She refers repeatedly to her 'summer jaunt'. That is certainly what it was, but her account is interlarded with information about trade, forestry, education, and the arts. Everywhere she goes she notices the situation of women:

> it seemed to us strange indeed to see women cleaning the streets; huge broom in hand they marched about and swept the paths, while a whole gang of female labourers were weeding the roadways.
>
> Women in Suomi do many unusual things; but none excited our surprise so much as to see half a dozen of them building a house. They were standing on scaffolding plastering the wall, while others were completing the carpentering work of a door; subsequently we learnt there are no fewer than 600 women builders and carpenters in Finland.

A later chapter gives tabulated lists of all the jobs done by women.

When she touches on this subject it is usually linked with her admiration for education in Finland – universal, comprehensive, and co-educational:

> The men and women enjoy great freedom. Educated in the same schools, they are brought up to ignore sex; the young folk can go out for a whole day together, walking

or snow-shoeing, skating or sledging, and a chaperon is unheard of.

The equality extended beyond this: '[t]o be a school teacher in Finland is, as said before, almost the highest honour to which man or woman can attain, and every one speaks of this calling with the greatest respect'. In this brave new world Tweedie, for all her riding astride, was more likely to appear prudish than controversial. She and her sister, swimming at Sortavala, insisted on 'bathing-dress' and cap; onlookers, believing that they were drowning, launched a rescue. Their concern for their luncheon-basket at times becomes obsessive.

They followed an anti-clockwise route around Finland from Helsinki, leaving finally from Hanko. After seeing Helsinki they took a steamer, the *Kaiser Wilhelm*, to Viborg, and from there drove to join a Finnish family party at 'Ilkeäsaari'. They travelled on to Valamo, and then went by train to the Festival at Sortavala; when they resumed their journey they were astonished that the passengers sang almost continuously during the whole seven-hour journey to Antrea. ('Can there be such a thing as a musical train?') The train from there to Imatra was so slow that some cyclists who had started at the same time got there long before them.

She did not fail to be rapturous about the Imatra falls ('Such a scene enters one's very soul'), but was at the same time very contemptuous of the electric lighting, and of the modern bridge. Needless to say, she and her party stayed at the Cascade Hotel – 'Oh! the joy that night of being in real hotel, with a real brass bedstead and a real spring mattress.'

From Imatra they returned by steamer to 'Ilkeäsaari' for the midsummer bonfire. It was a thundery day with the temperature 96°F (36°C) in the shade. Here, as elsewhere, she was embarrassed by the large bag of rugs and fur-lined coats which she had brought with her from England to guard against the cold of the far north: 'during the whole of June, July and part of August we never undid them once nor opened our umbrel-la.' Perhaps she had read *Vignettes from Finland*, with its ac-count of summer frosts.

There followed a thirty-six hour trip on the *Concordia* to Savonlinna. Because tourists had taken all the accommodation they lodged for a few days in the castle, 'such fun, and so de-lightfully romantic':

> We explored dark chambers with a candle and matches, we cooked coffee on the stove for breakfast, and boiled eggs in an enormous tea-kettle, aided in our pleasant toil by two smiling much-interested watchmen, and afterwards ate our meal among tangled shrubs in a courtyard shaded from the sun's heat by a linden tree.

The castle gave full rein to Tweedie's vivid imagination as she dreamt of historic scenes that the ancient stones had witnessed, and convinced herself that there were ghosts at her chamber door.

At Punkaharju there was no problem with accommodation, although it was also crowded with tourists: Tweedie had tak-en care to book in advance at the hotel, but two different ac-quaintances from the steamer, concerned for her comfort, had also booked for her, so the hotel was expecting three parties of English ladies.

Their next stop was Kuopio, for the start of their tour 'Through Savolax in Carts' to Kajaani. In Sortevala they had seen a performance of *Anna Liisa* by Minna Canth, which she describes in detail. Her interest in the author increased when she reached Kuopio; '[w]e inquired where she lived, and found she had a drapery store'. Tweedie's admiration for a widow who 'can find leisure and energy to look after her shop' as well as bring up her children and make her name as a writer must have reflected several strands in her own life, and she was dis-appointed to find that that Minna Canth was not in town.

The tour had been arranged by 'the kindness of the Governor of the district', and his son ('the Baron') escorted them on the drive from Kuopio to Iisalmi, in a carriage with a hood. They travelled sixty miles 'by a route soon to be followed with railway engines', so Tweedie was one of the last travellers to experience this post route, and to describe a Finnish post-house. She marvelled particularly at the seemingly impossible feat of getting their carriage, ponies and themselves onto the small ferry boats.

The party increased to six at Iisalmi. They changed from the carriage to three carts to carry them and their luggage to Kaajani: 'The most primitive of market carts in England,' she writes, 'could not approach the discomfort of this strange Finnish conveyance.'

'[T]o understand anything of a land or its people,' Tweedie claims, 'is to leave the tourist route and peep into its homes for oneself'. The description of a typical post-station (majatalo), north of Kuopio, she offers as 'merely a peep at a Finnish home, in which just such a scene is enacted every day'. For more than a century British travellers had been staying in Finnish post-houses, but few of them noticed and described as much as she did:

> In the kitchen-dining-room was a baby in a cradle, and another sort of crib was hanging from the ceiling by cords, the infant lying in a kind of linen pocket on a pillow.
>
> We were much amazed to see a patent process by which the infant in the cradle was being fed. It was a wooden crib, in shape like an old German one, and at one side of it projected an arm of wood curved round in such a way that it came up from the side of the cradle and bent almost over the child's face. Great was our amazement to find that a cow horn was fixed into this wooden arm, so that the thin part of the horn reached the baby's mouth, while the thick part stood up three or four inches above the hole

in the wood in which it was resting. Was it a toy, we mar-velled, because, if so, it seemed remarkably dangerous to have anything so hard in such near proximity to a baby's face, but great was our surprise on closer examination to find it a feeding-bottle!

The horn was hollow, and on the thin end was a primi-tive teat of linen, through which the baby was drawing the milk poured in at the top of this novel feeding-bottle.

In a corner of the same room was a wonderful frame on rollers to teach a child to walk. There was a small round hole through which the infant was pulled, so that the polished ring supported it under the armpits, from that rim four wooden pillars slanted outwards, being bound together at the bottom by other pieces of wood securely fixed to four rolling castors. In this the child could move; and the little brat rolled about from side to side of the uneven flooring, securely held up in its wooden cage. A small child of five was peeling potatoes, specially dug up in our honour, beside a wooden bucket, while a cat played with a kitten, and a servant girl – for well-to-do farmers have servants – made black bread in a huge tub, the dough being so heavy and solid that she could not turn it over at all, and only managed to knead it by doubling her fists and regularly plunging them to the bottom with all her strength. Her sunburnt arms disappeared far above her elbow, and judging by the way the meal stuck to her she found bread-making very hard work . . .

It was a primitive dinner, but with fresh fish and eggs, milk and cream, no one need starve, and we only paid fivepence each for our midday meal, such a sum being fixed on the tariff. Our dear comfortable old hostess was fascinated by our presence, and sat smiling and blinking beside us all the time, her hands, folded over her port-ly form below the short straight cotton jacket she wore, were raised occasionally to retie her black silk head-covering. Again and again she murmured – 'Englantilila-jet' (English-woman), and nodded approval.

Moving on, they enjoyed an idyllic scene as they 'rowed over the wide waters of Maaniker [Maaninkajärvi], as still as a mirror, to the little white church'. Their boat leaked alarmingly, but they splashed ashore to enjoy the view from the bell tower. Tweedie condemned the proliferation of the *Aussichtsturm* (viewing towers), here and elsewhere in Finland, as 'a bane of existence to strangers'. After this little diversion they resumed their journey, stopping off at several 'torps' (peasant houses) and 'savupiritti' ('smoke cabins'):

> In we went to see a chimneyless cot. See, did we say? Nay, we could not see anything until our eyes became accustomed to the dim light. It was a tiny room, the stove occupying almost half the available space; there was no proper chimney; the hole at the top did not always accomplish the purpose for which it was intended, consequently the place was black with ancient smoke, and suffocating with modern fumes. The floor was carpeted with whole birch boughs, the leaves of which were drying in the atmosphere as winter fodder for the one treasured cow. For the cow is a greater possession to the Finn than his pig to the Irishman. The other quarter of the room contained a loom, and the space left was so limited we were not surprised that the dame found her little outside kitchen of much use. Two very small windows (not made to open) lighted the apartment; so how those folk saw during the long dark winter days was a mystery to us, for they made their own candles they said, just as English folks formerly made dips, and we all know the illumination from dips is uncertain and not brilliant. Still smoke, want of ventilation, and scarcity of light did not seem to have made

them blind, although it had certainly rendered them pre-
maturely old.

At Lapinlahti the proprietor spoke 'excellent English', and
served them a memorable meal:

> Whether that meal at *Lapinlahti* was specially prepared
> for our honour or whether it was always excellent at that
> *majatalo* we cannot say, but it lingers in remembrance as
> one of the most luxurious feasts we had in the wilds of
> *Suomi*.

> The heat was so great that afternoon as we drove to-
> wards *Iisalmi* – two or three inches of dust covering the
> roadways – that we determined to drive no more in the
> daytime, and that our future expeditions should be at
> night; a plan which we carried out most successfully. On
> future occasions we started at six in the afternoon, drove
> till midnight, and perhaps did a couple or three hours
> more at four or five in the morning; think of it!

> After peeping into some well-arranged Free Schools,
> looking at a college for technical education, being invited
> with true Finnish hospitality to stay and sleep at every
> house we entered, we drew up at the next *majatalo* to
> *Lapinlahti*. It was the post-house, and at the same time a
> farm; but the first thing that arrested our attention was the
> smoke – it really seemed as if we were never to get away
> from smoke for forest-burning or cow-milking. This time
> volumes were ascending from the *sauna* or bath-house,
> for it was Saturday night, and it appeared as if the popula-
> tion were about to have their weekly cleansing . . .

> Our host, a finely-made young fellow, fondly nursing a
> baby of about two years old, seeing our interest in every-
> thing, was very anxious we should join the bath party, and
> begged Baron George to tell us of its charms, an invitation
> we politely but firmly refused. He showed his home. When

we reached a room upstairs – for the house actually possessed two storeys – we stood back amazed. Long poles suspended from ropes hung from the ceiling, and there in rows, and rows, and rows, we beheld clothing, mostly under-linen. Some were as coarse as sacking; others were finer; but there seemed enough for a regiment – something like the linen we once saw in a harem in Tangier, but Tangier is a hot country where change of raiment is often necessary, and the owner was a rich man, while Finland is for most part of the year cold, and our landlord only a farmer. The mystery was soon explained; the farmer had to provide clothing for all his labourers – a strange custom of the country – and these garments were intended for eight or nine servants, as well as a large family. Moreover, as washing in the winter with ice-covered lakes is a serious matter, two or three big washes a year are all Finns can manage, the spring wash being one of the great events in their lives. The finer linen belonged to his family, the coarser to the labourers, and there must have been hundreds of articles in that loft.

When we left the room he locked the door carefully, and hung up the key beside it. This is truly Finnish. One arrives at a church; the door is locked, but one need not turn away, merely glance at the woodwork round the door, where the key is probably hanging. It is the same everywhere – in private houses, baths, churches, hotels; even in more primitive parts one finds the door locked for safety – from what we know not, as honesty is proverbial in Finland – and the key hung up beside it for convenience.

Our night's lodging disclosed another peculiarity; – nothing is more mysterious than a Finnish bed. In the daytime every bed is shut up. The two wooden ends are pushed together within three feet of one another, kaleidoscope [*sic*] fashion, the mattress, pillows, etc., being doubled between; but more than that, many of the little

154

beds pull also out into double ones from the sides – altogether the capacities of a *Suomi* couch are wondrous and remarkable. Yet, again, the peasants' homes contain awfully hard straight wooden sofas, terrible-looking things, and out of the box part comes the bedding, the boards of the seat forming the *soft* couch on which weary travellers seek repose, and often do not find it! . . .

We had to rough it while travelling from *Kuopio* to *Uleåborg*. Often eggs, milk, and black bread with good butter were the only reliable forms of food procurable, and the jolting of the carts was rather trying; but the clothes of the party suffered even more than ourselves – one shoe gradually began to part company with its sole, one straw hat gradually divided its brim from its crown, one of the men's coats nearly parted company from its sleeve, and the lining inside tore and hung down outside. We had not time to stop and mend such things as we might have mended, so we gradually grew to look worse and worse, our hair turning gray with dust, and our faces growing copper-coloured with the sun.

Undaunted by the dust, they remained in 'the best of health and spirits', but they had to 'rough it' at one post-house where 'everything was filthy, and we felt sick at heart while drinking milk and coffee at the place'. 'Reader, pity our plight!' she concludes after being so hungry that she had to 'eat some of the native rye bread'. Another feature of 'roughing it' was the bedbugs: they disgusted the ladies, whereas the mosquitoes only annoyed them. Tweedie concludes an account of a bad night at another post-house graphically:

In the morning we peeped at the nice linen sheets; sprinkled on the beds were brown-red patches, here and there as numerous as plums in a pudding, each telling the horrible tale of murders committed by English women.

Comfort was near; a few days later they hit town:

> Kajana at last ! What a promised haven of rest after trav-
> elling for days in springless carts, happily through some of
> the most beautiful parts of Finland.

After explaining the techniques and economics of tar-making,
Tweedie describes her journey from Kaajani down to Oulu by
tar-boat. After a demonstration run in the governor's 'private
tar-boat', they took a small steamboat to Vaala, 'where our own
tar-boat was awaiting us'. Their tar-boat 'had been ordered',
and since they were a party of six with luggage, it can hardly
have had space for any tar. Twenty-eight hours later they arrived at Muhos, and transferred onto a little steamer for Oulu.
There is a whole chapter devoted to 'Descending the Rapids',
where Tweedie describes the excitement and the spice of danger, yet the central episode for her seems to have been not the
breathtaking dangers of the descent, but the loss of her tea kettle. As they picnicked near Pyhäkoski the spirit-lamp suddenly
exploded, igniting the tea-basket, which a quick-thinking member of the party threw into the river. 'Our tea was lost, and our
delightful basket, that had travelled in many lands, destroyed.'

Shortly after this a dense fog descended, and since they could
not continue the journey that day, they headed for a nearby
farmhouse:

> [W]hile the others worked, the writer made the accompany-
> ing hurried sketch [see Frontispiece] by the daylight of
> midnight at the 'Haven of Refuge', as we christened our
> new abode. The kitchen, or general living-room, was, as
> will be seen by the sketch, typically Finnish. The large oven
> stood on one side furnished with the usual stone stairs, up
> which the family clamber in the winter months, in order
> that they may sleep on the top of the fireplace, and thus
> secure warmth during the night.
>
> On the other side we noticed a hand-loom with linen

in it, which the good housewife was weaving for her family. Before it was a wooden tub, wherein flour for making brown bread was standing ready to be mixed on the morrow; in front of it was a large wooden mortar, cut out of a solid tree trunk.

The light was dim, for it was midnight, and, although perfectly clear outside, the windows of the little gray house were so few and so small that but little light could gain admittance.

This but added to the weirdness of the scene. It all seemed unreal – the dim glow from the spluttering wood, freshly put on, the beautiful shining copper coffee-pot, the dark obscurity on the top of the oven. The low ceiling with its massive wooden beams, the table spread for the early breakfast – or maybe the remnants of the evening meal – with a beer-hen full of Kalja [beer], a pot, rudely carved, filled with piimeä or soured milk, and the salted fish so loved by the peasantry – there all the necessaries and luxuries of Finnish humble life were well in evidence.

The heat was somewhat oppressive, for in those homesteads the windows are never opened from year's end to year's end – indeed, most of them won't open at all. In a corner hung a *kantele*, and as this romantic chamber, with its picturesque peasant occupants and its artistic effect, merely wanted the addition of the musical songs for which Finland is famous, and here was the very instrument hanging upon the wall, the farmer most kindly offered to play it for us.

After Oulu the party had planned to travel into Lapland, but 'felt degraded, mentally, morally, and physically' by the bugs and mosquitoes; wanting no further 'horrors', they took the coastal steamer south to Turku. 'Travelling through the interior and Northern parts of Finland,' she had concluded, 'is roughing it indeed'.

The boat stopped off at the coastal towns on the way, but Tweedie records only one trip ashore:

Wasa is celebrated for its beautiful girls; and remembering that during eight or nine weeks in Finland we had seen no pretty peasants, and only about as many good-looking girls of the better class as could be counted on the fingers of both hands, full of pleasant anticipation we went on shore to see these beauteous maids – and – there were none. The town was deserted, every one had gone away to their island or country homes, and no doubt taken the pretty girls with them. At all events they had left *Wasa*, which, to our surprise, was lined by boulevards of trees, – quite green and picturesque, stone houses here and there, and an occasional villa – so if we did not find lovely females, we at least beheld one of the nicest-looking towns of Finland.

Her comments on Turku are confined to the mummies in the cathedral, and the crayfish in the market:

We saw marvellous mummies – all once living members of some of the oldest families in Finland; there they lie in wondrous caverns in the crypt, but as formerly tourists were wicked enough to tear off fingers and so forth in remembrance of these folks, they are now no longer shown. However, that delightful gentleman, the Head of the Police who escorted us about *Åbo*, had the mysterious iron trap-door in the floor uplifted, and down some steep steps – almost ladder-like, with queer guttering tallow dips in our hands – we stumbled into the mummies' vault. The mummies themselves were not beautiful. The whole figure was there, it is true, but shrivelled and blackened by age. The coffins or sarcophagi in which they lay were in many cases of exquisite workmanship.

Tweedie is the first British traveller to mention crayfish; 'It was at *Åbo* we were introduced to one of the greatest delicacies of Finland':

> It was really amazing, in the market-place at *Åbo*, to see the large baskets filled with these little crayfish. Think of it, ye gourmands! They were not sold singly or even by the score, but by the hundred; and a hundred of them cost fourpence. When one remembers the enormous price paid in Paris for *bisque* soup, and the expense of *écrevisse*, generally, one feels what a fortune ought to lie in those baskets.

Despite her enthusiasm, she does not describe actually eating them.

Tweedie's jaunt ends in Hanko, 'A Fashionable Watering Place'. A Russian squadron was in town, and 'the Admiral kindly invited us on board'. She complains about the prices ('No-one with a slender purse should go') and describes the Sunday ball and the casino, characterising the town patronisingly as

> A dear, sweet, reposeful, health-giving, primitive place, spoilt by gay Russians and would-be-fashionable Finns, who seem to aim at aping Trouville or Ostend without the French *chic*, or the Parisian *gaieté de coeur*!

She seems in this *adieu* to be aligning herself with the 'unfashionable Finns', those she met more than those she travelled with. Neither here, nor anywhere else on her tour, does she sound like a penniless widow.

Tweedie was one of the first British travellers to take an informed interest in Finnish social and political issues. The successive editions of her book, up to 1913, were 'brought up to date in every way possible'. For example, the revised edition (1900) adds an Appendix on the Tsar's 'February Manifesto' of 1899 and the Finnish Reply. Her interest in many aspects of 'the new nation', especially education and the position of women, both of which she recognised as far in advance of England, was long-lasting. Finland 'is now "knocking at the door" of nations,' *Through Finland in Carts* concludes; in the 1913 edition she adds these final words: 'Finnish women are the most advanced in the world today. All honour to them, and all congratulations to their wise men. Great women help to make great nations.'

It is a subject she returns to, in some way or another, in almost every chapter, as in the following contemplation:

> In other pages we note the tremendous work women are doing on every side. It may, of course, arise from the fact that the Finns are poor, and, large families not being uncommon, it is impossible for the parents to keep their daughters in idleness, and as no country is more democratic than Finland, where there is no court and little aristocracy, the daughters of senators and generals take up all kinds of work. Whatever the cause, it is amazing to find the vast number of employments open to women, and the excellent way in which they fill these posts. There is no law to prevent women working at anything they choose.
>
> Amongst the unmarried women it is more the exception than the rule to find them idle, and instead of work being looked upon as degrading, it is admired on all sides, especially teaching, which is considered one of the finest positions for a man or woman in Finland. And it is scientific teaching, for they learn how to impart knowledge to others, instead of doing it a dilatory and dilettante manner, as so often happens elsewhere.
>
> We were impressed by the fact of the marvellous energy and splendid independence of the women of *Suomi*. Of course, there may be cases of hysteria and some of the weaker feminine ailments, which are a disgrace to the sex, but we never came across any.
>
> All this is particularly interesting with the struggle go-

ing on now around us, for to our mind it is remarkable
that so remote a country, one so little known and so un-
appreciated, should thus suddenly burst forth and hold
the most advanced ideas for both men and women. That
endless sex question is never discussed. There is no sex in
Finland, *men and women are practically equals*, and on
that basis society is formed. Sex equality has always been
a characteristic of the race, as we find from the ancient
Kalevala poem.

In spite of advanced education, in spite of the emancipation of women (which is erroneously supposed to work
otherwise), Finland is noted for its morality, and, indeed,
stands among the nations of Europe as one of the most
virtuous.

Tweedie was one of the first English travellers to pay serious attention to the sauna; the word itself is first found in English in
her book. 'A Finnish bath,' she wrote, 'once taken by a man or
woman, can never be forgotten.' Her enjoyment seems to have
increased even further in retrospect, since the first words of the
1913 edition are completely rewritten: 'It is worth the journey
to Finland to enjoy a bath; then and not till then does one
know what it is to be really clean.' She and her sister bathed
at almost every opportunity on their travels, although English
modesty prevented them from joining the locals at the farm
near Lapinlahti. Her addiction to baths could not be satisfied
by the sauna alone. At Kajaani she took the waterfall bath, a
small wooden cabin erected beside the rapids through which
part of the river was diverted:

> How shall we describe it? It was a small room about 8
> or 10 feet square, with a wooden floor and walls. The top
> of the wall facing us did not join the roof by about a foot,
> so as to enable the water to rush in, and the bottom of the
> wall behind us did not reach the floor by another foot, so

as to allow the water to rush out. Some half-dozen stairs descended from the platform on which we stood to the floor below, but as the only light came in where the falling water was always dripping, the walls were soaking wet, and therefore quite black. It was dull and mystic to say the least of it. Once the full force of the water was turned on by the large wooden arm, it poured in with such tremendous force from about 10 feet above, that in a moment the floor below was a bubbling, seething, frothing pool, and as we descended the steps into this bath, now some 2 or 3 feet deep, the force of the stream was so great that we had actually to hold on by the rail of the stairs to keep our feet at all on the slippery floor below. It was a lovely sensation. A piece of bacon bubbling about in the fat of the frying-pan must experience something like the same movement as we did, bobbing up and down in this rapidly flowing stream. It almost bumped us over, it lifted us off our feet, and yet, as the water swirled round us, the feeling was delicious, and its very coldness was most enjoyable after the heat outside, and the dust we had travelled through.

In Kuopio she heard about the ant bath and would not be satisfied until she had tried that too:

> Into a dear little room I went, and lo, the hot water in the bath was brown! while, floating on the surface, I saw a small linen sack, shaped like a pillow-case, securely tied at the end. The cushion contained the ant-heap, on which boiling water had been poured, so that the animals were really dead, the colour of the water having come from their bodies.

As she completed her bath – she took a douche just to be on the safe side – a whole procession of curious ladies came to look at her. She overcame her initial indignation as she reasoned, 'I had come to try a strange Finnish bath which interested me –

why should they not come to see a queer Englishwoman if it amused them?'

Through Finland in Carts is a milestone in the history of travel-writing about Finland. Tweedie is still just recognisably in the line of the pioneering travellers, but as a representative Victorian lady she often feels violated, and is forever scolding the Finns – for bad sanitation, for uncleanliness, for poor punctuality and for disregarding personal privacy. She is troubled by the open-door policy in inns, by the absence of blinds or curtains, and especially by naked bathing. Every day she encountered practices and customs which puzzled and surprised her.

One of her recurrent complaints about the Finns is that – apart from the sauna – they never wash. She never reconciled herself to the impossibility of getting hot water for washing; the maids could never be persuaded to provide anything more than a small basin of cold water, and there were problems even in a large hotel when they thought they had settled their request with the manager:

> After a few minutes we heard a knock on the door (the door actually possessed a bolt, or he would not have knocked), and on opening it we found the landlord. 'Pardon, Madame, but do you want the hot water to drink?' 'No, no,' we answered: 'to wash with.' He looked amazed; evidently he was more accustomed to people drinking tumblers of hot water – a somewhat rare occurrence at half-past seven in the morning anywhere, we should have thought – than he was to our requiring it for washing purposes.

Soap, too, was a problem; when their last piece was 'reduced to a sliver' Olga went hunting, and eventually returned not with 'beautiful pink scented soap . . . made in Paris or London', but

> a hideous brown brick made in Lapland . . . when we began to wash, this wondrous soap which had cost so much

trouble to procure – such hours in its pursuit – was evidently some preparation for scrubbing floors and rough household utensils.

She praises Finnish eggs, as she does the milk and cream, but could never procure any salt, and had to learn a new life-skill when eating them. At one post house there were

hot eggs, but no egg-cups, of course. We bumped the round heavy end of the eggs, and stood them up on our plates, native fashion, and felt we had learnt a trick that might be useful when egg-cups fell short in England!

'An endless source of amusement to the natives was the Englishwomen eating jam!' In Vaasa, after they had been to the baths, they tried to order some cloudberry jam:

'Hjortron? But there is no meat.'

'We don't want any meat; but the ladies would like some jam with their coffee.'

'Then shall I bring you cream to eat it as pudding?' she asked, still more amazed.

'No,' was the reply, 'they will eat it spread on bread and butter.'

'What! Hjortron on bread and butter!' the waitress exclaimed. 'Impossible!'

Tweedie's chauvinism is redeemed by her humour. However critically she looks at the Finns, she is usually aware that to them she too must often appear comic or eccentric. For example, wherever she went she was troubled by the lack of curtains, which meant they were awoken very early by the sun. In their lodgings at Sortevala she and her sister asked for their beds to be made with the pillows at the foot, so as to be shaded from the direct sunlight. The servant was very perplexed, and finally tackled their host, asking 'Is it part of the English ladies' religion to sleep the wrong way round?'

C. J. Cutcliffe Hyne

Tweedie's repeated claims that her discomforts could be characterised as 'roughing it' seem laughable when set next to the journey taken by Charles John Cutcliffe Wright Hyne (to give him his full name) in the following year. His *Through Arctic Lapland* (1898) is quite unlike any of the thirty-odd novels which constitute the bulk of his literary output (only *The Lost Continent: The Story of Atlantis* ever surfaces nowadays). He wrote no other travel books, claiming to have made only £8-15-6 from *Through Arctic Lapland*, and to have 'decided then that my country's travel books could be written in future by pens other than mine'. He would not have lacked material for further such books, since he travelled extensively, often as a game-hunter, in Europe, North America, Brazil, Mexico, the Amazon and the Belgian Congo. These travels provided material for his novels; one of his stories has been seen as a source for Joseph Conrad's *Heart of Darkness*. He had once rented an estate above the Folden fjord in Norway for shooting and fishing and had spent about a fortnight with a Sami family, developing a genuine interest in their way of life.

'His books,' writes Hyne's biographer, 'are written in a bracing tone, with frequent expressions of contempt for weaklings and whiners, and of belief in hard work and the salutary effect of the school of hard knocks.' Hyne's companion, Cecil Hayter, was an amateur artist, and provided the illustrations for the book; the only information I have found about him was that he later wrote a number of stories about Sexton Blake, an adventurous and fearless detective. This pair took on Lapland with some panache.

Hyne, like Rae, was an individualist and an improviser; the idea of an expedition came when 'one night in someone's billiard room we had talked vaguely over "going north and doing something up there"'. Rather than pottering along to Foyle's bookshop to get Murray's *Guide*, he went to the British Museum, where he found that 'had stumbled across the one bit of Europe which has not been pilloried on paper at one time or another'. So it was that he and Hayter set off for 'that unmeddled-with country, Arctic Lapland':

> [d]rawing from our own ignorance, and from the united ignorance of others (most freely and generously bestowed), we mapped out the details of the campaign with glibness and ease.

The plan looked simple enough on the map: it was to cross Lapland 'from north to south, and take to the seas again at the head on the Gulf of Bothnia'. There were 'plenty of villages – the map marked them with clearness and precision', and 'reindeer meat, salmon, rye bread, milk, cheese, and butter would be always procurable from the natives'. Every one of these assumptions proved to be ludicrously naïve and optimistic; Hyne came to describe the map-maker as 'a mis-director of the blackest class'.

The travellers sailed from London to Norway, landing at Vardø, beyond the North Cape. Hyne belonged to that race of Victorian travellers who always get their way, who outface their guides and servants, and who meet with cool aplomb whatever difficulties and hardships confront them. When they were promptly told that their chosen route, especially the central part, was impossible except in winter, he simply took no notice: 'Vardö could not be expected to know much about a journey which was never done,' he reasoned. By this time (1896) the railway had reached Tornio, and an excursion into Lapland would soon become a bolt-on extra to the standard tour, involving little diversion or inconvenience. Hyne's account of his journey offers an antidote to this sort of comfortable tourism:

the Lapland which he describes seems as remote and genuinely more dangerous even than that traversed by the eighteenth-century travellers.

They took the coastal steamer across Varangerfjorden and up Jarfjorden, passing whalers, stopping off at fishing villages, and finally switching to canoe as they approached the Finnish border. Soon 'the real troubles of the of the journey had fairly begun'. Chapter IV promises 'pungent Comment on the Habits of Finnish Carriers': their idiosyncrasies rivalled those of Rae's boatmen:

> Never were such carriers. They were all able-bodied Finns, though one (and he was the strongest) had a hump like a Brahmin cow, another had a hare-lip, and the head-man possessed a most virulent squint; but they were the most impracticable creatures that ever slouched over the face of the earth.

The idealised picture of Lapland (perhaps developed during the earlier visit to Norway) was evaporating rapidly. The 'two-roomed log-hut of a Finnish farmer' was not a promising start: they 'had to wade a river to reach it', '[t]he farmer had but one cow, and she was not in milk', the garden consisted of a few drills of 'unenergetic potatoes', and 'they could give us nothing to eat'. Hyne did concede that '[t]he water was good'.

The slow trek with the hopeless bearers ended when they came across a canoe; although it 'leaked like a basket', they kept it afloat until 'the navigable water ended for good' and they were then back on foot, through a dreary, dead and blighted forest. Suddenly they came upon

> a log-house painted dragon's blood red, and a bay beyond whereupon rode a masted boat. That one house made up the town of Ischinlisvuoni, the northernmost port of Enere See.

The boat was from Inari, and would take them there after some necessary repairs. They 'took possession of one of the two rooms', where they found that they were stared at continually, 'as though we had been performing animals'.

It was time for everyone to take the 'Finnish vapour bath', but the English guests declined. In another account he discloses that 'Hayter and I tried these Finnish baths, and our natural shyness always produced shouts of merriment'. As the bathers returned to the house, they presented a picture of life in that remote place which Hyne catches beautifully:

> All through that evening, and till three o'clock the next morning, the bathers in every stage of undress, from the complete to the partial, were sitting about in the kitchen which was next our room. It never seemed to strike any of them that the sight for alien eyes might be a trifle quaint. At the great white Russian stove a woman was cooking circular cakes of rye with a hole in the middle, and threading them on a stick as fast as they were baked. Another woman was roasting coffee, and a man beside her was grinding the beans as they were browned. Half-clad children were sprawling about the floor, and two or three were asleep in a corner. A naked man was contemplatively browsing on tobacco before the stove, and a woman was treading at a spinning-wheel in the middle of the room. By the window our two boat-men squatted on the ground with palm and needle, mending the split sail, and beside them the hump-back was playing jigs on a cheap accordion. These were all Finns. The only two Lapps in the place were supping in a corner, off curdled milk and flinty rye cakes.

After paying off the Finnish porters, not without problems, they were concerned to find that their 'two boatmen were Finns also'. They need not have worried:

> they were incomparable boat-sailors. In the course of our

voyage occasion came more than once when there was need for handiness and quick decision: and South-coast yachtsmen, bred in racers, could not have beaten these inland sailors from the north.

Napier would perhaps have been surprised that the Finnish seamanship which he so admired could be found as far north as Lake Inari.

The lake itself was for Hyne 'somewhat of a disappointment; the scenery was unexciting', and there was no 'shootable game'. The lake fishermen were much more interesting:

We came across these lake-fisher Lapps at intervals, and often sat and chatted round their camp fires. I remember well the first of these savage entertainments. Our eyes caught a slim blue drift of wood-smoke rising up from the farther side of an island. We ran down, hauled our wind, and sailed up to it. We were welcomed ashore with easy cordiality. There were three Lapp canoes nuzzling the foot of a black rock, and on the crown of the rock were their crews of four men and three round-faced, good-humoured women. They cleared the place of honour for Hayter and myself, and we sat down in the smoke drift from the fire, where the mosquitoes could only raid us with difficulty, and we listened to the politics of the lake: fishing was good here and bad there; this man had finished eating that lame deer he killed in the early spring; that man's canoe had been beached in a gale, and smashed like an egg.

One lady indeed wanted to know about the outer world. She was a portly young person, whose globular red face beamed with a healthy animal cheerfulness. She had stubby hands, and a figure which resembled a corn sack, well filled, and stamped down. She carried a neat brass wedding-ring slung to her neck-handkerchief, and had a most educated taste in tobacco. She filled her pipe with shavings from my plug of negro-head, lit it with a brand from the fire, and then absorbed the smoke in an ecstasy. It was enjoyment to watch her pleasure: she puffed that pipe to the uttermost ash, and the vapour circled amongst her smiles. Then the spirit of inquisitiveness, and perhaps of envy, took her, and she wanted to know if this beautiful, this exquisite tobacco was the common smoke of my country.

To weakly avoid an hour's complicated explanation, I admitted that it was.

And could English ladies have as much of it as they wished?

With distinct truth I answered that no stint was put upon them in the matter.

At Inari they had a letter of introduction to the priest, Pastor Hinkola. He was absent,

but Fru Hinkola and her brother, the postmaster, took us in charge, and strangers in a strange land were never more hospitably entreated. We had all our meals at their table, and if we did not sleep under the parsonage roof, it was only through our own refusal to trespass farther on their kindness.

They were not cheering, however, about our chances of getting through across the country to Kittila. It was never done in summer; there were no roads; the mosquitoes and the swamps were almost impassable; horses or reindeer were utterly out of the question; lakes and rivers lay in the way, over which it was very doubtful if we should find ferriage even for ourselves; and, finally, it was distinctly improbable that we could get carriers to pack our goods beyond the first stage or two.

The only possible route to Kittilä, they were told, was by canoe:

And we should see, what? Well, we should have an excellent view of several hundred miles of river-bank. And we could post onwards with horses either to Kittila or else directly down to the sea, in comparative luxury and comfort.

This had satisfied Rae, but would not do for Hyne: '[w]e had not journeyed that far, however, to exploit future tourist routes'. He ignored all warnings, and simply ordered carriers for the morrow.

'In the meantime we looked about us.' Hyne gives an account – both impressionistic and informed – of 'the chief city of the Lapps', Inari:

> There are twelve hundred people in Enare, but as the town-limits are some seven miles across, a stranger looking at it from the landing-place might reasonably put down what he saw from there as a small straggling village of new log-houses set down near a spired, red church. The houses were closer once and older, but one of the periodical fires broke out during a gale a few years back and swept the whole place away, so that it had to be entirely rebuilt . . .
>
> A few of the Lapps of Enare town keep unostentatious stores, where they sell sewing-cotton, gun-powder, cone-sugar, axes, and coffee-beans, all of which have been brought up by sledges during the winter from Helsingfors, Uleaborg, and the towns without the Arctic Circle. But the import traffic is small, and the reindeer, which form the only export, are driven down alive to the markets. The community is self-supporting: it catches and cures its own fish; produces its own milk, curd, rye-meal, and dried meat; weaves its own woollen cloth and checked cotton wear; builds its own houses, boats, sledges, and churns; makes for itself spoons, casks, bowls, balers, all from the native birch-wood; brings forth its own young, and buries

its dead with a roofed-in sledge for a coffin.

The community hinges on the parsonage, the largest house in the place, the only house which has an upper story, which is weather-boarded without, and which has the nakedness of its logs covered by a ceiling within. Here are the brains of the place, the Law of the place, the post-office, the only library. At the parsonage they had two hundred books; and English literature was not neglected. There were translations of Messrs. Stanley Weyman, Fergus Hume, and W. Le Queux, in sumptuous pictured covers. It was there we got our Russian roubles changed to Finnish marks.

Before leaving Inari Hyne, disappointed at not having found anything in Lapland to shoot, sold his rifles:

We sold the Marlin for the price it had cost in London town, and threw in the cartridges as ballast to the bargain. It was the postmaster who bought; and in the joy of his purchase he put the Marlin to his shoulder, aimed at a hut some fifty yards away, and pulled trigger. The result was surprising. The bullet went in at one side of the hut and out at the other, and as the inhabitants happened to be within at the time, they came out hurriedly, and looking distinctly worried. The postmaster was only acquainted up to then with the penetrative power of the local weapon. So this performance of the Marlin made him dance with delight.

He describes the next stage in two graphic chapters entitled 'Into the Land of Horrible Flies'. At Menesjärvi, which was 'nothing more than the squalid huts of one small family', they were offered the best accommodation – the couch in the dairy. They preferred the floor, ate curds, and opened a tin.

We tried pulling the heavy blanket-sacks over our heads

and getting off to sleep that way. But the result inside was a choking Turkish bath, and as the mosquitoes got in also, we did not get much profit that way. We tried leaving our heads outside the sacks, and protecting them with hats and veils, but that was a more dismal failure still. And finally we were reduced to lying on our backs and keeping our faces in the midst of a halo of pungent, stinging, ship's tobacco-smoke.

In the meanwhile we had not been left in our lonesomeness. Almost the entire time we had one visitor or another staring as though we had been strange and slightly amusing animals . . .

A weird crew they were too, this audience at Menesjärvi, and it was hard at times to persuade ourselves that we had not gone to sleep after all, and that these were merely the people of fever and nightmare. They were most of them deformed.

From Menesjärvi they hired a canoe. At first, after the 'horrors of the night', 'the canoe carried us as though it were the delightful vessel of a dream':

We might have been rowing by some river-side park on the Thames, the cultivated growth of ages, the daily care of a hundred gardeners. There were graceful foliage trees, and trim, well-favoured shrubs, and clumps of flowers, and lawns of the pleasantest green, all repeated faithfully in the still mirror of the water. It was hard to keep in mind that human foot did not tread these banks once in a dozen years.

Soon the sun went in, the mosquitoes returned, and the travellers were brought from their 'brief, pleasant dream back to some of the cruder realities of Arctic Lapland'. The stream gave way to marsh, and after some days they had altogether lost their route, as far as they had one. Their direction was generally southwards, but they took one deliberate diversion, to meet the 'herder Lapps'; Hyne gives a very intelligent account of many aspects of their life. They were especially interested in witnessing 'some practical sorcery'; 'we wished to see the drum brought out. And a genuine active curse performed,' he wrote, but all this proved to be too delicate a subject. 'Our grimy host grinned and shook his head.' 'I am inclined to believe that the whole business has died out,' Hyne concludes; the population 'are moving with the times. Many of them can read, and some can write.'

> Finally, after wallowing painfully through another quagmire of still more horrible wetness and filth, we came upon a river, deep, swift-flowing, and two hundred feet from bank to bank. And this, unless the map was crowning its petty perjuries by the most cruel, colossal lie ever scratched upon paper, was the Repojoki.
>
> Ivalomati, if it existed at all, was obviously on the farther side, and it behoved us to cross with as little delay as might be. But here came another difficulty. We proposed to build a raft to carry our goods piecemeal, and swim it across to the other side. But the Lapps, with the usual contrariness of those who live in a country of water-ways, could not swim a stroke, and refused flatly to be towed over, floated by a log. So there was nothing for it but to build a raft which would carry passengers, and to this pleasing business we set our hands without further talk.

Making the raft with one small axe was a test of their ingenuity – Baden-Powell writ large – but it just about held together until their ninth and final crossing, when it disintegrated (the subject of one of Hayter's best illustrations). After further hardships they arrived finally at Ivalon Matti:

> the village we had looked for for so long, a place made up of one small house of logs, one squalid barn with yawning

sides, and an adult population of three souls – a woman and two men.

Even Hyne, usually completely imperturbable, was affected by the mosquitoes here, recording that 'we passed that night in a condition bordering on frenzy'. In fact, the central part of Hyne's narrative reverts vividly and repeatedly to the sufferings inflicted by mosquitoes, dragonflies, bluebottles and horse flies; it was a new circle of Hell. A few days earlier he had recorded that their hands were 'the size of boxing gloves', and that Hayter had had to cut his way out of his trousers because his legs were so swollen. There were, of course, no carriers to be had; they finally persuaded the three from Inari to continue as far as Pokka, where they found 'a long slack-jointed Finn, with one ear missing and a face as unemotional as a slab of board', who reluctantly sold them food.

> A woman brought it in – rye-cake and a double handful of small pieces of raw fish, semi-dried, and a tub of thick sour milk. As an afterthought she produced a wooden spoon, which she thoughtfully licked clean, and set beside the repast.
>
> With regard to that brown rye-cake of Lapland, I brought a piece home to England, which my dog saw and annexed. He is a fox-terrier of lusty appetite, and he tried to eat it. He tried for a whole afternoon, and finally left the cake alone on a lawn, very little the worse for the experience. His master, at Pokka, did better. He was sick with hunger, and devoured two great slabs of the cake, and with it a handful of the stinking fish . . .

'It is curious,' Hyne comments, 'to note how the Lapp and the Northern Finn contrives to make his food unappetising . . . they go to the far extremes of decomposition.'

Their 'host' indicated that 'Küstula' [Kiistala] could be reached by boat so they set off full of hope, but soon the river petered out, and became 'absorbed into a vast green quagmire'. Returning from 'this fiasco', they found a new caravan arrived, 'two sturdy down-country Finns, and a weird Lapp with lank, black hair, and yellow, pock-marked face'.

These were the first travellers of any sort we had met in all Arctic Lapland, and we marvelled at what could be their business. Presently the two principals came out of the dairy-bedroom and talked with us. The elder was a huge man, deep-bearded and heavy-paunched, with a frown on his face and few words to spare. The younger was aged perhaps thirty, had a cut-away chin, and brimmed with words. We tried one another in a whole continent of languages, and finally pitched upon Latin as the only one we had any working knowledge of in common. It was on both sides schoolboy dog-Latin of the most canine variety, and because of the difficulties of pronunciation we could not interchange ideas even through this medium by word of mouth. So every syllable of our chat was scrawled with a stub of pencil upon the rough-hewn door of Scurujärvi farm.

'Potesne nobis dicere,' we wrote, 'si possibile est invenire equum nos portare de Kittila ad mare?'

And the man with the cut-away chin replied, 'Currus est in Kittila.'

'Estne via bona?' we asked.

'Est via, sed non bona. Sed via est.'

They soon found out for themselves just how bad the road was, but with the help of two boys and a reindeer sledge they got through the swamps to Kiistala, 'a fine settlement of quite a dozen farms'. Here they 'drove up to the biggest house', where they 'must have drunk a bucketful apiece' of icy water from the well, were received by the 'Squire' of Kiistala ('He was a Finn, and yet he was civil and kindly,' Hyne adds cryptically). They enjoyed the 'unspeakable luxury' of real beds, in a comfortable room, with a 'mosquito bar'. It was the beginning of the end of their Lapland journey.

From this point Hyne's narrative gathers pace as they travel through the inhabited parts of southern Lapland. The Squire, who had his own business to conduct in Kittilä, offered to take them. He had a fine canoe in which he steered them excitingly down the Ounasjoki, 'a river as wide as the Thames at Richmond, but vastly swifter'. It quickly carried them the sixty-three miles to Kittilä.

> The houses of the little town are scattered picturesquely on either side of this road, and are for the most part stained dragon's-blood red, or turmeric yellow, with white window-sashes. They have a fine taste for colour in Kittila. All the better houses are enclosed within their own neat fences, and of its sort it would be hard to find a more comely townlet. Even the shops are no disfigurement, and they are more than twenty in number – quite one-third of all the houses. They display no signboards, and they do not exhibit goods in the windows to give possible buyers cheap views from the public thoroughfares . . .
>
> A marvellous tidiness pervades everything. All is kept in good repair. Not a shingle is displaced from the neat brown roofs, not a scrap of the farm middens is allowed to straggle. There is no litter anywhere. And yet these people are Finns of the same race as those squalid, listless savages we had been living amongst only a few days before.

They could have continued down the Ounasjoki to Rovaniemi, but in fact they posted south from Kittilä, for the first time travelling in some comfort; the 'posting system' was a welcome change, and 'a triumph of quiet routine'. Suffering seems to have purged Hyne of his disdain for comfort, and contempt for 'future tourist routes': he allowed nothing to hinder their comfortable and orderly progress towards Rovaniemi He is the first Englishman to have described the capital of Finnish Lapland:

> Under a scorching sun next day we went out to look at the town. There is one main street of unobtrusive stores in Rovaniemi, with dwelling-houses lying back on one side, and the river swirling along in rapids at the other. At one end of the town was a hospital, each little room with its own white stove; and next it was a curious campanile in the form of a pagoda of brown, white, and yellow, with roofs of dragon-scale shingling, and a lofty, slender vane, whilst the Lutheran church, for which this campanile rang its bells, was a hundred yards away. This church was rather a fine old building, in cruciform, with its yellow walls striped with white, and a white cross high above the silver-gray shingling of its roof. On the church door were posted the private earmarks of the reindeer owned in the neighbourhood.

After their tour they 'went back to the post-house again for a meal – it was fine to be at a place where one could get food for the mere buying'. Hyne and Hayter were among 'a few choice spirits' invited down to the riverside by the landlord, to share some smuggled caloric punch, from a bottle with two inches of dead flies at the bottom. It was here that he learned how it came about in Rovaniemi that 'quaint scraps of English had dropped upon our ears': there had been a Welshman living in the town for ten years, who had coached the locals in English. As they raised their glasses 'each Finn's *repertoire* of English consisted of a fantastic soul-curdling oath'. 'We made many friends in Rovaniemi,' Hyne writes, 'and left the town with real regret.'

On the final stage of their Finnish travels, as they approached the Gulf of Bothnia:

We zigzagged back and forwards across the river as the road came upon the ferries, and we passed log-booms, and log-rafts innumerable. The air was sweet with the scent of hay. Wild raspberry trees grew by the wayside with the fruit but not yet ripe.

The land of horrible flies was far, far behind them as they glimpsed Tornio ahead 'through masses of harebells which made the ground as blue as the sky'. There were no more adventures before they embarked, like Rae before them, at Salmis, but for Stockholm rather than for Oulu.

'We were always hungry,' records Hyne, looking back on this journey. Concrete bread, rancid fish, and soured milk had fallen well short of their naïve expectations of fresh farm fare in Lapland. They had brought with them only canned delicacies (*Pâté de foie gras*, larks in aspic, and other 'trimmings'), which sometimes had to provide their only food. Of the milk he wrote: '[t]he scheme is a bit like our treatment of port, if you come to think about it. We call it maturing.' Elsewhere, he remarks coolly that '[t]oasted lemming has a tang of ferret'. Despite this diet, he records no illness during their journey; in fact 'the people took for granted that the wandering Englishman was a highly skilled physician, surgeon, oculist and dentist'. Hyne prescribed placebos to the great satisfaction of the locals, and even extracted ruined molars with an old pair of pliers.

Harry de Windt

If Hyne's experiences had made Tweedie's jaunt seem, by comparison, like a Sunday ramble, the next traveller restores the balance: Tweedie appears quite adventurous and enterprising in comparison to Captain Harry Willes Darell de Windt, whose *Finland As It Is* was published in 1901. He is the first of several writers who emphasise the ease and comfort of travelling in Finland:

> [T]he great charm of Finland lies in the fact that one may explore the wildest districts in comfort, if not in absolute luxury. The following trip, for instance, can easily be accomplished by the most delicate invalid of either sex, with the exception, perhaps, of the drive from Uleaborg to the head of the gulf of Bothnia.

As an aid to comfort he lists the principal hotel, chemist, doctor, bookseller, and 'rod and gunmaker' in each town.

De Windt's other travel books (*The New Siberia, A Ride to India, Through Alaska to Bering Straits*) imply a writer in the devil-may-care mould of Hyne, and a biographical sketch does indeed present

> an enigmatic man, described as handsome, and possessed of a strong will. His travel books capture all of the excitement of travel in the hostile and little-charted territories that he chose to explore.

In the friendly and well-charted Finland of 1900 he often sounds more like a bon-viveur, one who whimpers because of a wet day in Hämeenlinna.

He was stranded in St Petersburg in late July 1900 because

of the temporary closure of the Trans-Siberian Railway; he had set out from Paris for New York *by land* via Siberia, Bering Strait, and Alaska. He claims in his Preface that he wrote about Finland at the suggestion of an English bookseller in Petersburg, who complained of being 'pestered every day for books about Finland', and of a stranger with whom he had travelled from Berlin:

The man's nationality was a puzzle, for he spoke English without a trace of foreign accent, and French and German with almost equal facility. At first I put him down as a Pole, for his hatred of Russia was aired with a recklessness that occasionally caused me some anxiety. To-night the mystery was solved. 'You have time on your hands,' said my mysterious friend, as we sat down to dinner. 'Why not visit my country? What is it?' he laughingly added, adjusting his napkin previous to an attack on a savoury plate of 'bortsch.' 'Ah! to be sure, I have not told you. Why, Finland!'

Eighty miles away from the miseries of a St Petersburg summer de Windt awoke the next day 'in another world' – a fine hotel in Vyborg:

Its windows overlook a scene more suggestive of sunny Spain or Italy than the Frozen North. The picturesque town nestling against a background of pine forest, and blue waters of the harbour sparkling under a cloudless sky, the wooded islets with their pretty villas, the ruined castle of Viborg, with its crumbling thirteenth-century battlements, and last, but not least, the general air of life and animation are indeed pleasant to contemplate after the drab, dreary streets of the Russian capital. Viborg is, perhaps, the least imposing of all Finnish towns, for many of its dwellings are built of wood, which, however, is generally stained a dark red colour, cleaner and more cheerful-looking than rough, weather-bleached logs. Pleasant also is it to saunter through the picturesque old streets, to ransack the silver shops, and come suddenly upon a market-place, lying in the shadow of quaint old gabled houses, where the rosy-cheeked peasants, carts and cobbles, and canvas booths packed with fruit and vegetables recall some old-world town in far-away Brittany. Everything has a cleanly, bright appearance, and the fresh, pine-scented sea-breeze is grateful indeed after muggy, inodorous Petersburg.

He could not have had a more enticing introduction to Finland than an invitation from a 'well-to-do Finn' to a ball at a villa 'situated on a beautiful lake':

When we embarked, towards 5 p.m., on the little steamer chartered for the occasion, we found her decks crowded with ladies in ball-gowns, and most of the men in the orthodox white tie and swallow-tail, although one unconventional youth had adopted light grey trousers and a cerulean scarf. But everyone on board, old and young, were gay, good-humoured, and scrupulously polite, for there is no country in Europe where a stranger of any nationality meets with such cordial hospitality as in Finland.

De Windt lifts the description of the Finnish ball from a longer and more circumstantial account in his *Siberia As It Is* (1892); this sort of conflation perhaps goes with being a 'professional author'.

At Imatra

the comfortable hotel overlooking the falls is one of the best in Finland, which is saying a great deal. The restaurant was crowded, many of its occupants being in evening dress, for this is a fashionable summer resort of the best people in Petersburg. After dinner some strolling musicians enlivened the hours until bedtime, and I listened for the first time to the national instrument of Finland, the 'kantele,' a kind of zither, which admirably accompanies the wild, weird songs of the country. Finnish music is not unlike Hungarian, and is generally of a sad description, in the minor key. Some of the melodies I heard at Imatra were very beautiful and charmingly rendered, for Finlanders are born musicians, and musical festivals are frequently held during the summer months in all parts of the country.

Savonlinna lacked the comforts of Imatra, but had another attraction:

A loud peal at the rusty bell placed for the purpose at the waterside summons the janitor, who paddles across in a crazy-looking skiff to convey us to the castle.

His description is a good deal less fanciful than Tweedie's. Punkaharju, where he came across British tourists for the only time, provided 'one of my most enjoyable days in Finland, for the heat was tempered by a cool breeze, and the lights and shadows cast by lazily drifting cloudlets enhanced the calm, peaceful beauty of the island.'

Taking a roundabout route to Helsinki, he took the steamer from Savonlinna to Mikkeli, 'a pretty, sleepy little town' not previously recorded by the British. He had all day to wait for his train:

I found a primitive little restaurant, however, in some shady gardens where one could breakfast and dine in the open, and where I dawdled away the day pleasantly enough until nightfall brought the welcome whistle of the mail train.

It might have been worse, for Mikkeli was at its best, and in holiday garb on the occasion of some national feast. The restaurant was gaily decorated with bunting, paper lanterns dangled from the trees in anticipation of an illumination, and the tables around mine were occupied from midday until dusk by merry groups of people with their gaily dressed womenfolk and a sprinkling of the military from a neighbouring garrison town. During the afternoon a band enlivened the proceedings and a brisk trade was done by neatly clad waitresses in coffee and cakes, foaming bocks, and an amber-coloured beverage comprising wild strawberries and crushed ice. I found the latter consisted of 'mjod' and a cunning mixture of liqueurs – a seductive and apparently innocent drink, of which, however, one might easily take too much on a hot summer's day. My stock of tobacco being exhausted, I purchased, for the first time (with some misgivings) a Finnish cigar. To my surprise the tobacco, though somewhat coarse, was excellent and the cigar absurdly cheap at about 2½d. A few days later, at Helsingfors, I bought some cigars at the factory of Borgstrom and Co., at 25 marks a hundred, which would certainly have fetched 8d. apiece in Bond Street. I mention this fact in order that smokers may save themselves the expense of bringing their own tobacco into Finland . . .

As I left towards nine o'clock for the railway station, preparations were being made for an impromptu dance. Lights sparkled from the dark pines, and now and again a rocket would shoot into the starry heavens, to fall in a shower of diamonds over the lake. It was a pretty, homely scene, and although the gaiety was unrestrained, it was almost childlike in its nature and absolutely devoid of any objectionable feature. A snugly lit compartment and snowy sheets awaited me, and I turned into bed not sorry, after all, to have wasted a day at Mikkeli in such pleasant company.

The view from the train to Helsinki showed that it was not only the lakes that made Finland so attractive:

The line from Mikkeli traverses a fair and prosperous district, as unlike the monotonous scenery over the border as the proverbial dock and daisy. Here are no squalid hovels and roofless sheds where half-starved cattle share the misery of their owners; no rotting crops and naked pastures; but snug homesteads, flower gardens, and neat wooden fences encircling fields of golden grain and rich green meadow land. To travel in Southern Finland after Northern Russia is like leaving the most hideous parts of the Black Country to suddenly emerge into the brightness and verdure of a sunlit Devonshire.

Helsinki, 'the streets full of life and animation', was another pleasant contrast to Russia, especially as seen from the Observatory Hill:

From this point Helsingfors is seen at its best, the golden dome of the cathedral towering over a mass of spires, fire towers, and white buildings, set off by greenery; the quays alive with the bustle of locomotives and steam cranes, and the busy harbour crowded with craft of all kinds, from the grimy whaler to the white-sailed pleasure yacht. I can plainly distinguish my open window at the 'Societetshuset,' and beneath it the market-place, a bright patch of colour, with its gaily coloured booths, fruit, and flowers; while inland, beyond a confused mass of masonry and verdure, the picture is framed in pine forest, studded at intervals with shining lakes, for all the world like bits of crystal sunk into a piece of dark enamel.

Then back again for a saunter through the streets to while away the time until an evening at the theatre shall end the day.

De Windt notes with approval the female students in their caps – 'the women of Finland have reached a stage of emancipation as yet unknown in any other country'; he admires the exhibits in the Atheneum, and relates an anecdote about Bobrikoff.

An unnamed Professor, his guide in Helsinki, insisted that he visit Hämeenlinna, which turned out to be the low spot of his journey – 'dingy,' 'grimy', 'crude', 'cheerless' and 'melancholy' are among his chosen epithets – and it rained all day. He took an early train for Tampere, where he was astonished that that the 'Manchester of Finland' should be one of its 'prettiest towns'. Although he made the factories a particular interest, the town itself attracted him:

> The first thing that strikes a stranger in Tammerfors is the amazing number of bicycles. In Helsingfors almost every fourth inhabitant cycles, but here the percentage must be even greater. During the short walk to my hotel from the railway station I was, more than once, nearly annihilated at the crossings. When the automobile craze reaches here, I shudder to think of the results. Meanwhile, everyone uses the wheel – men, women, and children – even babies who should be in arms instead of mounted on a 'byke' . . .
>
> After the gloomy (not to say dirty) hostelry at Tavastehus, I was prepared to find dubious board and lodging here. It was therefore an agreeable surprise to find that the 'Societetshuset' was, although a one-storied wooden building, quite equal in every respect to the Helsingfors hotel, indeed, the apartments were even more luxurious. One does not expect to find bedrooms with brass beds, cheerful chintz curtains, and white furniture (*à la* Maple, in fact, down to an electric reading-lamp) in the heart of Finland, but to-day all these comforts awaited me, and many more. At the same time, there was a quaint mixture of modernism and the primitive, peculiar to this country, and not without its charms.
>
> Notwithstanding its up-to-date surroundings, the methods of the place recalled old coaching days, for the rosy-

cheeked wife of the proprietor personally attended to my wants, and mine host himself waited at table, and like a Boniface of old, produced a flask of rare Bordeaux from an innermost bin in honour of his English guest. There are no huge hotels in Finland, none of the glare and glitter of the Swiss and Italian 'caravanserais,' where you are known as a number instead of a name. On the other hand, you will almost everywhere find cleanliness, comfort, and civility, and in continental palaces of travel the latter article, at any rate, is only too often measured by the length of your purse.

To give an idea of the kind of price prevalent at Finnish inns, here is the menu of a well cooked and served little *déjeuner* to which I sat down on arrival at Tammerfors:

SOCIETETSHUSET

TAMMERFORS

Nota

	M.	P.
1 Bulloin (agg.)		50
1 Chateaubriand (Potattia)	1 :	30
1 Kompott		40
1 Rodwinn	3 :	–
1 Kaffee		30
1 Cognac	3 :	–

Total: Marks 8 : 50p

Does it reveal more about De Windt, or about Finland's prices, that drink accounted for nearly three-quarters of his bill?

His first view of Tampere had been like a glimpse of a socialist Utopia:

I arrived on a Sunday to find the factories closed and the streets crowded with holiday folk. The Finns are a pious people, and on Sundays until midday the streets of their towns resemble a desert, for everyone, save dogs and policemen, is in church. During the afternoon the park, combined with a military band, seemed to be the great attraction. Here I found the *élite* and employees of the commercial world assembled discussing coffee and ices under the trees around the bandstand, and laughing and chatting in the shade and coolness, amidst fountains and flowers. Mill-owners, with their wives and daughters, artisans and factory girls, all were enjoying a day of rest and pleasure together with an utter absence of the prim snobbery that in any other country would have drawn a social line between the classes and caused uneasiness and restraint.

From Tampere his principal excursion was to Nokia, a name then completely unknown to the outside world. Part of the high road was used as 'a fashionable driving promenade'.

The Rapids of Nokia are nearly five miles long and rush through a narrow, picturesque gorge of a wild beauty, somewhat marred by a prosaic paper manufactory, which to-day was of course inactive. The mills are worked solely by water power . . . We drove into the town again at dusk past the park, now gaily illumined by electric light, and down the principal street almost blocked by sauntering wayfarers. This thoroughfare is named the Kopmans-Gatan, or rather written so, for unless you pronounce the word 'Chapman' no one will understand you. The Finnish Manchester is evidently not a dissipated place, for by 11 p.m. the moonlit streets were wrapped in silence and repose. I therefore retired early, and soon fell asleep to a lullaby common enough in Finland: the soothing sound of falling water.

On the train to Tampere he had met a dairy farmer, whose wife spoke English, and he spent a day visiting their large farm, viewing the dairy, buttery, and stables, and ending with dinner:

we sat down in his pretty little dining-room, with its tinted walls, proof engravings, and French windows opening on to the garden, to as dainty and well-served a meal as you could enjoy in the Champs Elysées; for the snowy napery, bright silver, and bowls of cut flowers were more suggestive of Mayfair than a lonely farmhouse in far-away Finland! Everything was perfect – from the dish of freshly caught trout that commenced the meal, to the wild strawberries and iced junket with which it ended. Indeed, the time passed so quickly amid these pleasant surroundings that night had fallen when we adjourned to the verandah for coffee.

There are scores of descriptions of meals at Finnish farms, but nothing else remotely like this.

In the next chapter de Windt is in the restaurant at the Hotel Central in Vaasa, 'the prettiest town in Finland', breakfasting on tea and eggs, 'the former a vile decoction apparently composed of senna and hay!' 'Never drink tea north of Tammerfors,' he advises, adding that 'the coffee is excellent, even on the borders of Lapland'.

In Vasa nearly every street is a boulevard, and the town is almost surrounded by a beautiful park, a favourite resort in summer. Greenery is the prevailing note, for nearly every private house has its garden with shady trees and flowers. The public buildings are unusually fine, the roads excellent, with pavements of solid granite, and there are good shops and at least two very fair hotels. This is, in short, a prosperous-looking yet rather sleepy place . . .

The shops in Vasa are distinctly good, far better than those usually found in an English town of the same size and importance. In the principal street, for instance, you may purchase anything from an automobile to a celluloid collar as easily as in London or New York and at much the same price. The furniture establishments are especially good and up-to-date, and customers are accommodated on the 'hire system' . . .

Having occasion to purchase a clasp knife, I strolled into a cutler's shop on the way home, and was offered one of Sheffield make for ten marks. 'We have much the same thing for three,' said the shopman, adding modestly, 'but it was made in Finland.' As an experiment I decided upon the latter, which proved to be as good and durable as any article of the same price that I have ever bought in England.

The train timetable required an overnight stay at Seinäjoki station (de Windt admired Finnish stations) to arrive the next day in Oulu, 'the city of tar and timber', and a hotel where his 'sumptuously furnished bedroom was suggestive of the "Ritz" in Paris'. His breakfast the next day was distinctly Finnish, though, including 'smoked salmon, dried reindeer, and *cheese*'. 'I made many friends in Oulu,' he writes. A 'delightful companion', Captain Hansen, showed him the town, not only the timber yards and tar stores, but the prison, 'a really remarkable establishment' ('The penal system of Finland is wonderfully well organised'). He also hosted, in de Windt's honour, a 'royal repast', inviting the great and the good of the town:

> It was past midnight when we separated, and I walked home to my hotel in the pleasant moonlight, wondering whether there was another country in Europe where an absolute stranger would meet with such spontaneous and kindly hospitality.

He could have taken the comfortable steamer to Tornio, but 'wishing to see something of the remoter districts' he posted by land, very much to his cost. This journey recalls the eighteenth-century travellers' experiences, but back to front: whereas they found the posting system impeccable, but the board and lodging execrable, de Windt found that '[p]osting facilities in Northern Finland are as execrable as the accommodation is first class'. His experience at 'Kolkarra', the first stage north of Oulu set the pattern. He had to wait two hours for the post-master to appear:

We surveyed each other at first in silence, for my know-ledge of the Finnish language was restricted to a couple of words, learnt from Hansen: 'Heyvonen soukala,' which signifies 'Get horses quickly!' The sentence, however had no effect whatever until a silver coin was prominently dis-played to lend it force. My friend then rose and strolled out of doors and into the yard, where I followed and watched him as he stood in the rain scratching his head, appar-ently for inspiration. After a while he splashed through the mire to a neighbouring shed, from which the body and shafts of a 'karra' were slowly and laboriously extracted. A couple of rickety wheels were then produced from an-other outhouse, and a shock-headed lout summoned from a hay-loft, where he had evidently been taking it out in slumber. Then a second instrument of torture was with some difficulty put together, and I waited with some inter-est for the means of locomotion, which had to be searched for, then caught, and then brought back in triumph from a neighbouring meadow. Finally, after a delay of exactly three hours, all was ready for my journey to the next sta-tion, Shippolara, and I took my seat by the shock-headed lout, wondering whether I might, with luck, reach my des-tination within a week.

Things got no better at Huttola: '[i]f at Tolonen there had been a dearth of horses, Huttula could at any rate boast of a plague of rats, some of them of unusual size and audacity, and I passed a wakeful and miserable night'. A bright spot was Virkulla, with a restaurant-class meal and an intelligent and hospitable host, but by the time he had dragged his miserable way into Tornio, which was 'the picture of desolation', he had seen more than enough of the 'remoter districts'. A few years later MacDougall travelled this route by train.

Despite de Windt's challenging experiences during his last few days in Finland, the country had no more appreciative, articulate or better informed advocate in this era. He summed up his experience in his autobiography, *My Restless Life*:

a delightful trip, and one which I can heartily commend to the reader in search of beautiful scenery, pure air, and novelty combined with cheapness. I once imagined that the Grand Duchy was a bleak and barren land, and was therefore agreeably surprised to find a country dotted with prosperous and progressive towns, and far more up-to-date than Russia in its appreciation of hotels, schools, telephones, and other blessings of modern civilisation . . . The Finns are a kindly people (so long as you don't talk Russian) and their country is a Paradise for the angler or cyclist – especially the former, for the fishing is the best (and cheapest) in Europe. And I was received, even in the smallest villages, with free and lavish hospitality.

'Paul Waineman' (Sylvia MacDougall)

No one who has heard of Väinämöinen, the central character in the *Kalevala*, will have any difficulty in spotting that 'Paul Waineman' is a pseudonym. It was the pen name of Sylvia Mac-Dougall, who recounts in her memoirs, 'I was born in Finland, the land of a thousand lakes, where heartstrings are buried deep in the soil.' Her father was a wealthy Swedish-speaking Finn, Emil Borgström, and her mother was of Scottish descent. She spent her early childhood in Yussupoff Villa, a mansion in Kaivopuisto, a site now occupied by the British Embassy. When she was ten her mother brought the children to England to be educated, and the family lived a leisured and privileged life in a beautiful old house, Provender, in Kent, wintering in Nice or Algiers. She lived there until her death in 1962; her daughter, Nadine, married Prince Andrew of Russia, and their daughter, Princess Olga Romanoff, now lives there.

'I never took writing seriously,' she confessed, but during a visit to Rome she wrote a novel, *A Heroine from Finland*, which was published in 1902. Frequently reprinted, it was followed by more novels with Finnish settings: *By a Finnish Lake*, *The Song of the Forest* and *The Bay of Lilacs*. MacDougall's privileged upper-class background and her limited narrative talents restrict the interest of *A Summer Tour in Finland* (1908), yet it breaks significant new ground on several occasions. She broadly followed Tweedie's route, adding an excursion to Kangasala, now a tourist spot, and to Tornio, which was now accessible by train; the primitive drive north from Oulu, which de Windt had thought unsuitable for ladies, and indeed for himself, was now obsolete. '[T]he most timid lady traveller,' she writes, 'could with the fullest confidence essay a tour in Finland . . . A tour round the Isle of Wight would not be fraught with less peril.' Helsinki now is 'just the place for those in search of good restaurants, good hotels, good bands, and jolly little excursions which even the least energetic may undertake without undue fatigue.'

She was accompanied by her sister-in-law, Edith MacDougall, and their 'summer tour' was exactly what the phrase implies: a leisurely holiday without worry or danger. Her tour, taken by steamer and by train (no carts for her), was principally a round of country-house visits; she at times seems more concerned with dropping names than with discovering Finland. Sharing very little ground with the other British woman travellers of the period, she writes quite a lot about fairies (a dozen times), and deplores every aspect of female emancipation:

> The daughters of good families, who would have swooned a generation or two ago at the thought of soiling their white fingers with work, are now discontented unless they can get a place in some bank or office. This intense desire to be independent is the most surprising outcome of late years, and has been the utter ruin of society . . . Only the other day a handsome young girl, the daughter of a wealthy family, boasted to me that she had never worn a decolleté frock in her life. 'In Finland we are above such vanities,' she said laughingly.
>
> That girl was a type of the Finland of to-day.

She is clearly unhappy, too, about the fine schools which so impressed many visitors at this time:

> The board schools of Finland are models of excellence, and I have often wondered what ordinary little peasant children can do with so much knowledge crammed into their brains.

(The answer is, I imagine, that they made modern Finland.) As for politics, it would be interesting to know how the later history of Finland was regarded by one who wrote that 'socialism is bad enough anywhere, but in this land where every lake and forest is impregnated with old traditions, it is a sin'.

Her route from Vyborg to Imatra was through the Saimaa Canal, and despite a bad meal at the inn at Rättijärvi she was full of enthusiasm. Hers is the only detailed account we have of passing through the locks:

> At Juustila, then, we disembarked and changed into the canal steamer. I found a place as far forward as possible so as to obtain a good view of our ascent. I remembered that we had no less than two hundred and twenty-five feet of water to climb before we reached the first bay of the Saima lakes. One thinks of a canal, usually, as a straight, narrow slit of water between flat-lying shores, but the Saima Canal is one of the most beautiful water-roads in the world. It changes its aspect continually, now widening, now narrowing, as it gradually unfolds itself like a silver ribbon thrown with unstudied grace – here between cliffs of granite, dark and mysterious, there through mile after mile of the richest verdure. Then come exquisite woodland scenes, which fairies must surely haunt in the moonlight, and we pass under long aisles of immense trees, stretching their branches across the channel that separates them, forming a canopy of green above our heads.

> Before you have time to take in the beauty of that natural archway the ribbon twists again, and pastures, intersected by ditches aflame with wild flowers blazing in a very flood of sunshine, meet the eye. The canal has enriched these pastures, bringing moisture to the grass and making it almost as green as an English meadow. Cattle graze close to the water's edge, and in the distance the log-built walls of a humble cottage homestead show up against the background of the forest.

. . . the steamer glides into a kind of cavern, and the massive, ironbound gates through which one enters are slowly closed. The water is black in the shadows of the high walls on either side. All the light and the sunshine seem to have been left behind. Facing us similar gates stand threateningly in our way.

Suddenly an unseen hand pulls away a shutter in the mighty barrier, and through the opening a tongue of water almost like a flame leaps forth. One by one a dozen shutters open and the water dashes forth from each, in a cascade of foam, surging down upon us.

Our steamer rocks to and fro, and beads of perspiration gather on the brows of the sturdy sailors as they hold on for grim death to the ropes that bind the steamer to the sides of the lock, to steady the vessel in her ascent. The waters sobbed and hissed. At last the tension is lessened, the battle is over, and the water, trembling and moaning, endeavours to calm itself. The sailors relax their hold and throw the ropes up on the banks. Slowly the great doors open and we enter another cavern, if possible deeper and more dismal than the first. It is like going back into prison, and one thought that beyond those doors liberty and sunshine were waiting.

This was only the second of many rungs of the 'ladder of water'. There was then a three-hour journey by diligence to Imatra, announced by a 'distant rumble' two miles ahead. 'The conceit of man is so great that he has tried to improve Imatra,' MacDougall laments. She stayed at the hotel overlooking the falls, and, like Tweedie, deplored the tasteless developments: the suspension bridge, and the 'stiff little formal paths along its banks'.

She saw what were by now the popular tourist sights of the area; Punkaharju made the deepest impression, and called forth her purplest prose. Her longest excursion took her by steamer to Joensuu, where she found the 'Societetshuset', deserted, musty, and shabby; after some exploring, she sat down at a table overlooking a neglected garden. After a while

I distinctly heard footsteps. They came heavily down the garden-path, and into my sight there came the very fattest woman I have ever seen in all my life. Barnum's fat lady would have been slim and fragile by her generous side. She did not glide, but panted past my line of vision, and disappeared up some wooden steps leading from the garden to an old-fashioned wooden door that I had not noticed until then.

For one moment, as the door opened, I saw within a gleam of copper utensils shimmering in the light of an unseen fire. Then the door shut to with a heavy thud. But that brief glimpse had wonderfully encouraged me, I felt certain that shining copper belonged to a kitchen, and that my substantial ghost was its high priestess.

I waited some time in the hopes that some one would break in upon my solitude. Then I boldly carried out my attack, which ended by my finding myself behind that mysterious door in the presence of its ruler. At closer quarters she was somewhat alarming, and at first utterly refused to cook me anything.

I had not hit upon the usual hour when the ordinary inhabitants of Joensuu have their baser appetites satisfied. The entire staff of the hotel had finished their work for the day.

However, in the end she relented, and said she would do what she could. With that I had to be satisfied, and retired again to my table and the cruet-stand.

Expectancy lent wings to time. I had heard the voice of my charmer screaming orders to some one, so at least she had managed to catch one of the absent staff. My curiosity became still keener when down those wooden steps there came a young woman, wearing what probably was the height of the fashion in Joensuu, but which considerably startled a humble being like myself. What struck me most in that remarkable get up was a pair of high-heeled, lemon-coloured leather boots, surmounted by a short magenta skirt in dips and ends – flounces, I believe, is the proper name. This apparition, looking, alas! distinctly sulky, walked across the garden to a shed, swinging disdainfully a small wooden pail in her left hand. I had only time to wonder what she wanted there, when she reappeared leading a cow, and in the midst of the tall rank grass began milking violently into that pail. I felt most awfully sorry the cow. After that, 'things' kept on happening.

The fat cook waddled down herself to the garden, and evidently disturbed an unseen hen, or more likely a dozen by the noise. She returned majestically, holding something concealed in her apron. Anyway, I had the satisfaction of knowing that the eggs were newly-laid. A small boy appeared suddenly upon the scene, bent almost double under an immense block of crystal clear ice.

During all these divers preparations my curiosity became doubled as to what the meal eventually would turn out to be.

I must own that I was quite prepared to be disappointed, and therefore felt doubly dumfounded at the repast set before me. To commence with, I had a piled-up dish of delicious miniature lobsters (crayfish), a delicacy to be found in most parts of Finland. After that they placed before me an immense omelette filled with fresh asparagus heads. The maker of that omelette deserved the Order of the Garter. The chef of the café Anglais in Paris could not have beaten it in excellency, and I speak from experience. The omelette had hardly vanished before a splendid salmon trout with hollandaise sauce succeeded it. Then, lastly, I was offered a brimming bowl of wild strawberries set on ice, accompanied by a gigantic jug of whipped cream.

Time had sped quickly, and when I reached the steamer the steam was already up, and a clock close by struck eleven. Only an hour short of midnight, and still one could have read the smallest print without any difficulty. I think that was the first time I realized how far North I was.

The steamer took her first to Savonlinna, then to Kuopio, stopping regularly for fuel:

One helper did not belong to our crew, but had apparently crept up somewhere between the stacks of logs. He was a bare-footed lad with rosy cheeks and flaxen hair, and I should think not more than seven years old. This small morsel of humanity gravely demanded of the captain whether he required an extra hand, and when he was answered in the affirmative, he set to work with a comical seriousness that was delightful to watch. He worked away like a Trojan, and ran to and fro with logs as big as himself. Sometimes he tottered beneath their weight, but his little naked feet gripped the deck with a fierce tenacity, as he regained his equilibrium.

Some ladies on board noticed the plucky little fellow and made a small collection of caramels and pennies, which the captain presented to him on our departure. But the little Hercules became crimson with vexation and stuck his hands in his little knickerbocker pockets with defiance. Those caramels were belittling his manhood, and he resented the attention with all the fierceness of his proud Finnish blood. No persuasion would make him accept them, and eventually the captain gave them in charge to a man standing by.

In Kuopio MacDougall paid homage at the 'small wooden house' where Minna Canth had lived and died.

On the train to Kajaani, admiring the engineering feat of the new railway, she imagined how this remote and uninhabited area would one day be populous and prosperous. At Kajaani station there were four cabs, and hers came second in the race to the 'tourist hotel', where there was room only for the victor. She begged accommodation in a private house, so was able to spend some time sight-seeing before the 'the real climax to a holiday in Finland' – by tar-boat to Oulu.

> The tourist boats for descending the rapids go only twice a week, and tomorrow was the day. During the summer season, places in this boat are usually booked well ahead, as the boats can only take a limited number of passengers. Otherwise, if the tourist boat is full, intending travellers would have to content themselves with a place in one of the ordinary tar-boats, that until quite recently were the only means of descending the Uleå River.

In the ten years since Tweedie had taken this trip it had clearly become an established part of the tourist 'experience', rather like a sleigh ride with reindeer in Santa's Lapland today. These were tar-boats without the tar, and 'appeared quite luxurious compared to the very cramped and dirty quarters to be had on an ordinary tar-boat'. Each boat was checked by an inspector before setting off. Only at busy times, when all these boats were booked, did tourists have to go native, and travel in a real tar-boat!

In Oulu little impressed her; 'nothing can prevent it from being hopelessly ugly'. She made a quick excursion by train to Tornio, where it seemed that the swallows were the only other foreign visitors – 'during my whole journey in Finland I was never so reluctant to quit any place as that little grass-carpeted town hidden on the borders of the eternal snow'.

MacDougall's next stop was Tampere; her disappointment with the hotel was nothing in comparison to her indignation when she viewed Simberg's frescoes in St John's Church:

If all the inhabitants of Tammerfors rise up and stone me the next time I visit their town, I must say that, as a temple of Christianity, I have never imagined anything further removed from all preconceived notions of what such a building should be than their Church of St. John! The name is the only Christian thing about it.

The interior is a gigantic rotunda, reminiscent of a Roman theatre, with an immense gallery encircling it. Below the gallery is a deep frieze of solid grey granite, upon which is painted a huge garland of thorns, dotted with crimson roses.

This garland is held up at regular intervals by absolutely naked boys, painted life-size. Some are bending beneath their burden, some are erect, some are swaying, some have roses against their naked flesh, and others are cut with thorns.

This astonishing production is the work of a Finnish artist, and is meant to represent the sorrows of life, and how some mortals bear it erectly and some are crushed beneath their burden.

The Resurrection fresco also attracted her attention, especially the 'man of herculean proportions heading that procession':

He is attired in the simple garb of Adam, minus the fig-leaves. As a study of anatomy for medical students, that man is drawn with a master hand, but in what way he is deemed to lead your thoughts heavenwards completely puzzles me. The pastor must be glad that in the pulpit his back is turned to him, and probably the pastor's wife keeps her eyes discreetly downwards.

A few years Renwick later wrote of the same church '[t]he very memory of it makes me shudder'.

The next day, '[a]s the train stopped at the little roadside station of Kangasala the civilization of Tammerfors might have been a hundred miles off': 'Certainly there were no signs of progress here. In fact, as the train steamed off again, I half thought that I had been stranded here by mistake.'

Before leaving for Turku, she accepted an invitation from Colonel Hugo Standertsköld 'to dine and sleep that evening at Karlberg', his 'princely country seat' – perhaps the grandest estate in the country. Here she was 'almost bewildered by the luxury of my surroundings'. The house burnt down in 1928, but the park – Aulanko, outside Hämeenlinna – remains as one of the most famous in Finland. This was the grandest of her country house visits, but by no means the only one; the recurrent epithet is 'princely'. Between Turku and Hanko she tasted luxury with aristocratic families at Brinkhall, Svartå ('I had the honour of occupying the State Bedroom'), Fagervik, Åminne, and Billnäs. Her lingerings left her almost no time in Hanko before boarding the *Arcturus* for England.

MacDougall felt that these visits had enabled her to get to know Finland properly:

> My opinion is that no tour of a country is complete unless one has seen some of the old homes, wherein the generations of men and women who have made the history of their land have lived and died.

The other woman travellers at this time had had rather different notions of what made a complete tour: Clive-Bayley was 'anxious to see something of the people'; for Tweedie '[t]he way to understand anything of a land or its people is to leave the tourist route and peep into its homes [small, Finnish-speaking farms] for oneself'. These women represent, essentially, two very different opinions as to who 'made the history' of Finland.

Alexander MacCallam Scott

'I have made the collection of books about Finland my hobby for twenty years,' wrote Scott in the Preface to his *Suomi: The Land of the Finns* (1926). These books, together with 'various journeys through Finland, and . . . innumerable personal encounters', were the material for this extremely entertaining miscellaneous book about Finland. In 1908 he had published *Through Finland to St. Petersburg* 'to provide the visitor with a concise guide'. Although mainly informational, his book evidently comes from experience and affectionate appreciation; his accounts of Finnish art and architecture are especially knowledgeable and convincing. His personal experiences are largely concealed, and can only be glimpsed in some of his descriptions. Once, at least, he escapes into first-person narrative:

> The world seemed suddenly to have grown young again as, on the first morning, I ran down the steep path among the pines to plunge in the sweet, limpid, tideless waters of the Gulf of Finland. The scent of the pines, the rustling of the reeds, the lapping of the ripples, the warmth of the sun, and the cool freshness of the water – they are unforgettable. The Isles of Greece have nothing to offer more exquisite.
>
> With the advent of summer, this miraculous resurrection, the people experience the ecstasy of joy of a captive suddenly released from an underground dungeon. Everything is new, and fresh, and strange. They live in the open as simply and naturally as a primitive race who have not yet eaten of the fruits of the tree of knowledge. One seldom sees a bathing costume, even of the meagrest description, in Finland. In the towns the men's and the women's

bathing-sheds are separated by a few hundred yards. In the rural districts mixed bathing is frequently indulged in by the peasants. And yet there is practically none of that 'Peeping-Tom'ism which the elaborate toilets of the fair bathers in more sophisticated lands seem to attract. One Sunday Consul Cook carried me off in a motor-boat to explore the island suburbs of Helsingfors. Sometimes as we shot through a narrow sound we could discern a file of men walking stark naked through the pine-trees down to the water's edge, or sunning themselves on the rocks. It was as if the woods were once again peopled with fauns and the rocks by Tritons. Passing another island we surprised Diana bathing with her attendant nymphs. They heeded us not. In our puffing, throbbing motor-boat, that triumph of modern civilisation, we sailed straight into Arcady, back into the youth of the world and the primal age of innocence.

It is surprising to discover that the man behind this poetic and fanciful picture of Finland was a career politician; Scott became a Liberal MP in 1910, switching to the Labour Party in the 1920s, and he wrote the first biography of his friend Winston Churchill (1916). His political interest in Finland is limited, perhaps because in 1908 he was writing of the 'lull' before Stolypin: '[s]ince November 1905 other counsels have prevailed'. On the question of women's rights he has more to say. He was a very active and vocal member of the anti-suffrage committee of the Liberal party, and, MacDougall apart, the only British writer about Finland not to have admired the advanced position of women. Like most of the writers of the time, he quotes from the *Kalevala*, but ingeniously turns it to his own purposes:

The Pohjola wedding is one of the most popular episodes in the *Kalevala*. All the preparations were made upon a heroic scale, and they are all described with a wealth of detail. The ox that was slain was greater than the Wonderful Derby Ram. It waved its tail in Karelia and bellowed in Tornei. A squirrel ran for a month between its horns, and 'it is not there yet.' Never was there such a brewing, and never was there beer so powerful. The wedding hall towered to the skies. When the cock crowed on the roof you could not hear it on the ground, and when the dog barked at one end of the hall you could not hear it at the other. The whole population of Northland, rich and poor, young and old, was invited to the wedding. After the feasting come the songs of farewell and advice. The Rainbow Maiden's farewell to her old home is very simple and affecting. The song of "Osmotar, the Bride Adviser," contains a whole system of domestic economy and prudent maxims for housewives. An old beggar woman sings a doleful tale of an evil husband, and a crabbed old man tells how nagging wives should be treated. The husband, too, is exhorted to be kind and gentle with his young wife. If she prove disobedient he is to bear with her whims for three years –

> Teach one year in words of kindness,
> Teach with eyes of love a second,
> In the third year teach with firmness.
> If she should not heed thy teaching,
> Then instruct her with the willow,
> Use the birch-rod from the mountain,
> In the closet of thy dwelling,
> In the attic of thy mansion;
> Strike her not upon the common,
> Do not conquer her in public,
> Lest the villagers should see thee,
> Lest the neighbours hear her weeping.

It is to be feared that, in these days, when ladies are

elected Members of Parliament in Finland, some of this advice has become obsolete. Nevertheless it is an honoured custom to have these bride songs repeated at the marriages of the country folk. They are regarded as hardly less essential than the religious ceremony.

Scott and MacDougall published their books in 1908, so both probably describe experiences from 1907. It is tempting to imagine them meeting, and deploring mutually the liberties being claimed and taken by Finnish women.

Rosalind Travers

In August 1908 Rosalind Travers was on the boat to Finland; the passage quoted above would have provided her with some provocative reading. Aged thirty-four, she was travelling to take her mind off a broken love affair, but there were more pressing reasons for what she repeatedly refers to as her 'exile': her political activities had greatly embarrassed her upper-crust parents, who had requested her 'to leave home on account of my participation in a highly-respectable, orderly and dignified Women's Suffrage procession the year before'.

Travers describes meeting on the boat 'a far-off cousin' called Celia, who became her companion during her time in Finland. I suspect that this is a playful attempt to relocate *As You Like It* in Finland (aligning her *Letters from Finland*, 1911, with the mood of her collections of poetry: *The Two Arcadias*, 1905, and *Thyrsis and Fausta, a Pastoral*, 1907), and that Celia is a fictional character onto whom she could transpose some of her own radical excesses, without further discomfiting her family. In her account, therefore, it was Celia who was exiled: '"Well, if I must," she said, "I'll go to the only civilised country in Europe, the one place where women have got their full rights. Let us pay a visit to Uncle Keith in Finland."' It was 'Celia''s involvement with political dissidents which, according to Travers, led to her virtual ejection from Finland after ten months; in the light of Travers's later allegiances and activities it seems certain that she is describing herself.

Her experiences in Finland profoundly altered the course of her life, as F. J. Gould writes:

> Much struck by the sturdy Social-Democratic life and manners of groups of Finnish women and men, she

returned to England, determined to find out the quality of Socialism in her own native land.

She lectured 'with great success all round the country on the Finnish situation'. *Letters from Finland* went to the publisher in April 1911, and in the same month she and Aino Almberg founded the Anglo-Finnish Society, of which she was the first secretary. In July 1909 she attended an anti-Tsar rally in Trafalgar Square, wishing to join 'the denunciation of the imperial enemy of her beloved Finns'. There she met the famous English socialist, H. M. Hyndman, founder of the Social Democratic Federation. She formed a close attachment with Hyndman, thirty-three years her senior; they married in 1914, a year or so after his wife's death. She wrote to him (12 January 1914), 'remember that we owe it to Finland that we ever met at all'. They worked together in political causes until his death in 1921. She completed her volume of memoirs, *The Last Years of H. M. Hyndman*, and shortly after that she committed suicide.

Her *Letters* are written to several friends in England and elsewhere, and although the names and addresses (towns such as 'Andredswold') are fictional, it is possible that they were actual letters, and that she was using them to structure her own responses to Finnish experiences, and to present what she had learned. *Letters from Finland* is rather more than a travel book: Travers's writings, like Clive-Bayley's, anticipate the books about 'the new nation' which proliferated after Finland's independence.

She was greeted by 'Aunt Karin and Uncle Keith' at their summer residence, Himelholm, situated on Jusserö, a little island near Suomenlinna, overlooking Helsinki. She noted that there was no church 'and – more wondrous still – no public house'. Travers was a zealous teetotaller and temperance worker.

After well-informed sightseeing in Helsinki, including 'two rather bewildering visits to the Athenaeum' to view Finnish paintings, she set off on an autumn tour, mainly by train, to

Turku, Tampere, Oulu and Tornio. From there she took the post route – still in existence in remote parts – across to Kajaani, and returned to Helsinki by way of the popular beauty spots of Eastern Finland. She stands apart from the other woman travellers of the time, travelling out of season, and generally alone. Her 'aunt' seemed quite unruffled by her plans:

> 'It's rather a wild idea, and none of our English nieces have done such a thing before; but your German will carry you through the towns well enough – and if you get left in the lurch anywhere, you must just turn to the post office, or the bookseller – or the pastor. Only, promise me that you won't go down any of the rapids.'

Travers has a small niche in this history as the first British cyclist in Finland. From the hotel in Tampere she cycled out to Kerpola to view the paper factory; her cycle 'possessed neither bell, brake, nor gear-case, the chain came off at intervals, the road-surface was remarkable, and my skirt was too long':

> The road, as I say, was interesting, both in material and scenery. It was made of cobblestones, as big as my two fists, within the town limits, and of nothing at all in the country. Here it was generally black and very wide, having two separate lines of ruts (one to go and one to come), and two precarious footways. (Yet this, they say, is a cycling district!) To cross from one side to another in pursuit of the best surface took both skill and foresight, but passers-by were very kind, and would step out of the way for me. And the country was lovely, *lovely!* The road led between two lakes of marvellous clearness and 'skiey grain,' gleaming among birch woods that were pale golden overhead and mossy green below. Then came stretches of pine forest with ruddy undergrowth and cheery little houses, then lake-waters again, islands, marsh-meadows, distant shores looking for once quite blue, nearer slopes strewn

with villages, and the deepest, most cloudless autumn sky over all. (Also in places the blackest, most shameless mud under-foot!)

Tampere did not much put her in mind of Manchester; she reflected:

Were I a female factory hand, I am sure that I and my children would have a better chance of health and comfort at Tammerfors than in any English industrial city . . . [M]y later years would not be darkened by the hideous, helpless melancholy of slum-life, the dread of unemployment, and the long sense of a losing fight against Society. Nothing like a slum is to be found in Tammerfors.

Her reaction to St John's Church was very different to Mac-Dougall's; she remarks simply of the notorious altar fresco, 'I cannot imagine how it should arouse other than religious feelings.'

In Tornio she was astonished that a town with two thousand inhabitants could boast two banks, a town hall, schools, a hospital and a local paper, not to mention bookshops:

But I must not overlook the three bookshops of Torneå! They exist, mind you, for the primary purpose of selling books, not stationery, nor silver inkstands, nor postcards, and I begin to fear that Finland is very much ahead of Southern England in 'book-learning.' Do you think I could find three real bookshops in Riversguard, or even in the whole of Andredswold? Or should I easily come across foreign books, in two languages, for sale in Exeter or in Gloucester? . . . Yet at Åbo and Tammerfors all sorts of current French and German books were immediately attainable; and though Torneå could not produce these, it had an extensive library of Finnish translations from other languages. In the window of the smallest bookshop, near the Public Garden, I saw at one and the same time Finnish renderings of Herodotus, of Shakespeare, and of Tolstoy. You might call it an epitome of Finnish culture.

She took the steamer to Muhos ('but pray don't imagine that Muhos is a *place* – it is just some five houses, a landing-stage, and a telephone branch') and then followed the post route to Kaajani. As she was travelling upstream she had no temptation to break her promise not to go down the rapids. The inns, thanks to the Finnish Tourist Association, were now excellent, but the actual transport was in remote parts little changed from the eighteenth century: 'a small, springless, two-wheel cart which had forgotten what paint was, a confidential old horse in a string harness' driven first by a schoolgirl and then by 'a small boy, whom I could have put in my pocket'. She stopped at Teerelä, where she got information from the pastor, who was operating a threshing-machine on his glebe. She gives an exciting account of a contest between five young lumber men who 'proposed to shoot Talvi-koski, not in boats – though that even would be an act of skill – but standing upright upon bare, untrimmed water-sodden logs, guiding themselves with their iron-tipped poles.' Near Vaala she saw a traditional savupirt-ti (smoke cottage) and 'a mysterious and monstrous stack of wood, partly covered with layers of earth and grass, standing upon a raised brick platform. This, I learnt afterwards, was an old-fashioned tar-furnace.' The next morning she was taken to see the tar-boats setting off for Oulu.

Later on I parted regretfully from Fru Splander [the 'dear, communicative body' in the telephone office]; and took the steamer for Kajana. Now I am in the beaten track of tourists and hotels – but oh! some day I'll come back to the wilderness again! What a kindly, honest folk they seem, these far-away Finns! Slow they are, certainly – their best friends admit it – but what demand is there for hurry or punctuality in places like Riehki or Teerlä? And a certain stolidity about the natives is not unwelcome to a traveller. By the time they have begun to wonder at your strangeness, you are past; and if it ever *did* occur to them to exploit you, the notion would not arise till you were miles away! Certainly I could not have been more fairly treated; I was ignorant of the road, the tariff, and the language, so they might have cheated me times and again but my bills for travelling and lodgement from Uleaborg onward are about a third of what they would be in civilized parts.

She is enchanted by Kajaani, and by Tynne, a schoolgirl who guides her 'in a mixture of Swedish and German'; avoiding tourist sights, she watches children's games and describes their dances. The day concludes with a magical, epiphanic moment:

Down in front of me was little Kajana, all gaily red and white and brown in a clearing of pale fields; beyond, east and west, were five great grey lakes and a line of low hills. Over all the country lay forest, like a shaggy fell. There was hardly anything to be seen but forest, where lakes were not – dark green woodlands spotted and streaked with tawny gold. Such a strange land!

From Kajaani she took the train to Mikkeli, where her impressions make strange reading for anyone who knows the modern town:

I intended only to stay the night at Mikkeli, but finding that the little town commanded half a dozen lakes and miles of hilly woodland, I remained there over Monday. There is nothing to be seen in the guide-book sense. A good many excellent wooden houses, a town-hall in stone, an ugly Lutheran church in red brick with a spire, and an equally ugly Russian church with lead cupola and gilded balls. Outside Mikkeli the country roads lead through pine

forests, up hill and down dale. There are little lakes, grey
and round and still, set in birch trees and tawny reeds,
with high rocks frowning into them and quiet meadows
leading down to the brim. Further on, streams of peat-
brown water go purling and sparkling under faded wil-
low-shrubs, and cattle, with their pleasant bells, come
wandering through the pines to splash there and drink.
Then you find the usual red-painted, wooden farm-house
in a grassy clearing, where dogs lie about in sunny corners,
and heavy, fair-haired girls go to and fro. Nothing new –
all very simple and remote and Finnish – but strangely
happy-seeming in the September light, which has here,
long before mid day, the quality of mellow afternoon.

Travers has the ability to describe the unspoiled countryside
without either idealising or sentimentalising it; the reference
to a 'guide-book' marks her as a traveller who has bucked the
tourist trend.

On the steamer from Mikkeli she was 'the only foreigner,
and the only woman, at table with the captain and seven solemn Finns'. She thought she was going to Lappeenranta, but
the boat actually went to Savonlinna. Unperturbed, she did the
usual sightseeing there, walking several miles in the rain along
Punkaharju. She was, predictably, unimpressed by the 'expensive and depressing' Cascade Hotel at Imatra. Finally heading
east towards Helsinki, she recorded the first British experience
of Lahti, 'a very growing place', where, in a strange episode,
she reduced a teenage mugger to tears with a stern speech in
English.

She spent the winter in Helsinki; a resident now, she adven-
tured into parts of the city which tourists did not frequent even
in summer:

More snow fell a week ago, and the weather is now
clear again and sharply cold. The pavements were covered

three feet deep, but all this is now shovelled off and piled up alongside, so that you walk by miniature Alps, six and seven feet high. What remains does not scrunch under your feet, but gives a high, indescribable sound: 'the snow screams,' people say, and this is a sign of the great cold.

Ski-ing is now good, so I set off exploring again one afternoon among the isles and bays to the north-west. Beyond Mejlans [Meilahti], beyond even Fölisön [Seurasaari], I think, there was a little point with a dozen red and white cottages clustering among the firs. As I drew near the most outlying of these little homes a woman came down to fetch water from a hole in the ice. She looked weary and troubled, but said "God-dag," to which I responded, adding the original remark that it was cold. She was a Swedish-Finn, so I enquired the name of this hamlet and what sort of people dwelt there, and presently we were chatting as if she were a Sussex woman by her garden gate. She asked me to come in and warm myself a moment, and I gladly complied.

It was a little, dark, poverty-stricken stuga, with a few strips of carpet on the floor, scant furniture, and a stove. Near this was a low bed, where lay a tiny, fair-haired child, perfectly motionless, watching us with unastonished eyes.

'That is my little girl,' said the woman. Looking gravely down upon her, she added, 'She's dying, so they say.'

The child was perhaps seven years old. She lay folded in her own thoughts and visions, not suffering, not frightened, but disregardful of all life. Perhaps she was so near the edge that she could see across, and it was more interesting than anything here. . . .

But, turning to the mother, I could only feel the unreason, the monstrousness of the fate that allows a young child to die – and the pity of it! I said futile things, and we probably cried together.

'It was the rickets and weakness,' she told me. 'If she could have got better they would have taken her into the Cripples' Home at Berghåll [Kallio]; for there's little room here, when the other children are back from school. She couldn't thrive, somehow, after we came; and I never liked the place; my home was near Esbo. Perhaps, when it is all over, my brother will take us away . . . I've had my share of trouble. My husband went with a fishing village on the ice last year, and the floe broke loose, and he was drowned . . .'

We talked for a while, the poor mother and I; and presently I gave her what little material help she would accept. She thought the child took notice of me, so I held the tiny, cold, unanswering hands in mine for a time. Then, since we fancied that it brought a look of pleasure to those strange eyes, I left my bright-coloured scarf spread out upon the bed. I promised, vaguely and uselessly, to come again; but when I went yesterday, the cottage was deserted, and all traces of life were gone.

Travers found her own accommodation in town, but dined frequently with her relatives in Mikonkatu. She learned Swedish, and by the time she left in early summer had become very well informed about Finnish cultural, educational and social practices. In particular she learnt a lot about 'the growth and development of Feminism in Finland' partly through meetings with Helena Tott-Jürgens, one of the leaders of the Women's Movement:

> It seems, then, that the women in Finland have obtained all and more than they are asking for elsewhere. I naturally enquired, 'How did they get it? and how does it work out?'
>
> 'They got it by deserving it!' cried Helena Tott.

There are twenty-four entries for Tott in the index of *Letters from Finland*.

Travers was moving now in circles which were of interest to the police, and which led to her enforced departure. The British Consul calmly explained that 'a certain Russian personage' had made it clear that 'Celia' ought to leave Finland while she could still do so voluntarily:

> unless the lady would undertake promptly to leave the country – her recent highly suspicious actions with regard to the island and fortress of Sveaborg, together with her known frequentation of the houses of disaffected persons and her distribution of forbidden literature, would absolutely oblige the Russian Government to take proceedings against her as a spy.

It was now 1909, and Stolypin was in charge.

Henry W. Nevinson

In September 1910 a group of British journalists was 'invited by leaders of the Diet to visit Finland'. Of these only Henry Nevinson seems to have published an account; his extended letters to the *Nation* are reprinted with a few alterations in *More Changes More Chances* (1925). A noted war correspondent, Nevinson had long been a critic of Russian imperialism, and so was a natural supporter of the Finnish cause. He had been an early member of Hyndman's Social Democratic Federation, but did not find it radical enough. His took a political interest in education and and supported the Suffrage Movement to the extent of carrying banners and making speeches. He viewed Finland with a socialist's approval:

> Two passions occupied the people's mind – education and patriotism. In every village or small town I could be sure that the most important buildings would be schools. Elementary schools, commercial schools, technical schools, Lyceums or classical schools, deaf-and-dumb schools, gymnastic schools, – a town that would escape notice in our country would have them all. And in no other country was such equal opportunity for every kind of knowledge, livelihood, and work given to women. Even then, all women over twenty-four had a vote on equal terms with men and could sit in the Diet if elected, as about twenty were.

At midday on 16 September the British journalists were present at the historic occasion when 'the Finnish Diet assembled, as was thought, for the last time in freedom':

> From a side door near the throne, strangely dressed officials then preceded a swarm of Russian military and naval

officers, sparkling and tinkling with medals bestowed for every reason but victory. They stood in a glittering band beside the throne, and before the steps a stout, squat figure became conspicuous in the brown tunic of Russian undress. It was tyranny's representative, Governor-General Seyn, a man of evil repute in Finland already as one of Bobrikoff's agents in the darkest days. In a harsh and challenging voice he read a Russian decree announcing that the Tsar had again called the Diet together, and then he stood glaring at the President, as though expecting defiance.

Many expected defiance, for it was known that demands would be laid before the Diet calling for the election of members for the Russian Duma and the Imperial Council, a contribution to the Imperial defence, and the granting of special rights to Russians in the country; and these demands had not been signed by the Tsar as Grand Duke of Finland, but only by the Council of Ministers in St. Petersburg. But, standing unmoved before the Governor-General, the Diet's President in one brief sentence acknowledged the Grand Duke's message, and the ceremony was over. The officers rattled out; with the members of the Diet I passed gratefully into the open air, and only the two-headed eagle remained, clutching its orb and sceptre.

In *The Nation* this account had been given the title 'A Scene from the Finnish Tragedy'.

Nevinson spent more than a week in Finland, but records only a few, brief impressions: whimsical ('[p]erhaps an old castle may stand on an island rock') and practical (a pulping-mill and 'an iron-works in full blast'). Different from either was a shooting party which hunted an elk, 'the whole business being as cruel and bloody a sport as I have ever witnessed'.

Sir George Renwick

Renwick, who made his reputation and money in shipping, sat for many years in Parliament, a Conservative with a very liberal outlook. In his first travel book, *Romantic Corsica* (1909), he wrote of 'a beautiful and romantic little country as yet virgin to all but a few of the great host of travellers and tourists'. This description also fitted Finland, in most ways a far cry from Corsica; it is Renwick's taste for solitude and primitive rural scenes which links *Romantic Corsica* with *Finland Today* (1911). Like Boswell before him, Renwick admired the sturdy independence of Corsica, and respected its political struggles. The same feeling imbues some of his writing about Finland: he is sympathetic towards Finnish national aspirations, though less stridently so than Travers. It was in *Romantic Corsica* that he wrote: 'I was converted to a belief in women's suffrage while in Finland – the first country to give women parliamentary votes and to send women as members to Parliament – long before the question seriously vexed England.' It is curious that this elderly Conservative MP should have supported women's suffrage, while Scott, the young Liberal, opposed it. In *Finland Today*, which contains 'A Word of Preface' from Nevinson, Renwick writes of 'this brave little nation', with a hint of condescension towards 'a splendid little nation at a sombre period of its history'. He visited Finland in 1906 and 1909, but his book is based also on 'a lifelong interest in the affairs of the Grand Duchy'.

As well as describing beauty spots which had become popular during the age of the steamer, Renwick has chapters on the people, history, politics, sports, literature, music, art and architecture of Finland. 'There is much more in Finland than "sights",' he writes; he enjoyed tramping in the wild countryside, as he had in Corsica. On his way from Pori to Tampere he took what he intended as a morning walk from 'Tryvää', which finally took him him sixty hours. On another occasion he records arriving at the inn at Pihlajavesi to catch the train after a forty-eight kilometre walk from Virrat.

Renwick's travels offer a strong antidote to the torpid tourist culture which had developed in the later nineteenth century. 'Not to know the sublime silence of Finland's forests,' he writes, 'not to wander by paths where human foot seldom treads, is not to know Finland.' We see him turning away from the standard attractions: in Tampere he recommends Kangasala, but as a good walk – 'only twelve miles or so . . . an ideal day's tramp'. 'I think that the best way to know Finland really well,' he muses at Liminka, 'is to explore such out-of-the-way places, to take an unbeaten path whenever it is possible to do so': his steamer makes an unscheduled stop to land him at Koli – 'like being put down on a desert island', while at Vaala he sacrifices 'some degree of comfort' by opting for the non-tourist version of the tar-boat. Tornio for him was the perfect unspoiled place, and he sees the danger of writing about it: 'I hope readers of mine will not go in such numbers as to make it a "popular" resort.'

He describes several towns hardly glimpsed by most tourists: 'I strolled into [Lahti], a delightfully spick-and-span place, with straight and broad streets with a touch of the Garden City about it.' Several writers mention stopping in Kuopio; he alone describes his visit:

> To see Kuopio in all its beauty it is necessary to climb Puijo Hill, from which a view extending far over town and lake and islands to the dim purple of distant swelling uplands, a marvellous sight, can be obtained. I wandered up the path late one evening, and, just as the sun was setting, climbed the tower which decks the summit. There I sat chatting with the keeper, drinking coffee and munch-

ing hard *knäckebrod*. How picturesque, in the glow if the evening, are the red tints of a Finnish town, for the Finn prefers red as a colour. Particularly does red predominate in Kuopio, and it sets the town off nicely among the green of vegetation and the blue of the lake.

Kotka, the pig long forgotten, was now a huge port, with massive saw-mills; it impresses him, but he prefers Hamina, 'delightful and restful after aggressively new and active Kotka'. As for Porvoo: 'to go to the grand duchy and not to see Borgå is like going to Italy and missing Florence'.

Renwick vividly describes shooting the rapids at Mankala. Further north:

> I found a heavily laden tar-boat at Sotkamo, and the crew of one of them, three men, thought it an excellent idea that I should come with them to Kajana. But when I saw the boat I was, I must confess, a trifle afraid . . . I was assigned the post of steersman.

When the crew hoisted the sail they went to sleep, but for Renwick it was too novel an experience 'to be wasted in sleep'. This, and Mankala, were preparation for his tar-boat adventure from Kajaani, the best of many British accounts from the period; he enthusiastically relives the experience, rather than simply recording it:

> The steamer I took from Kajana to Vaala, a journey of a little over four hours, carried an unusually large number of people, so the captain said, and it was evident that the special boat in which tourists descend the river with some degree of comfort was going to be rather crowded.
>
> 'Look here, my friend,' said an American as he and I sauntered among the quaint huts of the little township, 'guess you and I will do the trip in the old way, right now, and not wait for that special boat.'

This motion was carried unanimously, and off we went to the harbour, where boat after boat was putting off into the stream. We soon struck a fairly handsome bargain with the crews of a couple of laden tar-boats, an inspector advising us that it was best for them not to carry more than one additional person. We tossed a markka in the air to decide who should go first, and I won.

'Guess we'll meet at Muhos!' shouted the American as my boat gradually allowed itself to catch the current. The steersman holds the steering-pole lightly, that pole upon which our safety depends. It is four or five yards long, and cut to oar shape at the end which goes into the water, and is tied loosely to the stern of the boat. Thick as it is – the handle end is six to eight inches thick and it broadens out towards the other – the force of the water in mid-torrent makes it quiver like an aspen. The pilots, every one of them licensed, are men of iron nerve and enormous strength, and they require every whit of both they can muster. The crew of the boat I went in consisted of two men and their wives; both men and women in the course of the long journey take turns at rowing.

I sat amidships and with a tarpaulin, a rug, and a mackintosh made myself comfortable for the seven or eight hours' journey down-stream. I had just settled down when the rowing ceased and the current caught us in its fierce grasp.

'The Niskakoski; nine miles long!' one of the women shouted in my ear as we dashed along on the first reach of the foaming waters; but the exciting part of it is only six miles. And what a six miles it is! One pays no attention to the land on either hand; the churned-up waters, only a matter of inches away, fascinate one's eyes; it is impossible to give heed to anything but those hissing waves. The noise, too, is terrible, the sensation of speed – we did six miles in about ten minutes – an extraordinary one. A rock in front! One rises in one's seat and holds one's breath, waiting, nerve-strung, for the shock. But the boat swerves and sways, and the rock is far behind before you can think what has happened.

Swish! A huge wave breaks over us, and, just as we recover from it, another and another. Every second seems to be charged with sensation which would have served for an hour, but the strangest experience of all is when the boat glides out into calm water again. The smooth river seems unreal, and as the oars, worked by strong arms, carry the heavily-laden boat along one wishes for raging waters.

At first the river banks are low, but soon they rise and tower on high. Below the first cataract the landscape is delightful, and on the beautiful day I made the journey the country on both sides was exquisite. Many tiny cottages were to be seen, and there is a good deal of cultivation. Often, too, one can see a returning tar-boat crew pulling their boat up-stream. Two or three tug away at it while another, by the aid of a pole, prevents the vessel from being damaged against the rocks. The crew are generally barefoot, and at times the path is very rough, but they seem to be accustomed to it. On the calmer stretches of the river and on the lakes they are able to row or sail, but for a great part of the return journey, which may last three or four weeks, the boat has to be hauled.

What a peaceful life must be lived in those little farmsteads among the pine-trees! Crops and flocks are the only concerns. The outer world may do as it pleases; here but little of its hubbub penetrates. The two women of the crew, I thought, looked at the peaceful scenes with longing regard, for what a different life was theirs! Three voyages to Uleåborg and three hard return journeys is their work during the short northern summer, and it is generally a race against time to carry out their task. Then follows the long,

dreary winter in their little eastern village or isolated homestead. The hardship of it all is writ deep in their faces.

A lesser torrent – Ahmakoski – is negotiated, followed
by another spell of rowing. Then, after Utakoski, six or
seven miles farther down, the river broadens and takes
the water of the Utos on the right hand. Utajärvi Church
is seen, and soon afterwards the pretty little village of
Merilä, where, I was told, there is a tiny inn and where
the journey may be broken. On we went, however, and
Sotkakoski was soon behind us. Then a dull roar could be
heard; it got louder and louder.

'What is that?'

'Pyhäkoski.'

Phyhäkoski, the Sacred (or Holy) Rapid, extends for
twelve or thirteen miles. The pilot nerves himself for the
battle, for Niskakoski is child's play compared with what
is now near. The Sacred Rapid is at first narrower than Niskakoski. Between high, tree-clad banks we rush; swish,
swish goes many a wave over us, but oh the joy of that
evening dart down the torrent! The sun tinted the water
with every possible hue.

'Why!' one of the men exclaimed, 'the torrent does not
throw waves over us but rainbows!' That is the spirit in
which to appreciate Pyhäkoski.

Then, for a short space, the raging waters seem to take
breath. The boat glides easily along, sweeps gracefully
round a corner, and then faces the wild torrent again. Just
as one is beginning to compliment oneself on having excellent nerves comes an experience that would make one
shiver with fear if there were only time, but it is all over
before one quite realises what has taken place.

On we dash at the rate of about half a mile a minute –
straight for a sheer wall of rock which stands out and nar-
rows the torrent's passage, so that the waters are churned

into a raging whirlpool. We rush as though to destruction on the rock; suddenly the pilot throws his whole strength on the rudder, and when we are about a quarter of a length from the rock the boat swings with terrifying suddenness round the rock, seems to fly over the hissing whirlpool, and reaches the waves that dance for joy beyond its dangers. For some seconds one's heart seems to stand still; one looks round to see if one is really safe, and there is to be seen once more, as the boat hurries along, beautiful banks of trees and a glorious evening sun.

When the torrent is over and we can talk in comfort again, I am told some of the horrors of that part of the descent. To turn too soon may mean to be sucked down into the raging depths, for it is only by darting over at the utmost possible speed that the whirlpool's power is overcome. For the pilot to be a second too late in throwing every ounce of his strength on the steering-bar would mean being dashed to pieces on the rock – the Pälli, it is called – and being thrown helpless into the waves. Safety hangs on the decision of an instant.

He and the American stopped at 'a fairly good little inn at Muhos' and decided 'to tramp to Uleåborg the next day as we were told it was beautiful country. It was – and we took two days to it.' They stopped off at a *savopirtti* where an old couple, '[h]appy, hospitable folk', offered food which was 'almost beyond us', but the provisions from their rucksacks which they offered in return 'were objects of wonder and admiration', especially the Huntley and Palmer biscuits. They stayed at a small inn, 'bathed long and thoroughly in the river' to clean themselves of bugs, and breakfasted at Liminka. Here the salmon was so much to their taste that they lingered, and 'set out to explore the neighbourhood in leisurely fashion', taking the evening train to Oulu, with dinner in 'a magnificent Societetshuset', and 'the most seductive menu I have come across in Finland or out of it'.

Ernest Young

Ernest Young taught science and geography at the John Lyon School, Harrow, becoming Headmaster in 1906, and moving in 1911 to head the new Harrow County School; he was an admired educational innovator, still honoured the school's history. Somehow he found time to visit Finland, and to write *Finland: The Land of a Thousand Lakes* (1912). He must have been an excellent geographer, for it is hard to believe that he had not spent a year or two in Finland, so well has he understood and incorporated all his material. The chapter on education begins: 'No one who knows anything of the Finns will deny that they are the best educated nation in the world', suggesting that he might have gone there for 'professional development'. This chapter is unmistakably written by an educationalist.

Young's Preface makes clear that he is providing information, something which he thinks, incorrectly, has been ignored in books about Finland which have described 'those parts of the country seen by the writer, or . . . personal experiences of travel'. On just a few occasions, however, Young forgets his self-imposed discipline and gives a first-hand account. The Imatra rapids were one sight which stirred him to a vivid personal response:

> The noise is appalling and can be heard, under favourable circumstances, at a distance of five or six miles. At first it is heard as a low rumble; then it deepens to a prolonged moan, and as one nears the scene of the tumult it is the uproar of a great storm that knows no rest.
>
> No photograph and no words can give any idea of the scene, for it is impossible to reproduce the roaring of the waters or the splendour of the jewelled mists that hang

over the surface and of the columns of glittering foam that rise, sometimes to a height of twenty feet, as the maddened river tears its way down the slope. Masses of swirling treacherous green dash themselves against the rocks and break into cascades of sparkling diamonds. The dark pines bend over to listen to the tumult, and the boulders shiver again under the force of the impact. The water never rests, never subsides; and, beautiful as it all is, it is still more terrible as a type of the cruel, pitiless destructive forces of unrestrained nature. Its grandeur suggests violence, its still backwaters treachery and death. The river becomes more peaceful where it expands, seems even to wear a cruel smile of contentment, as if satisfied with its powers for ill. Another hundred yards or so and it breaks into bigger wavelets, chuckling and crowing like the very incarnation of evil.

You turn away your eyes to the trees and the rocks upon the banks, almost glad to give them some repose after the bewildering, dazzling, tormented, writhing mass of foam. There are the companions of the stream, motionless and silent, living their lives peacefully and patiently, undisturbed, unhindered, on the very brink of destruction. Just as you are making up your mind to depart, a mass of water dashes against a rock and is hurled back to meet the galloping billows from behind. In the conflict, walls and pillars of water are ceaselessly shattered into foam, and then rise and fall, form and reform, as they hurry madly to the open space beyond.

Young gives the first British account of travelling in Finland by motor car. On a lake steamer heading for Kuopio, a fellow traveller said, 'Come to my town, Nurmes; it is a fine town and there is a man who has a motor car – sixteen horse power!' So 'we slept on board and the next morning arrived at Nurmes', where 'we borrowed a boat and rowed across a lake to the home of the man who possessed the sixteen horse-power machine'. The owner courteously offered to drive them to the next stage of their journey later in the day:

> . . . we waited in the house of another acquaintance that we had made on the boat. Here we were entertained with all the delicacies that the little town could provide, and we were almost sorry when the hour arrived to bid our courteous host and his charming wife adieu. The ride in the car was exciting enough in its way. The horses, everywhere, were terrified by the sight of so unusual a vehicle in this lonely part of the world, no matter how slowly we went. The driver worked hard with the hooter and gave long and noisy warnings of our approach, so that the peasants were able to get down and hold on to the heads of their restive steeds. Chickens and dogs ran deliberately from side to side of the road courting a destruction that the courtesy and skill of the chauffeur prevented them from suffering. The cows simply stood stock still in the road and refused to budge until we were right under their noses, when the smell of the petrol or the throbbing of the engine converted them into models of agility and speed. It is only under the influence of an automobile that the cows will condescend to show their powers of leaping fences and ditches.
>
> The roads were good enough; in places they were even excellent, though the gradients were often rather steep, and our sixteen horse-power Darracq needed a little persuasion, and once or twice a little assistance, in getting over the tops of the small hills, for the roads seemed to run straight from point to point as though gradients were of no consequence to the engineer who made, or the peasants who use these northern forest-roads. At times the roads run for sixty miles through almost unbroken forest, where the silver of the birch and the red of the pine take new

tints with the passing of every cloud, and where the throbbing of the engine and the whirr of the wheels seem but to
intensify the mystery and the silence that in part constitute
the attraction of the Finnish woodlands. There are many
dry spots among the heather where the luncheon-basket
can be despoiled of its contents, and where wild strawberries and raspberries by the thousand afford all the dessert
that man could long for.

Most of Young's first-hand accounts of Finland appeared not
in *Finland: The Land of a Thousand Lakes* but in magazine
articles. Seven of these were collected in *From Russia to Siam*
(1914); they are short sketches, with titles like 'A Visit to a
Finnish Farm'. One of the best of them, 'Out for the Day: a
Trip in the Backwoods of Europe', is set in Kajaani, where,
having a day to spare while his clothes were being laundered,
he decided to take a boat trip to Sotkamo. He was greatly puzzled by the timetable:

> The name of the place to which I wished to go was Sotka-
> mo. The name of the place at which I was stationed was
> Kajaani. Now in one and the same paper I found Kajana,
> Kajanum, Kajanista, Sotkamo, Sotkamosta, and Sotka-
> moon, and I was then unaware that the variations in the
> terminations of the names meant *to*, *from*, and other prep-
> ositional directions.

In his confusion he believed that he could complete the round
trip in a few hours. At the quay he found that 'the boat appeared to consist of two cabins and a funnel'; he went aboard,
a whistle blew, and they set off. 'There were few landing places
on the route, and the boat stopped only at rare intervals.'

> When we arrived at Sotkamo it was three o'clock in the
> afternoon, and I was hungry. So far I had had no food, as
> the palatial craft in which I was voyaging possessed no

buffet. I looked anxiously at the land. There was a church, a saw-mill, and a few mean houses. Now a church is not a good place in which to obtain food for the body, and the products of a saw mill are neither palatable nor nourishing. I determined to stick to the boat. It was bound for Ontojoki, and at the worst should be there in another two hours. I would wait and, if necessary, raid a cottage at the other end of the journey. There were people on the river besides ourselves – men sailing their fifty-foot tar-boats, and men, women, and horses on the timber rafts that were slowly finding their way down the stream. All these people must have bought food somewhere, probably at Ontojoki. We would go and see. We went and saw. It was about half-past five when we anchored in the desired haven, and all that was in sight was a timber depot. With the exception of one man, who received sundry parcels and barrels from our steamer, not a soul was to be seen. The cargo was unceremoniously tossed ashore, and then we prepared to return. The captain, imagining that I wished to disembark with the bags and the boxes, came to me and signified that I was to get out. The boxes did not belong to me, and I had not the faintest interest in their contents or their owners, so I did not budge.

'Ontojoki,' remarked the captain, in sonorous and fluent Finnish.

Pointing majestically to myself I replied. 'Kajana, Ontojoki; Ontojoki, Kajana.' I waved my hand first in the direction in which we had come, and secondly in the direction in which we were to return. Captain and crew burst into roars of laughter. It was past all their imagining why I should sit on their little steamer all day without food, merely to go back again, and I could not explain to them that I was merely waiting for my washing . . .

It was quite dark when we once more drew alongside the few boards that are called the quay at Sotkamo. The first mate tapped me on the shoulder, pointed to his mouth, and remarked in simple but eloquent language, 'Food shop.' I followed with an unwonted alacrity, for I am rotund. We stopped at the door of a small house. There my guide entered into conversation with a woman and two girls. They spoke in whispers though they knew I did not understand a word they were saying. What the mate told them I do not know, but they certainly found it very amusing, and had hard work to suppress their merriment. The proprietress of the establishment led me into a little back room and hastily banged the door. In the twinkling of an eye the place shook with laughter. I laughed too, for just at that moment I caught sight of myself in a looking glass. I forbear to describe my dirty face, and my wind-blown hair, or the curious combination of a panama hat and a big winter overcoat.

The food he was offered consisted of 'solid salt relieved with a flavour of fish', bread which was 'brown, sour, and hard, a kind of vinegar-soaked stone quoit', and oat-cake with 'the flavour of aniseed and the texture of leather', all of which he passed over. He dined finally on two slabs of sausage-meat 'of indeterminate character' and a large jug of milk.

I strolled back to the boat, but there was no one moving, so I entered the little cabin and stretched myself out on the bench. I soon fell fast asleep. When I awoke it was half-past three in the morning, and the hooter was being blown preparatory to making a fresh start. The next time I awoke it was five o'clock and I was back in Kajana. We had done the last part of the journey, about a quarter of the total distance, in an hour and three quarters. Altogether I suppose we had travelled about sixty miles, and we had spent eighteen hours over it.

Young found better refreshment on another day out, when he spurned the tourist hotel at Punkaharju to walk 'the whole length of the back of the hog':

About six o'clock I arrived at Punkasalmi, the station from which I proposed to return. The train did not leave till eight, and that meant no food at Nyslott till after ten. As far as I could see, Punkasalmi consisted of a farm-house and a station, neither of which was of any use to me. I struck into a country road and wandered on to a collection of small log huts not very far away. The first hasty glance revealed little that offered encouragement to a hungry man, but a more careful inspection discovered the word *Kahvila* attached to one of the cottages. My knowledge of foreign tongues, thought somewhat limited, was of sufficient extent to allow of the recognition of the word Kahvila as the local representation of *Café*. I opened the garden gate and walked timidly to the cottage door. I hesitated about knocking, because of my inability to explain my wants. But my footsteps had disturbed a dog, who set up an unpleasant demonstration, and brought a woman to the door. As she stood expectantly before me, all I could say was 'Café?'

Her reply was in the affirmative, and she motioned me to enter. Her little habitation contained two rooms, both of them spotlessly clean. In the first, or living-room, the most conspicuous object was an enormous brick stove. An elderly woman, evidently weak from age and sickness, was moving uneasily on a couch. Both the women were bare-footed. Round the walls was a white wooden bench. There were several tables and chairs, roughly fashioned of local woods, and there was a sweet, cleanly, rustic smell about the room. The heat from the stove was oppressive, and I was not sorry when I was shown into the second and smaller apartment.

Here, as in the first, there were a number of growing plants, a feature, as I afterwards found, of almost constant occurrence in all classes of Finnish homes. In the room into which I had been shown, were crowded many of the luxuries and some of the necessities of the family. It was evidently used as a bedroom, and the bed itself was made to slide up like a telescope in the daytime, in order to reduce the space it occupied. There was a sewing machine of American make, a bookcase filled chiefly with religious works, a whole gallery of family portraits, and many dishes of fresh flowers. The hat rack was the branch of a tree nailed to the wall. Indeed, one of the most pleasing things about this humble dwelling was the use made of the forest in furnishing the house. The walls and ceiling were of wood, unpolished, unvarnished, unpainted – absolutely beautiful in their simplicity and cleanliness. The floor had been polished, probably because the inhabitants of the cottage were in the habit of going about bare-footed. Birch had been used in the construction of a three-legged table, a four-branched stand for flower pots, sundry picture frames, and a towel rail. The wood was in the natural condition, with its silvery bark brightening and adorning the surface . . .

The coffee served was excellent. I do not exaggerate when I say that better could not be obtained in Paris. Thick cream and a plate of sweet bread and biscuits made up the rest of the decorations on the polished tray, and the cost of the meal was fourpence.

Young's appreciation of the traditional attractions of remote and unexplored regions is undercut by his picture of the future. At the same time that he was extolling Finland for being free of 'the tourist-ridden spots that are such an abomination in the better known lands of the Continent', he was imagining in practical detail the possibilities of a motor tour. The 'chief deterrent to a motor tour is the language difficulty, for it would take a lifetime to learn Finnish'. He envisaged a summer tour with a Finnish chauffeur and interpreter, who would be able to 'take the car from point to point' to meet those who had temporarily left it for a journey by lake steamer.

Charles Fillingham Coxwell

Coxwell was born in France and lived in Australia. He translated Russian literature and was also a published poet, though one would not guess this from the rather wooden style of *Through Russia in War-Time* (1917), which provides the final British account of the Grand Duchy of Finland. He was about to return to Europe from New York when the *Lusitania* was sunk, and as a consequence he became one of the first travellers to take the new 'safe' route by way of Archangel. He decided to take the opportunity to explore Russia, and to return home through Finland and Scandinavia.

After extensive travels in Russia he entered Finland from Petrograd, as it was now called. He makes a few unmemorable observations about Vyborg, Helsinki, Turku, and Tampere, but his accounts of the customs officials and bureaucrats are both comic and ominous. He had not been prepared for the problems he encountered at the Russian-Finnish frontier, and was actually sent back to St Petersburg where it took him three days to collect all the permits and waivers required to travel on into Finland. To his dismay he found later that Finland was as hard to get out of as Russia had been.

He took the train to Rovaniemi:

> To reach Rovanièmi, the northernmost point of the Finnish railway system, it was necessary to sleep at Kèmi, where a failure on the part of everybody to understand my object did not surprise me, since an Englishman's love of travel is incomprehensible to most subjects of the Tsar. The inn was full, but after supper a girl, carrying a lantern, led me to a house where, by passing through the kitchen, I reached a not uncomfortable chamber, as

to which, however, I at first experienced doubts, because the wooden bedstead, being built on a telescopic principle, was much contracted, and its capacity for extension did not at once reveal itself to an unimaginative mind. Next day, by a train that moved at the rate of fifteen miles per hour, I reached my destination, situated just within the Arctic circle. As for the country passed through, at first there were Christmas-trees and primitive dark grey log-houses with chalet-like barns to match them. Then came an undulating wilderness of broken granite, sparsely covered by scrubby birch-trees, already yellow-leaved in late September. It became necessary to explain my purpose at Rovaniemi station to the gendarme in charge, who examined every one's passport and my luggage carefully; nor did he seem to regard me favourably, being doubtless unable to decipher my papers.

Here Coxwell was told that his wish 'to gain a glimpse of Laplanders' would be better effected in Sweden, so he back-tracked to Tornio where he 'received liberal attention from the Custom House officials':

The examination was thorough, and lasted perhaps an hour. Once more it became necessary to battle for precious negatives, films, and rolls. Not quite liking to see un-opened and unexposed material thrown away, I announced in Russian that such and such film packs were 'novy,' or 'new.' Whereupon an unsympathetic gendarme solemnly asked, 'What is "new"?' a Socratic form of investigation with which I could not cope. But, with sardonic humour, he added he supposed 'new' was not 'old,' a speculation so much to his taste that he uttered it at least as often as I asserted that anything was new. After a while a superior appeared, who, with ability to speak French, displayed a reassuring and not ungenial disposition. When all spoils from my belongings had been set aside with view to a later investigation, I was searched in a considerate manner, and requested to attend at eleven on the following morning. Meantime, as the hotel was full, an apartment in a private house would be shown me . . . Next morning a stroll made me acquainted with this singularly calm and peaceful little town, composed of clean, white or tinted, separate wooden houses. In an atmosphere not only sunny but crisp, a walk through the comparatively spacious street, where grass grew at intervals, proved agreeable.

At the appointed hour he presented himself at the Customs House:

I answered questions and tried to shepherd my property. While any undeveloped film was forthwith confiscate, every negative underwent careful scrutiny . . . Meantime, at the officer's request, a linguistic genius who stood near satisfied himself that my correspondence and notebooks were innocuous. At last even the picture postcards were done with; whereupon, having lost little, I collected my scattered goods with a gendarme's help, and felt that I had been treated fairly and justly. At a barrier on a pier, passports were expeditiously restored to their owners, who could then embark in a small steamer for Harparanda, where, at the Stadt's Hotel, all very gladly partook of a meal.

Once in Sweden he headed north to visit the Lapps, travelling as far as Abisco before heading for England.

Coxwell is the last British traveller in the Grand Duchy of Finland to have left a published account. Before very long there would be a new wave of travellers, coming in search of the New Republic.

Epilogue

The mutation of explorers into travellers into tourists was steady and predictable, but still incomplete in 1917. Finland had by this date become well established as a popular, comfortable, and inexpensive destination for a leisurely summer holiday. The country had been opened up with the advent of the steamer, first on the routes from Stockholm and from Lübeck, then on the extensive lake system as far north as Kajaani, and finally on routes from England. During the second half of the century the railway network had steadily expanded to the major towns; the journey which Joseph Marshall made from Vaasa to Savonlinna in 1768 on horseback could have been made by train at the end of the following century. Tourism was a beneficiary of these developments, rather than a driving force.

By about 1912 published accounts of summer tours in Finland were becoming repetitive. The format of the books is easily recognisable: embossed covers, thick paper, and many photographs, often supplied by the Finnish Tourist Association. The growing list of popular destinations had become predictable; there were half-a-dozen accounts of Kangasala, Imatra, and the tar-boats, for example, to choose from for this selection.

The end of the century witnesses the paradox of tourists beginning to spoil places that they want to see by the mere fact of going there: MacDougall describes her arrival at Punkaharju, where there were already 'a score or more of excursionists . . . that a rival steamer from another direction had just deposited there'. Even at remote Helvetinjärvi Clive-Bayley found nothing to eat at the nearby farmhouse because parties of sightseers had emptied the larder. The paradox is seen most strikingly in the way in which the terrifying descent of the rapids from Kajaani to Oulu by tar-boat becomes just another tourist attraction (for Rae, in Lapland in 1873, descending the rapids had still been a local means of transport). Young writes:

> The tar-boats leave Vaala daily during the summer season. Those used by the tourist are provided by the Finnish Tourist Association. They are painted red and yellow, the national colours, and are comfortably cushioned . . . The greatest number of passengers that can be carried is twelve.

Vaala was a day's journey from Helsinki, so '[i]n order to enable tourists with only a short time at their disposal to experience the novel and thrilling delight of shooting the rapids, the Finnish Tourist Society have arranged a new interesting route down the Mankala rapids on the river Kymmene'. A hundred years later 'white-water rafting' is a much-advertised leisure activity in Finland.

There is perhaps no sadder sign of the change from travel to tourism than this, unless it be the transformation of Imatra. John Paterson, the missionary, visiting the falls in 1817, wrote that 'the whole scene was one of wild sublimity', but the roads were bad, the nearest village 'wretched' and the post-house 'the most miserable-looking place'; later tourists describe not wild sublimity, but an elegant, fashionable, over-priced resort. It was a new departure for travellers in Finland to be criticising luxury: while enjoying the ease and comfort of touring, they could disapprove of modern features – 'alas! year by year, the railway advances,' laments Clive-Bayley, who had explored Finland largely by train.

The changes continued after 1917, with motor buses filling the last gaps in the transport system; many of the recorded journeys in the 1920s and 1930s are by bus. Rail and bus connections opened up Lapland as the popular destination it had been in the eighteenth century. It would not be long before the motorcar was making its mark; Young's dream of a motoring holiday in Finland came true, although not for him.

The development of air transport would broadly mirror that of the steamer a century earlier, with airports being established in major towns from the 1930s, and flights first from Stockholm, then from further afield and within Finland. In 1938 V. C. Buckley arrived in Finland by air, to take a motoring holiday.

De Windt wrote of his hotel in Tampere that 'there was a quaint mixture of modernism and the primitive, peculiar to this country, and not without its charms'. In the next phase of the British discovery of Finland the quaint and the primitive more or less cease to be attractions. The independent Finland after 1917 was 'the new nation', and ushered in a new era for travel writing; foremost among the interests of British visitors would be the advanced social institutions, architecture, music, and the Winter War.

Appendices

1 Finnish Trains

From Ernest Young (1912), pp.197–200:

The railway ticket is printed in three languages, and there are no remarks about by-laws on the back. The notices in the train are in six languages – Finnish, Swedish, Russian, German, French and English.

The trains are unambitious in the matter of speed and the journey from Helsingfors to St. Petersburg – a distance of about 276 miles – is accomplished by the express trains in about fourteen hours, that is, at a speed of under twenty miles an hour. But what the trains lack in speed they make up in comfort and cheapness. The cars are excellent and the sleeping arrangements are such as are not open to any but the well-to-do in England . . .

A servant lights the lamps, one by one in each compartment from the inside, as the train tries to rush along. Electricity has not yet made its appearance, and when night falls you may as well go to bed, for it is impossible to read with comfort. The seats are covered with clean white linen covers, which are removed and washed when they are dirty.

The time-table is full of helpfulness. The directions as to symbols are printed in six languages. There is a key to the distances between the stations which can be used to ascertain the cost of the journey. There is a railway map that is of a comfortable size, and does not tear in pieces when it is unfolded; and there is a most ingenious diagram of each of the main lines and branches, by means of which you can see where you have to change, and how long you have to wait, if you wish to use any of the branch lines.

But the full beauty of the Finnish *Bradshaw* is not realised until you are hungry, when you look down the page and see a little picture of a knife and fork at the places where you can get anything to eat. The train stops at these stations an appropriate length of time. If the dinner-hour be near you may get twenty minutes, and it is

241

wonderful what can be done in twenty minutes, if certain dietary rules be disregarded. The food is spread out on a long table, with piles of plates, knives, forks and other articles. You help yourself and you can satisfy your appetite according to several tabulated schemes. By means of a printed tariff you see how much it will cost to have soup alone, or two dishes or three of the whole course. You eat as much as you choose of one dish if one dish be your choice, and when you go to pay, you are not asked how much you have eaten but how many dishes you have sampled. A full-course dinner of really excellent quality costs about two shillings. If you have coffee and cake you get one cup of coffee but the supply of cake is unlimited. A bottle of beer costs a shilling, but that includes as many sandwiches as you care to consume. If you be very thirsty and want a second bottle of beer you pay a second shilling, but this obviously conveys no advantages in the way of sandwiches.

2 The Priest and the Widow

Hamley's account (see p.81) continues:

> In the evening (so our allies told the story) they were discovered making their way back to the forts through the French lines, and were fired at by their sentries as spies. The priest was shot, and the lady wounded, though she had still resolution enough to drive on and make her escape. To give an additional spice of romance to the tale, they asserted that the priest was an officer in disguise, and the lady a man in masquerade. If this were so, there is no truth in outward signs, for she certainly talked small, had no traces of beard under her muffler, and must have been a very manikin in coat and breeches. Onwards we marched after this rencontre, without seeing anything more formidable than a group of old ladies in red petticoats, and with red kerchiefs over their heads, whom a long-sighted amateur pronounced to be Russians with helmets, until to his great discomfiture they came near, and manifested themselves to be of the unwarlike sex.

Hughes gives a different version (Hughes, pp.84–5):

> On the day of the landing of the troops, a Russian lady, I believe a Frenchwoman, but the widow of a Russian officer killed

by a shell from the 'Valorous' or 'Hecla,' was endeavouring to escape in a carriage, under the care of a priest. The first party they fell in with was a group of British officers, who called upon them to halt. The padre, however, only lashed his horse into a gallop; upon this, one of the officers dashed into a footpath in the wood, and, cutting off an angle of the road, appeared in front of the caleche with his rifle covering them. This time they halted quick enough. They were treated with all possible kindness, and, being noncombatants, were allowed to depart, with many good wishes, and a warning to stop next time when summoned.

This warning, however, was not sufficient. The next time they were hailed by a French sentry, and again the unhappy pastor, trusting the speed of the horse, went off at a gallop. The Frenchman fired, and they both fell; one of them, the poor woman, I believe, to rise no more. This unhappy story was related with many variations, but the version I have given is, I think, substantially true.

The story of the widow and the priest is an intriguing one, and has several features typical of war legends, as described by Paul Fussell in *The Great War and Modern Memory* (1975). Like all legends, it exists in different versions, and everyone believes their own to be 'substantially true'. What this one has most in common with such legends is that it is demonstrably not true. According to a modern Åland historian the whole population of Skarpans, the local parish, including the priest, had been evacuated before the war, and the town burnt, 'to prevent the enemy from using them as cover during an assault'. (Robins, 21.)

3 The Parson and the Pig

Captain Fanshawe wrote to his father after the second attack on Kotka in July 1855 (Fanshaw, p.327):

An amusing incident occurred on the night when the *Cossack* was left in charge of the access from the mainland to the Island of Kotka. The marines guarding the bridge-head were keenly on the alert, for a Russian attack in force was very probable. Suddenly at midnight the general silence was broken by a great commotion; the men stood to arms, and all eyes were strained into the darkness of the fir-wood on one side, or the glare of the burning barracks on the other. A few moments' tension, and the cause explained itself to be – a parson chasing a pig! The latter had been trying to escape from the burning building; the former had come from England in a yacht to witness naval operations in the Baltic. Piggy's fate was sealed, for the marines vigorously joined the chase, and all had roast pork for supper.

This was, of course the Rev. Hughes (see pp.84ff.), who wrote his own account (Hughes, p.222):

> I went forward a little way into the village to see whether the fire was likely to spread towards the ship, and as I went I beheld a lonely porker jogging down the road, and grunting dismally over his sorrows.
>
> Actuated by motives of humanity, I felt it my duty, if possible, to direct the suffering animal towards the bayonets of the marines; for it would have been too sad a circumstance if he had escaped, with his ribs half roasted and his hams prematurely smoked, to mourn in solitude in the woods, so I tried my best to keep him straight in the right path. The pig, however, like many of us, not knowing what was best for him, thought otherwise, and sheered off for the forest; after a fine hunting run of ten minutes, I turned him and got him back to the broad road, which he began to suspect would lead him to destruction, for he slewed port and starboard, and I had much trouble to keep him in the right direction; at last, however, I got him to the top of the little hill, under which the captain and marine officer were posting their men according to the manners and customs of war. 'Look out for the pig,' I shouted; and, in a moment, every man was under way, over rocks, under branches, up and down full gallop. Poor pig had a bad chance with them; a bayonet stuck in his short ribs, another in his gullet, and a Minie bullet pierced his heart. The body was brought in triumph to the boat. This pig belonged to the barracks.

There is a painting of the parson and the pig by Fanshawe in the National Maritime Museum at Greenwich.

4 The Finnish Prisoners in Lewes

Perhaps the most unexpected way in which Finland became known in England in the nineteenth century was by the arrival in the little Sussex town of Lewes of about 170 Finnish prisoners, captured after the fall of Bomarsund. They were described in the *Illustrated London News*:

> On leaving the Lewes station, Lieut. Mann gave the word of command, and the prisoners, having been formed into detachments, four abreast, proceeded through School-hill, Albion street, and East-street, to the prison. Lieut. Mann offered one of the officer's ladies his arm, which she accepted, her husband accompanying her on the other side. The officers followed the men. The pensioners acted as a kind of formal guard, walking with fixed bayonets, and a body of the East Sussex constabulary were in attendance. A large crowd of persons followed the captives to the prison; but there was no expression of any feeling on the occasion. The officers are intelligent-looking persons; and their ladies of attractive appearance.

The officers were paroled, and housed locally. *The Times* reported that 'several of the leading gentlemen had been introduced to the officers, and others had left their cards'. For the men a newly-built prison had been converted, cell doors removed, with workshops, a reading room, and even a tennis court. During their nineteen months of gentle internment they became very popular in Lewes, and their activities were reported regularly in local and national newspapers. The articles, especially wooden toys, which they made in their workshop were sold in the town, and to the many visitors to the prison. When the war ended in 1856 Lewes gave them a civic farewell, and the townsfolk lined the street to the station.

Twenty-eight of the prisoners died of tuberculosis in Lewes, and are buried in the picturesque churchyard of St John sub Castro, where a memorial, erected in 1877, known locally as the Russian Memorial, lists the names of all the dead. It was restored by the Soviet Embassy in 1957, and again, this time as a joint Finnish-Russian enterprise, in 2012. In 1997 an opera, *The Finnish Prisoner* by Orlando Gough, was performed at Lewes.

Notes and References

Epigraphs

Tweedie, 4. Travers, 159. De Windt, 9.

Preface

Tweedie, 343; *ILN,* 14 April 1855, 355.

Introduction

Rigby, *Quarterly Review* 76 (June 1845), 99. Norman, 7–8.
Tweedie, 1. *Handbook* (1839), Preface, v, 126; (1849) 341;
(1865), 272; (1868), 383; (1875), Preface. Sturge: Richard, 509.
English servants: repeated in the 1871 edition, xviii. MacDougall,
87–8. Whatley (1839), 7. Bunbury (1856), 65. Ryall, 276.
Renwick, 167. Hamley, 173–4. MacCallam Scott (1908), 22.
Tweedie, 232. Don, 11. *ILN,* 15 July, 1854, 47.
An analysis and extracts from the *Kalevala* are given as early as
1846 in Volume 2 of Henningsen's *Eastern Europe and the
Emperor Nicholas,* 163–208.

Embryo Qualities

Sulivan, 179. Sturge, 30. Evans ms. Renwick, 225.
Dr Pasi Sahlberg has pointed out to me that the Church had an
important role in ensuring that adult literacy 'has always been
quite high in Finland', but that this was no more than a basis for
the great changes in Finnish education in the 1980s.
Naval officers: e.g. G. M. Jones and C. C. Frankland. See *Not So
Barren,* 154ff.
Henningsen, 198. Sturge, 22. Napier (1857), 346.
Music: Hill (1854), 114. Clive-Bayley, 96–7. Tweedie, 83.
Renwick, 277. Bowring, *Westminster Review* (April 1827),
317–41. Dover Wilson, 62.
Sauna: An American, Paul du Chaillu, uses the word *sauna* in

1881 in *Land of the Midnight Sun* (II, 206). 'extraordinary spectacle'; see *Not so Barren,* 164. De Windt, 244–5. Bell, *Land of Lakes* (1950), 150. Frankland. See *Not So Barren,* 182. Gallenga, 111. Standish, 160.

Transport

Maxwell, 43. De Windt, 287ff, 27. Young, (1912) 201. MacDougall, 59. De Windt, 27. *Handbook* (1839), 121. Gallenga, 109. Bunbury (1857), 204. Tweedie, 204. Young (1912), 197. MacDougall, 100. Evans, ms. Rae, 95. Paul, 165. Young (1914), 297. Nevinson, 350. Clive-Bayley, 210, 199. Gallenga, 121. De Windt, 52. MacDougall, 59.

Board and Lodging

Clarke, see *Not so Barren,* 88. Whatley, *Handbook* (1839), 131. Sturge, 8. Rigby, 71. De Windt, 44. Evans, ms. Rae, 120. Tweedie, 242. Standish, 162.

Women travellers

Quarterly Review LXXVI I, 845 Sulivan. 258.. Young (1914), 286. Young (1912), 196–7. Travers, 5. Tweedie (1913). Clive-Bayley 262, 267–8. Travers, 96.

Political Background; Russification

Kirby, 24–6. Gallenga, 114. Mead, [9]. MacDougall, 6. Tweedie, 238. Hyne, 274.

Rev. Robert Bateman Paul

Paul, 163, 166–7, 182, 168, 170–1, 176–7; Turku: 179–83.

Thomas Whatley

Handbook (1839), 130ff.

Elizabeth Rigby

Sheldon [1], the more commonly attributed last words are 'The sun is god'; *ODNB*; Barrow: *Excursions in the North of Europe* (1834), 3; Rigby, 66–7, 71–9.

George Francklin Atkinson

Atkinson [iii], 42, 45, 50, 161–2; Helsinki,: 164–8; 'the slow canal': Goldsmith, 'The Traveller', 171; Turku: 170–4.

S. S. Hill

Hill, vi, 106; Turku: 108–11; Helsinki: 115, 117–18; progress: 109.

Selina Bunbury

Bunbury (1856), 25–6; Turku: 53–5; Helsinki: 66; 'nests' 93; Porter: see *Not So Barren*, 7, 106–7; war: 92; forest: 98–9.

The Russian War

Kirk, *History Today* 54 (8). Figes, 159.
Westminster, see *Hansard*: HC Deb. 8 March 1855, vol. 137, cc261–321. *ILN,*14 April 1855, 353. Ponting, 35. Napier, Greenhill and Gifford, 99. Bell, Embassy Website.
1854: pilot: Dodd, 165. Kalvenholmen: Embassy Website. *Augusta:* Dodd, 163. Sulivan, 160. Plumridge's Notice: reproduced by Hirn. English admiral: *The Englishwoman in Russia*, 295. Gifford: Greenhill and Gifford, 177f. Napier, 209. *Much Ado about Nothing,* I i.
1855: Fanshawe, 319. Dodd, 102. Greenhill, 336. Dodd, 48. Lambert (1990) 293.

Nature of the war
Padget, 97. Napier, 272. Hamley, 172. Dodd, 152. Fanshawe, 327. Sulivan, 195. *Henry V*, III vi. Hirn, 57. Padget. 103. Fanshawe, 327–8. Don, 80. Dodd, 178. ball: Embassy Website. Dodd, 180–1. Geneste, *ILN*, 11 August, 1855, 163. Hamley, 211. Napier, 302, 301. Napier: Greenhill, 99. fun and games: Graham, 301. Padget, 108, 111. advertisement: reproduced by Dodd, 164. Priscilla Napier, 156. Don, 79. Stockholm ferry: *Eclectic Magazine* Vol 33, 1854.

Captain Bartholomew James Sulivan

DNB; Sulivan, 174; Degerby: 168; his piety: ix; 210–11; sequel: 212; *Älgö*: 162–3; women: 179, 258; 360.

Colonel Charles Hamley

Hamley, 200; 197; 190–1; pastoral: see *Not so Barren*, 13.

William Gerard Don, MD

Don, 73–4.

Rev. Robert Edgar Hughes

1854: Hughes [1], 2, 63, 74, 88–9, 97–9, 122–3, 131.
1855; 210–1; Latin quotation: 'He has mixed peace with war, miserable lad.' Based on Horace, *Odes* V iii. 215–6, 218–20, [2nd ed.], 220–2; Maria Pupur, Embassy Website; Bunbury (1857), 262; Greenhill, 257.

Lord Dufferin

Lyall, 79; *Cornhill Magazine* NS Vol. V (November 1898), 598–600, 601; Lyall, 81.

Selina Bunbury

Bunbury (1857), 1, 187, 208, 209; church: 215; 225; bath-house: 252–4; 255, 259.

Joseph Sturge

ODNB; Richard, 506, 507; Sturge, *Report*, 6; Richard, 508,; Sturge, 12; Tampere: Sturge, 9, 12; Turku: 511; 'Enrick Julin' is Erik Julin Snr., the foremost businessman in Turku; John Julin, his second son, became a significant businessman and politician; investigations: Richard, 512, Sturge, 15, Richard, 514. Whittier: see Halmasvirta and Wilson, 29–31.

Edward Rae

Rae, 2–4; mosquitoes: 45; a parody of Byron's 'The Destruction of Sennacherib'; 71–5, 77; 'vapour bath': 80–1, 85, 91–2, 96, 99, 103, 108; Oulu: 114–15; Finnish: 75; Raahe: 118–20; 'Finomânes': Fennomans, the Finnish Party dedicated to promoting Finnish as the national language; Vaasa: 123–4.

Arthur J. Evans

Extracts are taken from the two ms. volumes of Evans's journal, transcribed by his step-mother, in the Ashmolean Museum, Oxford, and are reproduced by permission. I have tidied it up in many places, and introduced a lot of the punctuation, in order to make an easily readable narrative.

'The missing link': the phrase is first recorded as used by Lyell in his *Elements of Geology* in 1851. Edward Daniel Clarke, in Lapland in 1799, had anticipated the phrase, writing of a Lapp couple in Enontekiö that they 'might be considered as the long-lost link between man and ape'. (*Not So Barren*, 73). Scheffer; *The History of Lapland* by John Scheffer, an abridged translation of *Lapponia* by Johannes Schefferus, was published by Oxford, 1674. Evans had certainly done his homework! 'var so göd'ed us': a Swedish phrase of invitation. 'skreglig stark', 'fearfully strong'. Smelly reindeer-skin coat: Brown, 15.

Annie Margaret Clive-Bayley

Scott (1926), 141–2; Clive-Bayley, 8; Hongola has a useful website. Aprons: 143; first trip, 90, 99, 115, 126–7; second trip, 170–71, 179, 163, 182; post house: 211–13, 199, 205, 208, 194, 215; Valamo: 221–2, 228; Helsinki, 265–6; third trip, 293–4.

Ethel Brilliana (Mrs Alec) Tweedie

Through Finland in Carts went through three or four editions. Ryall, 281; Tweedie (1933), 110; (1912) 65; (1933) 111; (1900) 10, 18, 173; (1900) 149, 28, 194; Kuopio: 181, 223; the Governor was Gösta Aminoff, his son Juri Aminoff: 209, 230, 228–32, 235, 261–2; Lapinlahti: 242–6, 278, 246; Kajaani: 280, 298, 327–8,

3

330–1, 334–6. Women: 163–4, 163–4, [42], 53–4, 51–2; washing: 131, 211, 231, 309, 130.

C. J. Cutcliffe Hyne

Hyne (1931), 189; *ODNB*; Hyne (1898), 4, viii, 5, 6, 12, 54, 61, 67; (1931), 173; Lake Inari: (1898), 70–1, 77, 79, 80–1, 89–92, 98–9; Menesjärvi: 131, 134, 136, 164, 183–4; Ivalon Matti: 191, 194, 113, 209, 214, 228–9; Kiistala: 238, 250–1; Roveniemi: 272–7, 278; (1931), 85.
Note on the drum: it is historically very late to be expecting to find magicians in Finland, but interesting to note in *The Nigger of the 'Narcissus'* Conrad's Finnish Sailor: 'Wamibo's spells delayed the ship in open sea'. Conrad was possibly a reader of Hyne; see G. P. Winnington, *Conradiana* XVI (1984), 3.

Harry de Windt

De Windt, Preface; Baker [1]; De Windt, 7, 15–6, 20, 39, 56, 70, 73–6, 113–14; Helsinki: 128–9, 165–7, 169, 172–3; Vaasa: 192–5, 214–15, 225–6; north from Oulu, 242, 262, 273; De Windt (1909), 283–4.

'Paul Waineman' (Sylvia MacDougall)

MacDougall (1944), 1, 107; (1908), 6, 11, 75, 100, 215; Saimaa: 76–8, 87–8, 124–7, 149; Kajaani: 170, 178, 188, 197, 215; Tampere: 242–3; (Renwick, 66); 246, 258, 281; Clive-Bayley, 210; Tweedie, 230.

Alexander MacCallam Scott

Scott (1926), 13; (1908), 21–2, 207–8.

Rosalind Travers

Travers (1923), 1; (1911), 5; Gould, 16, 181; Mead, 12; Travers (1911), 34, 88, 109–10, 116, 123; Tornio: 133, 139–40, 144–5, 157, 159–60, 166; Mikkeli: 167, 168; Lahti: 195; Helsinki: 310–12 – I feel convinced that Travers is here describing 'The

Bibliography

Primary sources

Atkinson, George Francklin, *Pictures from the North in Pen and Pencil. Sketched during a Summer Ramble.* 1848.

Barrow, John, Jnr., *Excursions in the North of Europe. through Parts of Russia, Finland, Denmark, and Norway, in the Years 1830 and 1833.* 1834.

Bunbury, Selina, *A Summer in Northern Europe, Including Sketches in Sweden, Norway, Finland, the Aland Islands, Gothland, etc.* Vol. 1. 1856.

— *Russia after the War: The Narrative of a Visit to that Country in 1856.* Vol. 1. 1857.

Clive-Bayley, A. M. [C.], *Vignettes from Finland, or Twelve Months in Strawberry Land.* 1895.

Coxwell, Charles Fillingham. *Through Russia in War-Time.* 1917.

De Windt, Harry, *Finland As It Is.* 1901.

Don, William Gerard, MD, *Reminiscences of the Baltic Fleet of 1855.* Printed 1894.

Lord Dufferin, 'Bomarsund 1854, from the Deck of the Foam', *Cornhill Magazine*, November 1898.

Fanshawe, Alice, *Admiral Sir Edward Gennys Fanshawe.* 1904.

Gallenga, Antonio, *A Summer Tour in Russia.* 1882.

Hamlcy, Col., Charles, 'Aland – the Baltic in 1854', in *Travel, Adventure and Sport from Blackwood's Magazine.* Vol. 4 (n.d.), pp.171–214. (First published June 1855.)

Hill, S. S., *Travels on the Shores of the Baltic.* 1854.

Hughes, Rev. Robert Edgar, *Two Summer Cruises with the Baltic Fleet in 1854–55, being the Log of the 'Pet' Yacht.* 1855. Second edition 1856.

Hyne, C. J. Cutcliffe, *Through Arctic Lapland.* 1898.

Lunn, Sir Henry Simpson, *How to Visit Northern Europe.* 1896.

MacDougall, Sylvia [Paul Waineman], *A Summer Tour in Finland.* 1908.

Maxwell, John S., *The Czar, his Court and People: including a Tour in Norway and Sweden.* 1848.

[Michell, Thomas], *Handbook for Travellers in Russia, Poland, and Finland.* New edition, revised, 1865.

— Second edition, revised. 1868.

— Third edition, revised. 1875.

— Fourth edition, thoroughly revised. 1888.

Napier, Sir Charles, *The History of the Baltic Campaign of 1854.* 1857.

Napier, Elers, *The Life and Correspondence of admiral Sir Charles Napier.* 1862.

Nevinson, Henry W., *More Changes More Chances.* [1925.]

Paget, Admiral Lord Clarence E., *Autobiography and Journals* (ed. Sir Arthur Otway). 1896.

Paul, Rev. Robert Bateman, *Journal of a Tour to Moscow in the Summer of 1836.* 1836.

Rae, Edward, *The Land of the North Wind, or, Travels among the Laplanders and the Samoyedes.* 1875.

Renwick, George, *Finland Today.* 1911.

[Rigby, Elizabeth], *A Residence on the Shores of the Baltic. Described in a Series of Letters.* 1841. Vol. 2.

Scott, Alexander MacCallam, *Through Finland to St. Petersburg.* 1908.

Standish, Frank Hall, *Notices on the Northern Capitals of Europe.* 1838.

[Sturge, Joseph], *Report of a Visit to Finland in the Autumn of 1856. Confidential.* Birmingham Printed [1856].

Sulivan, Henry Norton (ed.), *Life and Letters of the late Admiral Sir Bartholomew James Sulivan, K.G.B 1810–1890.* 1896.

Travers, Rosalind, *Letters from Finland August, 1908 – March, 1909.* 1911.

Tweedie, Mrs Alec, *Through Finland in Carts.* New edition, 1900.

— ibid., Nelson Classics edn. [1913].

[Whatley, Thomas Denman], *A Handbook for Travellers in Denmark, Norway, Sweden and Russia.* 1839.

— *Handbook for Northern Europe; including Denmark, Norway, Sweden, Finland and Russia. New Edition, partly re-written, and corrected throughout.* Part Two: Finland and Russia. 1849.

Wilson, John Dover, *Milestones on the Dover Road.* 1969.

Young, Ernest, *Finland: Land of a Thousand Lakes.* 1912.
— *From Russia to Siam. with a Voyage down the Danube. With Sketches of Travel in Many Lands.* 1914.

Secondary sources

[anon.] *The Englishwoman in Russia; . . . by a Lady Ten Years Resident in that Country.* 1855.
[anon.] *Finland – 'The Land of a Thousand Lakes'. Description of Tours.* Hull, 1899.
[anon.] *Particulars of the Sailings of ther Finland Line of Mail Passenger Steamers.* 1914.
Baker, Karla, 'The Restless Life of Harry de Windt', Bartholomew Archive Blog.
Bell, Marjatta, 'The Crimean War in Finland', British Embassy website.
Brown, Ann, *Before Knossos . . . Arthur Evans's Travels in the Balkans and Crete.* Oxford, Ashmolean Museum, 1993.
De Windt, Harry, *My Restless Life,* 1909.
Dodd, George, *Pictorial History of the Russian War, 1854–5–6.* 1856.
Frost, Stephen, 'Ernest Young – He set the world within these walls', ebookbrowse.com/ernest-young-2006-pdf-d363259859.
Fellman, Ida, *Furuhjelms på Hongola gård* (website 2010).
Figes, Orlando, *Crimea: the Last Crusade.* 2010.
Forsgren , Tuuli, 'Finland – ett land av smultron?' in Red Heidi Hansson, Maria Lindgren Leavenworth and Lennart Pettersson (eds), *Regionernas bilder: Estetiska uttryck från och om periferin.* Umeå, 2010.
Gould, Fredrick J., *Hyndman Prophet of Socialism,*1928.
Greenhill, Basil, and Gifford, Ann, *The British Assault on Finland 1854–1855: A Forgotten Naval War.* 1988.
Halmasvirta, Anssi, and Wilson, David, *Henceforth is the Anglo-Saxon the Brother of the Finn! Poems about Finland 1634–2000.* Jyväskyla, 2003.
[Henningsen, Charles Fredrick], *Revelations of Russia.* 1844.
Hirn, Marta, *Från Bomarsund till Sveaborg.* Helsingfors, 1956.
Hyne, C. J. Cutcliffe, *My Joyful Life.* 1931.
— *People and Places.* [1931].

The Illustrated London News (ILN)

John, Angela V., *War, Journalism, and the Shaping of the Twentieth Century; The Life and Times of Henry V. Nevinson.* 2006.

Kirby, D. G., *Finland in the Twentieth Century.* 1978.

Kirk, Matthew, 'Crimea in Finland', *History Today* 54 (8), August 2004.

Lambert, Andrew D., *The Crimean War: British Grand Strategy, 1853–56*, Manchester, 1990.

— 'Looking for Gunboats: British Naval operations in the Gulf of Bothnia, 1854–55', *Journal for Maritime Research,* 6:1, 65–86 . (2004). To link to this article: http://dx.doi.org/10.1080/21533369 .2004.9668337.

Lurcock, Tony, 'From Travel to Tourism: British Travellers to Finland 1830–1900', in Marie Wells (ed.), *The Discovery of Nineteenth-Century Scandinavia.* Norvik Press, 2008.

— *'Not So Barren or Uncultivated': British Travellers in Finland 1760–1830.* 2010.

Lyall, Alfred, *The Life of the Marquis of Dufferin and Ava.* 1905.

MacDougall, Sylvia [Paul Waineman], *Let's Light the Candles. Memoirs.* 1944.

Mead, W. R., *The Anglo-Finnish Society 1911–2011.* 2011.

Norman, Henry, *All the Russias. Travels and Studies in Contemporary European Russia, Finland, Siberia, the Caucasus, & Central Asia.* 1902.

Napier, Priscilla, *Black Charlie; a Life of Sir Charles Napier.* 1995.

Ponting, Clive, *The Crimean War: The Truth behind the Myth.* 2004.

Renwick, Sir George, *Romantic Corsica.* 1909.

Reuter, J. N., 'Finland', in Williams, J. Fischer, *Memories of John Westlake* (1914).

Richard, Henry, *Memoirs of Joseph Sturge.* 1864.

Rigby, Elizabeth, 'Lady Travellers'. *Quarterly Review* 76 (June,1845), pp. 98–137.

Robins, Graham, *Bomarsund, Outpost of Empire.* Mariehamn, 2004.

Ryall, Anka, 'Europe's Northern Periphery and the Future of Women in the Travel Narratives of Ethel Tweedie', *NORA (Nordic Journal of Feminist and Gender Research)*, Vol. 17, No. 4, December 2009, pp.273–88.

Scott, Alexander MacCallum, *Suomi: The Land of the Finns*. 1926.

Sheldon, Julie, *The Letters of Elizabeth Rigby, Lady Eastlake*. Liverpool UP, 2009.

Stone, Ian R., 'Gentlemen Travellers in the North: Cutcliffe-Hyne's *Through Arctic Lapland*, 1898', *Polar Record* 40 (2004), pp.213–20.

Taylor, Bayard, *Northern Travel: Summer and Winter Pictures of Sweden, Denmark and Lapland*.

— *By-Ways of Europe*, New York, 1869.

Travers, Rosalind, *The Last Years of H. M. Hyndman*, 1923.

Tweedie, Mrs Alec, *Thirteen Years of a Busy Woman's Life*. 1912.

— *Tight Corners of my Adventurous Life*. 1928.

Williams, Hugh Noel, *The Life and Letters of Admiral Sir Charles Napier, K.C.B.* 1917.

Index of Places

This list gives only the principal accounts and descriptions.

CB editions

Founded in 2007, CB editions publishes chiefly
short fiction (including work by Gabriel Josipovici,
David Markson and Dai Vaughan) and poetry
(Fergus Allen, Andrew Elliott, Beverley Bie Brahic,
Nancy Gaffield, J. O. Morgan, D. Nurkse). Writers
published in translation include Apollinaire,
Andrzej Bursa, Joaquín Giannuzzi, Gert Hofmann
and Francis Ponge.

Books can be ordered from www.cbeditions.com.